D0850329

ROYAL HISTORICAL SOCIETY
STUDIES IN HISTORY
SERIES
No. 26

JULIAN S. CORBETT, 1854-1922

Historian of British Maritime Policy from Drake to Jellicoe

Recent volumes published in this series include

For a complete list of the series please see pp. 217-18.

JULIAN S. CORBETT, 1854-1922
Historian of British Maritime Policy from Drake to Jellicoe

Donald M. Schurman

LONDON
ROYAL HISTORICAL SOCIETY
1981

The Society records its gratitude to the following, whose generosity made possible the initiation of this series: The British Academy; The Pilgrim Trust; The Twenty-Seven Foundation; The United States Embassy's Bicentennial Funds; The Wolfson Trust; several private donors.

The author wishes to thank the Canada Council for two grants in support of research.

Printed in England
by Swift Printers (Sales) Ltd.
London E.C.1.

For Elizabeth Tunstall and Richard Corbett

and

in loving memory of
Brian Tunstall

CONTENTS

PREFACE

Julian Stafford Corbett was a great naval historian. He was for many years unofficial advisor to the Admiralty, friend of Lord Fisher of Kilverstone, and eventually the official historian of World War I. In addition, he was a tactical expositor of great competence and an expert on the traditional practices of blockade in wartime. Corbett's views on sea strategy are still canvassed.

This book is not a biography in any conventional sense. The nature of the evidence, the uneven manner in which Corbett's life intersected public events, together with the great variety of his interests, have made it undesirable to shepherd him step by step from the cradle to the grave. Although he was not a consistently important public figure, he was a very important public figure at eccentric moments in time. Corbett just fits Lloyd George's description of Kitchener — he was a searchlight beam which from time to time pierced the dark with devastating effect, and then disappeared. The exception to that judgement is, of course, his historical writing. His books are his major achievement and although they are discussed here, as they were in my *Education of a Navy,* they are better read than summarized. I have tried to show them as complementary source material fitting naval needs and controversies. The books are not all discussed in a similar or parallel way. I have shamefully neglected *Some Principles of Maritime Strategy* merely because its concepts are set out here in my discussion of the 'Green Pamphlet', and because the details that give the book strength are best read first hand and not summarized by a less expert hand than his.

As an historian Corbett brought forward a conception of military history as part and parcel of the general history of the state and of international politics. If Mahan emphasized that there were connections between sea war and national policy, Corbett, writing about Britain, showed just what those connections were. Respect for national traditions, traditions that were often uncovered by his own research, gave his writings a balance that is undeniable. Since his time, of course, parts of his work have been superceded by history that is more detailed. But even allowing for the inevitable fact that he has lost some matches to newer historians, it must be recognized that, as Brian Tunstall once put it, 'he invented the game'. He came to naval history as Mahan was beginning to link sea power with national power; he left it in a state where one could see how the relations between sea power and national power really worked.

His work was British, and he never claimed to be writing international history. However, he was yet constrained to show that the British exercised sea-based power in a responsible restrained way, not particularly because they were a more virtuous people, but because he had come to know the limitations, as well as the advantages that sea power conferred on its practitioners. It was precisely this judicious sense of the limitations of sea power that made his writings less popular than those of other military/naval writers. It is precisely this sense of limitations that makes it difficult for some to appreciate him today. The story of the Royal Navy is a success story, at least up to the year 1805, and Corbett handled this success story in such a way as to show that the greatest successes were tenuous, and the most potent strengths had limits. Therefore, difficult or not, his history was a superb achievement for a man who wrote in an age when the Royal Navy paraded its visible might, and chauvinism was infrequently tempered by judgement in military/naval writing.

It will be seen that these insights permeated his practical advice to the Royal Navy in the Fisher era.

Writing a semi-biographical, somewhat episodic, history necessitates stifling the temptation to write exhaustively about each situation. This temptation has been resisted and the criterion I have attempted to use has been 'does it reveal Corbett's viewpoint in relation to this recognizable historical event?' Thus I have not gone in much for scholarly controversy, nor is my account heavily laced with references to all the recent relevant literature. Where I have borrowed material it is acknowledged in the usual way in the footnotes. However, the overwhelming mass of the evidence is drawn from the Corbett papers, and the arrangement of the book reflects the strengths and weaknesses of this main source.

There are two exceptions to this general statement. One is that for the material on official histories I have used the Public Record Office extensively, and have followed the trail blazed by Stephen Roskill and A. Temple-Patterson. Roskill, indeed, generously loaned me papers that made my searches in the Record Office easier, and explained much that was hitherto hidden from me. The other exception is the work of Arthur Marder. His writings have shaped this period for anyone working in it and I gratefully acknowledge this fact.

In short, what I have desired is that Corbett's place in the 'Dreadnought' age should be made clear, and that his illuminating intelligence might shine out clearly. Although I have been critical of Julian Corbett I make no claim to have written without affection and respect.

Elizabeth Tunstall and Richard Corbett, Sir Julian's daughter and son, have unfailingly responded to every request for materials or information, and have shown great kindness to me and my family. Dame Margery Corbett Ashby, Sir Julian's cousin, gave me the benefit of her perceptive memory. Corbett's grandchildren, Gillian, Jane, Robert, Jeremy, and Julian all were interested in this book. To Julian, my close friend of some twenty years, it goes with special affection.

My greatest assistance came from the late Brian Tunstall. He appreciated the importance of his father-in-law's work, preserved and arranged the papers, and gave me unrivalled family insights and advice. If these pages have any virtues they often reflect his wisdom. I do not hold him responsible for the weaknesses. The chapter on 'The Tactics of Trafalgar' could not have been written without his comments, for, in my view, his knowledge about signalling and sail tactics had no rival in his lifetime. Peter Marsh Stanford kindly let me see his very able, but unpublished, manuscript on Corbett. Alan Pearsall, Kenneth Timings and Peter Kemp all expedited my researches at the National maritime Museum, Public Record Office, and the old Admiralty Library. I have profited from discussions with Alan Pearsall, Adrian Preston, Brian Bond, Michael Howard, Carl-Axel Gemzell, James Pritchard, Rowena Reed, Karen Logan, Brian Ranft, Christopher Lloyd, George Naish, Lucien Karchmar and Neil Summerton. In particular I would mention Barry Hunt and Nicholas d'Ombrain who shared their knowledge with me freely. Other people have saved me from many follies and helped to strengthen the work. The remaining blemishes are mine. Arthur Marder has generously encouraged and helped me. So did Lady Liddell Hart and the late Sir Basil Liddell Hart at States House where part of the manuscript was written. I am grateful to Mr. G. Cleare for access to the Slade papers, to Ruddock Mackay for some Fisher material, and to Stephen Roskill for his overwhelming kindness in sharing his World War I 'official' history researches with me. Much typing and proof reading was done by my late wife Janice, Kathleen Macdonald, Nancy Warren and Barbara Shane. The work was revised extensively during the summer of 1977 and without the assistance of my wife, Olive, it would have been impossible to complete. The late Trevor Reese helped greatly with the editing.

Finally, I am eternally grateful to Janice who believed the work to be important, and to Gerald Graham who shared that belief and never wavered in his support.

D.M.S.

1

EARLY LIFE AND FIRST TRAVELS

It was not until 1895 that Julian Corbett began his career as a naval historian; nor was it until 1900, at least, that he began the adjacent career of adviser to and publicist for the Royal Navy. Since he was 46 in 1900, it can be seen at once that his period of conscious and unconscious preparation for his life work was extensive. My first two chapters depict the slow development of an expert on naval history and strategy. The source material available for this purpose was uneven; for Corbett, like many other men, only began to preserve many papers relating to his own life when he had achieved a certain eminence. His father's business diaries, his own brief diary jottings, the 1880s and 1890s letters home, especially accounts of travel abroad, and his own novels and early historical writings, constitute the sources for the following survey of his first forty-five years.[1]

Charles James Corbett, Julian's father, came to London from Croft, in Lincolnshire, in the late 1840s. An architect by profession, he rapidly perceived that there were lucrative opportunities in the building trade in London. At this time businesses in London were not generally housed in the more or less functional office buildings common to the twentieth century. Corbett saw the possibility of altering this, and his technique was to buy up an older building, often a public house that was losing trade, gut it, and build office premises one floor on top of the other. By 1858, after a slow beginning, he could see that with a little luck, he might become a very rich man. In 1861 he was able to finance a large loan from the National Provincial Insurance Company and operate from a much larger and more secure financial base and from that time onward he constantly augmented his wealth. For the family this meant comfort and security.

When Julian Stafford Corbett was born on Sunday 12 November 1854 the family was living at 'Walcott House' on Kennington Road not

---

1 A general discussion concerning the sources for this book is to be found in the bibliographical note on p. 202. Most of the information contained in Chapter I, however, does not relate to Corbett's public activity as a naval historian, and specific references would take up space unnecessarily. The material is based on verbal information from the family: from family correspondence to be found in Box 3 and Box 8 of the Corbett papers in the possession of Mrs. Brian Tunstall, and from the *Diaries* of both Julian S. Corbett and *his* father Charles J. Corbett in the possession of Richard Corbett. Mrs. Tunstall and Richard Corbett are Julian Corbett's daughter and son.

far from the Oval. He was the second son born of a marriage that had been contracted in 1852. After an underlined *'Hurrah*!!!' Corbett noted in his diary, somewhat complacently, that 'Mr. Wagstaff said Lizzy behaved in a most satisfactory manner and that the child was a fine, and particularly healthy one'. The baby was christened at Lambeth Church on Friday 2 February 1855. David Alexander, a Manchester businessman was one of the Godparents. 'Julian stood the water without crying at all.'

Charles Corbett had married Elizabeth Stafford in 1852, and their first child, Charles, had preceded Julian by about a year. Julian was followed in time by three more brothers and a sister. In 1858, the family moved to Croydon, and finally in 1861, they moved to Imber Court at Thames Ditton near Kingston-upon-Thames, and this became the headquarters of family activity until the turn of the century. The father, an intelligent but unsophisticated man, found the metropolitan scene endlessly fascinating. He took his family regularly to view museums, art galleries, processions and notable events as they occurred. Both he and his wife were great walkers, and they liked to see and be seen in Hyde Park, or in the grounds of the Crystal Palace at Sydenham to which the family were regular visitors. The Corbetts felt it important to expose their children to cultural influences. Julian was taken to visit the British Museum at the tender age of seven. It was recorded that he was 'greatly delighted and not a little astonished'. The older Corbetts viewed such public events as the Duke of Wellington's funeral, a review of the Fleet off Spithead, the illuminations that marked the end of the Crimean War, the presentations of the V.C. to the veterans of the Crimea, a High Church service, where Corbett was stunned by the genuflections, and a grand review of the Rifle volunteers in Hyde Park in 1860 during the time of the Great French scare. Charles James usually concluded the description of such cultural sorties with the words 'much pleased'.

There were private pleasures as well. They particularly enjoyed the kind of overnight visits made possible by the facilities of the railroad. They exchanged visits on a regular basis with their relatives at Croft, Lincolnshire, and with the Alexander family, who were industrially prominent in Manchester. Many years later Alexander's daughter became Julian Corbett's wife. There were also other trips to various parts of the United Kingdom. After 1861, when they were more affluent, there were visits to the Continent.

From the early 1850s Charles Corbett was hospitable and there were occasions when as many as sixty-five people sat down to dinner at one of their entertainments. The more habitual pleasure, however, was the small intimate gathering of family and friends, when they ate and drank well, sang, and played cards far into the night. Perhaps the most noteworthy thing about the house in which Julian Corbett was brought up was the degree to which entertainments did centre around the family hearth, and the degree to which they involved a few select permanent friends.

Wealth did not make the Corbetts especially ostentatious, but Imber Court was a big house and played a very important part in all of their lives. Appropriately enough as the home of a future historian, the estate had historical connections with important figures in English history. It had been hunted over by Henry VIII when he lived in Wolsey's old palace at Hampton Court, and, in the seventeenth century, it was the property of Lord Dorchester, one time English Ambassador at Venice and Amsterdam, and was visited by Charles I.

Although there was some evidence in the latter part of the nineteenth century that parts of the old building survived, it was, when the Corbetts lived there, mainly an eighteenth century construction. The architecture was not particularly distinguished, yet the grounds were spacious and the situation was delightfully close to the water. It was in the roof of this building that Julian Corbett eventually began his literary career, indeed it served him as a study until the house was sold in 1900. The family also owned a property in the country called Woodgate not far from Hayward's Heath in East Sussex, where they went for shooting and to engage in other country pursuits. Imber Court has since become the property of the Metropolitan Police Force; and Woodgate in Sussex is in the hands of a former Prime Minister of Great Britain, Harold Macmillan.

The family life of the Corbetts was particularly close and it remained so for many years. At the centre of this family stood the elusive figure of Elizabeth Corbett. We do not know very much about her except that she was musical and that she was a woman of some intelligence. In letters to her Corbett always treated her as an intellectual equal. She remained the focus of all family activities until her death in 1892, ten years after that of her husband. It should be noted that Julian did not marry until after his mother's death. The intellectual curiosity and progressive tendencies that characterized Charles Corbett emerged in the children in an intellectual freedom that made them both liberal in outlook and Liberals in politics; but so far as accomplishment in the competitive world was concerned, their casualness bordered on indolence. It has been seen that it took Julian a long time to find his proper niche in life; in the same way it was true that his younger brothers never really settled into any occupation that could be described as other than 'gentlemen of leisure'. Julian's elder brother, Charles, was somewhat of an exception to this. After attending Marlborough and Oxford he settled into the family business, which he seems to have run successfully to the benefit of the whole family and its heirs. In later life, he was remembered affectionately by his family as an intelligent, and a somewhat indulgent parent, who encouraged intellectual curiosity and reforming ideas in the minds of his children, whom incidentally, he had educated himself. He seems to have been an attractive man. One of his children was Dame Margery Corbett Ashby, the well known suffragist, who made a distinguished international name for herself as a rational, competent, imaginative and effective advocate of women's rights. In the great Liberal political upset of 1906, Charles became Member of Parliament for Lewes, and he seems to have been on Lloyd George's list for a Peerage had the 1911 threat against the House of Lord's required implementation.

All the men of the family were diminutive in stature and modern and progressive in outlook. One of Julian's brothers, Herbert, or Bertie as he was known, was a great traveller. For a time he dabbled in real estate, then emigrated to America and he remained a global perambulator for the rest of his life. He had a good brain that he never used in any systematic manner. Frank was a charming lightweight, who had tuberculosis. Consequently he slept out a good deal and took plenty of exercise. His great contribution to the family life was the planning and construction of a series of artificial ponds at the Woodgate estate, on which family and friends all worked, and which still exist on the Macmillan estate. He had a flair for antiques, which he bought with some discrimination. He married a woman somewhat older than himself who was addicted to Christian Science. Edward, or Tod as he was called by the family, was marked out to be a doctor. He had a clever mind that could produce an answer to almost any direct question. Unfortunately it turned out to be an unorganized mind and he never fulfilled his intellectual promise. He is remembered in the family for his meticulous habits, such as maintaining a set of woodworking tools in immaculate condition. He was a fussy man whose real passion was yachting and he sailed regularly on the Norfolk Broads. Most of the family were anglers. Fish were kept in the ponds at Woodgate and regular visits were made to Scotland and Norway to cast flies on the salmon waters. Ada was the only daughter. Her son, Dennis Wilson, became an aircraft pilot who acquired an international reputation as the first man to fly the Irish Channel. He advocated the use of the monoplane long before the military forces of the crown could be persuaded of its ability to fly. This aviator was killed early in the first war in the Royal Flying Corps. Ada subsequently moved to Italy and spent most of the rest of her life abroad.

This family was not tuned in to the precision of thought that Julian's career required of him. None of them, subsequently, were really interested in his occupation. Julian's work was probably not considered very important because it was not commercially profitable. Scholarly pursuits were not regarded as measures of success in the family. For his part, Julian Corbett was touched by the same liberal reforming suffragist and disarmament viewpoints that characterized the public outlook of his family. Nevertheless, Dame Margery's support for female political rights was not without its moments of embarrassment for him, and it is certainly true that he could not afford to be an exponent of disarmament when he was working as a propagandist for the Royal Navy. However, it is important to bear in mind that Julian did not begin to succeed as a historical writer until nearly 1900, and up until that time he was, like the rest, a captive of his own cultivated, self-sufficient and leisurely home environment. For many years his home represented to him the highest standard of life and it was up to the rest of the world to attempt to meet that high example.

In August 1869, Corbett was sent to Marlborough College. Marlborough had had a reputation for being a rough place, but under the guidance of George Granville Bradley had managed to humanize itself somewhat in the 1860s. Bradley's speciality was the teaching of logical precision through the use of Latin grammar and he regularly secured a number of places for his boys at Oxford. The school encouraged 'country pursuits' as opposed to organized games. Bradley was particularly interested in military campaigns and he delighted in showing the boys the intricacies of the manoeuvres of armies of the past. Corbett did not have a particularly distinguished career at Marlborough, nor did he express affection for the school in later years.

Corbett went up to Trinity College, Cambridge, in the Michaelmas term of 1873, and he took a first class in the Law Tripos, which he sat just before Christmas 1875. Generally speaking, these were pleasant years. He had presented himself to Cambridge, as he later put it, 'to be moulded into a member of society'., and he assisted that process by exercising his undoubted social talents over a wide field, and by coxing boats on the River Cam as well as by excelling in his legal studies.

This relaxed approach to University life, in such a marked contrast to the tripos tensions that are so much more a feature of Cambridge to-day, was undoubtedly shared by most of Corbett's contemporaries. Accustomed to good living, they came to the University to live a life in contact with academic people, and not as pilgrims to an academic shrine. They were not easily impressed by ritualistic dons, formal meals, or hovering landladies. Judged by the standards of Imber Court, Cambridge was often found to be wanting. Certainly Corbett found many quaint customs not to his taste: especially was this the case with the town-gown disturbances that had come to mark the annual remembrance of Guy Fawkes. These he characterized as barbaric, as no doubt they were. He was also appalled by the apparent low level of interest in music. Furthermore, while he was forever enslaved by the charms of Cambridge architecture, he found the landscape surrounding the ancient town depressing. Corbett described it as 'somewhat of the Lincolnshire order, stand on a sheet of note paper and you see into the next county', a prospect that was no doubt pleasant for those who could appreciate 'extensive views', but one that he found boring. However, his attitude to the general Cambridge physical environment, like attitudes of countless undergraduates before and since, tended to fluctuate from adulation to revulsion in tune with the vagaries of the fenland weather.

Corbett derived great enjoyment from shell racing. His diminutive stature prohibited him from taking part in the strenuous side of that sport, but it ideally fitted him to cox an eight. He spent a good deal of time on the river Cam, and he was fortunate in his crews since his boat made four bumps during the May races of 1874, and the next year he coxed the First Trinity boat at Henley Regatta, in both the 'Grand Challenge' and the 'Ladies Plate'. He wrote ecstatically of Henley. 'I have been having a most delightful time of it up here. I have never spent a jollier time in my life. We are the lions of the place. That is to say boating people generally are'. Yet for all his success he was not a rowing fanatic, and on two separate terms he refused to go on the river, once because of the pressure of studies and once because the weather was such as to make the experience less than enjoyable. Furthermore, he seems to have gradually lost his interest in the sport after he went down from Cambridge. The river never did elicit from him that perpetual personal devotion that so often distinguishes those who row for their College.

Similarly his law studies drew sufficiently on his natural abilities to produce examination success, but the law did not command his undivided loyalty. Nevertheless, he subdued his other interests to such a degree, and applied himself to his studies with such mental intensity, that he took a First Class degree in the Tripos. Like most men and women educated there, Corbett had, or developed, a deep affection for Cambridge. Years later Sir John Fortescue, the historian of the

British Army, praised the effortless and erudite way Corbett guided him through the architectural and historical by-ways of the Colleges.

There was a split between his desire to be active, sporting and manly, and his other desire to be buried in books and devouring knowledge. Years later he wrote a novel entitled *For God and Gold.* In this piece of fiction his hero went up to Trinity College, Cambridge, in the middle of the sixteenth century and he steeped himself in learning in order to play his part in the defence of the Reformation. Corbett forced his hero to condemn retrospectively the Cambridge studious, pedantic way of life, and made him reflect that perhaps the activity of Sir Francis Drake's little finger was worth more to the Reformation cause in England than all the learned heads in Cambridge collectively. This may well have been the author's personal viewpoint at the time. Cambridge did determine that the life of a secluded don, was not the life for him. It had forced him to face life, if not to make decisions about life's problems. Fortunately he was well enough off for it not to matter much.

In 1877 Corbett was admitted to the bar and he spasmodically pursued a legal career until 1882. He also took lessons at the Slade Art School. This did not solve his career problem, but it reinforced a considerable talent for drawing, which from then onwards afforded a constant source of enjoyment as he supplemented his travels with careful sketches and amused his family with his gift of rapid caricature.

In 1878 he made a long trip to India, and then a year and a half later he visited North America.

Aside from the young Englishmen who went out to these lands as immigrants, or men determined to make their career as Government Servants, it was then by no means the custom for young men of means to supplement their education by travels outside the European area. Not only was the geographical range of the tours remarkable for the time, but the contrast between a subcontinent of teeming millions ruled by his own countrymen, and a continent being filled up and developed by ex-Europeans who prided themselves on their particular brand of political freedom was bound to strike a sensitive observer forcibly. Nothing could have been better calculated to broaden the viewpoint and increase the perceptions of a potential writer. Apart from the Canadian background that later illuminated his study of Canada during the Seven Years' War, Corbett never wrote directly on the history of these countries when he became an historian. Yet undoubtedly these wide-ranging travels had helped to produce that breadth of viewpoint so characteristic of all his mature work. More particularly, the letters he wrote home during the visits were his first real attempts at sustained descriptive writing, and they constitute, in a very real sense, his literary training ground. The letters are light, shot with sardonic humour, and they demonstrate an already easily flowing prose style. In the letters the comments on the political and social customs of the peoples he visited reflect keen powers of observation and, at the same time, they bear the marks of the young and still immature commentator and tourist that he was.

Julian Corbett and his brother Charles arrived in Bombay at the beginning of October 1877 and remained in India until April of the next year. Beginning in Bombay they explored the western Ghat mountains and then used the railway to travel eastward to the Deccan. Afterwards they went northwards to Jaipur, where they spent Christmas, enjoying the hospitality of the Maharajah. Early in the New Year they visited the Delhi area where they gazed on the remains of Mogul splendour, and, like most tourists, stood in amazement and entrancement before the breathtaking beauty and elegance of the neighbouring Taj Mahal. Lahore and the north they found forbidding because of the extreme cold. As Corbett said, 'they didn't leave England for that'. At Cawnpore and Lucknow they gazed on the scenes made famous or infamous by the Indian Mutiny, and then went down the Ganges by boat to Bengal, from whence they went overland to the base of the Himalaya Mountains, which undoubtedly impressed them more than anything else they had seen since leaving England. On the way back Julian was almost thrown into a mountain ravine by a temperamental donkey. After spending a few days in Calcutta they took ship to Madras, and journeyed through country redolent with memories of the brief brilliant resistance of Mysore to the relentless extension of British control in India, and so on southward to Travancore. A few days in Ceylon completed the tour and they took ship for Bombay and home.

The India they visited was an India held in firm subjection by the ruling British. While Disraeli might stir the imaginations of the more romantic of his countrymen, and of some Indian princes, by the declaration that the Queen had become Empress, people on the spot were under no delusion about the fact that behind the glamour lay military force, and memory of the mutiny was both green and cherished. While the courts of local princes might glitter with a splendour reminiscent of past days of glory, looked at more closely they gave off the decadent odour that always surrounds paid puppets. The movement that was to culminate in the independence of India had not properly begun and the age of Empire appeared to stretch ahead as far as the eye could see. Certainly the Empire brought peace, British justice, and the railway. But underneath all this, and apparently undisturbed by it, moved India's teeming millions, wretchedly poor, conservative, subdued, but strangely untouched by the European conquerors. This timeless people had seen conquerors come and go before.

Corbett found the size and immensity of India staggering, and, for him, much of the beauty of the scenery was due to its scale. The scale of its history was also vast and he observed that if the British were to choose Delhi as the Capital they would only be adding one more name to the list of great empires that had held court there. He appreciated the grand opportunity that India afforded to the sportsman, and he took full advantage of all the shooting chances that came his way, especially when good sport was well supplemented by luxurious arrangements by generous hosts.

When it came to making judgements on people, and on their clothes, work and personal customs, Corbett's standards demanded that they be natural and indigenous to their environment. In this respect India fulfilled his expectations. An exciting, different, eastern flavour permeated everything, and the 'naturalness' of it all enchanted him. He enthusiastically followed the sleeping and eating habits of the country. The waywardness and accomplishments of men and beasts he carefully recorded, along with his appreciation of the bizarre and the exotic. In his sketch books, the authentic daily life of India peeps out; in the graceful shapes of women in flowing saris, local agricultural implements, the rough faces of hired guides, and even the faces and forms of animals which seemed to have special Asian personalities all their own. Significantly the Europeans and their habitations are missing from his sketch books.

He considered the chief Indian fault to be untrustworthiness. To put it bluntly he found, in common with most of his countrymen, that 'thieving' was almost a national occupation in India, and one of his first reflections on board ship heading for home was that it was a relief to be free of 'the interminable struggle against being swindled'. In addition to a disrespect for the property and rights of others the Hindu also showed what Corbett conceived to be a lamentable lack of general community or political responsibility, which made any form of collective government difficult to conceive, much less operate. This apparent callousness was slightly offset by the kindness most Hindus exhibited to friends and relations in distress. Yet he felt that the defects of the Indian character were traceable not only to poor religious leadership, but also to the bad government under which the population had groaned for centuries. He thought that this was particularly true of Mysore, and he instanced the 'senseless wars' waged by Haider Ali and Tipu. This was a rather bad example since 'senseless wars' were by no means confined to Indian principalities in the eighteenth century, and since the main enemy of Mysore had been, after all, the East India Company.

That the Indians would ever be fit for self-government he considered unlikely. This was partly owing to the charming eastern tendency to resist uniformity. 'The East abhors uniformity, the West lives by it. Hence the West conquers the East and the East can't understand the West'. It was also a consequence of the natural antipathy of the conservative poor farmer to change or reform. It owed something to the lack of moral and political responsibility already mentioned. More particularly, however, Corbett traced political ineptitude to the naturally unmilitary nature of the Hindu, whom he likened to lambs who would be at the mercy of the first lions who moved against them if ever the British withdrew. For this reason the education for self-government that some people advocated would, in the long run, be wasted effort. 'Good government' could be given to the Indians and they could benefit by it, but if self-government depended on Europeanization then it would never come, since the Indians could never be made into Europeans.

It seemed to Corbett that British rule was likely to go on for an incalculable time. After all, he was a creature of his own times, and, despite certain wry reflections on his own reaction, he was proud to be a member of the conquering race. One could not help enjoying being treated as an important person. After being greeted with ceremonial courtesy by a local dignitary he, and Charles, 'swaggered'. 'I think I was meant for a King', he wrote, since it all seemed to come so naturally. Also it is clear that the brothers did not hesitate to make use of their birthright when the occasion seemed to demand it. For example when transport animals were not available in the hour of need, on their terms, Julian described how they simply 'requisitioned' what they wanted, blandly commenting that otherwise travel in India would be impossible.

Finally, he was in no doubt as to what provided the ultimate sanction for their style of travel in India, and indeed for Englishmen being in India in the first place. Government was not carried on by 'moral pressure', as some were keen in asserting, but 'by the rod'. Yet he was quick to note that even with force at one's back the moral purpose of the rulers themselves would not stand out for long against the immensity of India's problems and the lethargy that a long stay there seemed to breed. The British, he thought, owed their continued strength to the rotation system which systematically retired old lags and kept the Indians face to face with men who came out fresh, filled with enthusiasm, with the idea that they were born rulers, and with some capacity for hard work. It seemed to him to be one of the better features of Lord Lytton's governorship, that the demands of duty were enforced on Europeans, and Corbett noted the fact that Lytton kept the British hard at their work even in the hot weather. This had, he felt, impressed the Indian peoples enormously.

Thus Corbett left India with the consciousness of having successfully carried out a great personal physical adventure in a vast, exotic, and perplexing land. The experience undoubtedly fanned the intense fire of nationalism that smouldered within him, to emerge at a much later date. In the 1890s when it became fashionable for literary people to write of the glories of Empire he had undoubtedly a clearer idea of what 'Empire' meant than most of them. Furthermore it is interesting that the future naval historian should think highly of Calcutta because of its link with the sea. He commented on its strategic importance. The most important result of the tour, however, was that if Corbett was perceptive about some aspects of Indian life and the impact of alien cultures on each other, he was mostly impressed by the over-all value of what his countrymen were doing there. He concluded that English liberalism was not exportable to India.

2

AMERICA AND THE SEARCH FOR A CAREER

The same spirit of adventure and curiosity that drove the Corbett brothers to India in 1877-8, propelled them across the North Atlantic the following year. This time Charles and Julian took their brother Bertie with them. They travelled with their country neighbour Maurice Macmillan of the publishing family, leaving England in mid-July, and returning before the first of November. In a little more than three months they saw a good deal of the continent north of the Rio Grande. In the east they visited the cities of Boston, New York, Washington and Philadelphia in addition to sampling the scenic attractions of the White Mountains, the Lake Champlain-Hudson River area and, of course the mighty falls on the Niagara River. Westward they visited Chicago, still rebuilding after the fire, and moved on to the Rocky Mountains by way of St. Louis, Kansas City and Denver, Colorado. In the South they visited Nashville, Charleston, and Richmond. Despite this full schedule upwards of a week was spent in Canada moving, by rail and water, from Toronto to Kingston, Montreal and Quebec City.

As they had made their own way in India so they did in the New World. With the exception of family friends of the Macmillans in New York they travelled about on their own. The trip differed from the Indian one in that it was carried on at breakneck pace, for although they encountered primitive means of transportation, the visitors were never very far from the omnipresent railroad which always stood ready to hurl them into yet another part of the country. Indeed, the America they saw was one vast hotel-railroad syndrome and the few times that they escaped from this tyranny, such as at Niagara Falls, Quebec, and in the Rocky Mountains, Corbett was able to write his most vivid and entertaining descriptions. For he thought the America he saw in transit was the real America. This was, and is, a common tourist conclusion in all countries. Corbett's viewpoint also owed something to the fact that he was an Englishmen just back from the contemplation of his countrymen in the role of rulers of a teeming sub-continent. The people he had met there were not inclined to dispute the superiority, moral, scientific and political, that the rulers tacitly assumed. In India he was one of the conquerors, a subject of what was obviously the greatest Empire in the world. The people of India could therefore be discussed with tolerant good humour and with the easy superiority that the Englishman felt over the Asian. In the United States the people Corbett met were by no means convinced of any British superiority: indeed the United States as a nation had been founded on a rejection of England. For Americans the whole bedrock of their national pride required constant reminding that Europe in general bred an inferior kind of man. They, in turn, felt that Englishmen were members of a nation whose premier position was fast passing to the giant of the New World. This viewpoint was not only held by vast numbers of Americans, but often freely expressed by them in a way that was hardly calculated to appeal to English visitors.

Like many visiting Englishmen Corbett's views were conditioned by his preconceptions. Their tourist activity, in a sense, involved the verification of those preconceptions. In this sense Corbett was a conventional English traveller in America. Looking for bragging citizens in a too-free democracy besmirched by a lack of tolerance for aesthetic things, and with corruption omnipresent in their politics, he found them. His descriptions of New York, apart from apt descriptions of the physical site, reveal his prejudices. People he had never previously met opened conversations with him on a personal level; too much iced water was served with bad food; and American accomplishments were impressed upon him by people whose patriotic faith invariably outshone their store of accurate comparative information, and whose seriousness of purpose in speaking of local virtues was seldom tempered by the exercise of a sense of humour or self-criticism.

Corbett was impressed by the economic stir and bustle that was manifested on all sides, but he was appalled at the way respect for individual rights was too easily sacrificed on the altar of progress. In New York, for instance, the newly constructed 'elevated' railway, he deduced, was built by contract jobbers who showed scant respect for the property rights of others, or for the public welfare when it was not translatable into quick profit. Men who knew little and cared less about European transportation systems confidently asserted that such a phenomenon as their 'elevated' would soon be emulated by every up and coming capital in Europe. Boston, in contrast, he found more sedate and cultured. He was impressed by its architecture, the scale of Harvard University, and an art gallery which housed some of the best paintings he had ever seen.

Corbett did not find the South particularly interesting, or at least he formed no settled views concerning its place in the Union and the social differences that existed there. The negro did interest him strongly. He wrote, 'they are a delightful race these negroes; stupid, ignorant and coarse certainly, but still so good tempered'. It was wonderful, he thought, how they laughed and flashed their white teeth continually, especially when the joke happened to be against themselves. They made up somewhat for Yankee seriousness.

The West really captured Corbett's interest and secured his approbation. This more magnanimous feeling began to assert itself in Chicago. If America was a country devoted to hustling business activity, this phoenix rising from the ashes of a terrible fire exemplified all that was good and far-sighted in that ethos. Carefully planned wide thoroughfares, terrific economic activity, and rising buildings that were as grand as any in European capitals all pleased him. Furthermore, Chicago exhibited in its 'Exposition' a collection of etchings that reflected taste and discrimination. Even the customary visit to the slaughter houses did not lower the city in his estimation, for faint liberal humanitarian disgust at the bloody work of the charnel house was overborne by his liberal approval for the efficiency of the mass production methods employed.

The far west of the frontier was superb.

These western people are most delightful, quite unlike the Easterners. There is none of that swagger that is so unpleasant there. They are for the most part strong tall well-made men with rugged manly faces that are worth a thousand handsome ones as we understand it in effete Europe and they talk to you in a frank genial way as though they thought there could be nothing but good fellowship between man and man. I don't like my travels to make me think less of the old country but I can't help seeing how much better this is than the way in which we Englishmen, the young ones especially sniff at each other and put on some beastly affected airs when we meet. Now here when you are thrown in with a man, he at once begins to talk in a natural way that isn't familiar or deferential or anything but just natural as one human being to another. Very often he pulls out a great dirty card with his name printed thereon in huge capitals. This is if he has one, if not he says — my name's so and so, and I live on blank street — and hope you'll come and call. Then you give him yours which he reads out loud for his own instruction and says he's very glad to have met you. Then, he'll introduce you to the first friend of his he meets. His friend thrusts out his hand, generally up here taken from an ore begrimed coat and so dirty that the mould comes off on your hand. When he hears you come from England, he says he's very glad to have met you and instead of guessing that you've nothing like this in the old country he begins to tell you all he can that will interest you and takes apparently a keen delight in answering all your questions. You have no idea how charming all this is. People say it wouldn't do for all men to be equal but it seems to run here alright. You address a miner or a millionaire (and we have talked to some of each) equally as Sir.

It was travel itself that dominated his stay in the United States and his comments on the facilities were profuse and sometimes pungent. He had visited the Eastern States in the local holiday season, and then, as now, those Americans who could afford to travel were on the move. He had plenty of opportunity to observe them, and what he saw did not greatly appeal to him. At strategic places along the routes of travel there were stationed great wooden 'palaces' generally relatively larger than the other buildings in the community (and in Saratoga N.Y. that meant very large indeed). These buildings were devoid of architectural charm, and inside were hardly comparable to the select chalets available in Switzerland. They were the noisiest, most prominent, and crowded places in the communities. Not only were they filled with tourists who remained on perpetual parade, but their lobbies and writing rooms and lounges were filled with a good proportion of the local population who came to sit, stare, lounge, chew, and spit. It seemed to him that the American male was always chewing: tobacco was the preferred morsel, closely followed in popularity by toothpicks. In fact it seemed that the men nearly always had to remove something from their mouths before they could speak. With regard to spitting, that vile habit was so universal that it was a tribute to British digestive hardiness and the ultimate pressure of hunger, that the transatlantic visitors ate at all, since they generally passed through rooms featuring the art of expectoration when on the way to dinner. There was, in short, nothing attractive in coming to rest in one of these circuses after a day of travel or sight-seeing, and sitting down to iced water and too much food badly served.

The Canadian visit took Corbett into a part of north America that was more like England in many ways. Indeed Toronto produced one of the only favourable comments on hotel food that appears in the correspondence. The buildings there, he felt, were much more solid and permanent than the American ones, and he had high praise for the architecture of the University of Toronto. On the other hand he could see that Toronto, Kingston and Montreal did not give that 'go-ahead' impression of American cities; indeed Montreal seemed to be a city in a state of decay rather than of growth. The Canadians appeared to be slower than the Americans at everything, and this extended even to their physical movements.

There were good things. Niagara surpassed what he had seen in India. He came to the Falls in the rain, and the combination of wet weather and excessive commercialization made a bad first impression, but as the weather improved and the falls were viewed from different angles his opinion changed, and his growing feeling of awe is clear in both his letters and his sketch book. On the way to Montreal the party spent a day amongst the Thousand Islands just east of Kingston, and the solitude, beauty and grandeur of that wilderness struck him forcibly and permanently. He easily succumbed to the old world charm of Quebec City, where an antique charm was enhanced by the majestic sweep of the St. Lawrence river. Impressions heightened by patriotic memories produced more of a sense of mood than he felt his pen adequate to convey. Corbett, of course, was later to make Quebec City a strong focal point for his *England and the Seven Years' War.* That his visual experience of this place helped him in writing the relevant parts of his book there can be no doubt — but in 1879 he wrote home that Wolfe had made his attack on the Beauport Shore, east of the city, the day before his forces scrambled up the slopes from Anse du Foulon, an assertion that was false. He was not yet an historian: just a tourist sorting out impressions. Yet he had acquired romantic memories that were to prove useful in the future.

Julian Corbett left the United States understanding a good deal about its physical make up, and about the looks, habits, sights and sounds produced by its population — but apparently without having seriously considered the deep political problems that its inhabitants faced and had fought over. In fact he had seen North America through a spasmodic viewfinder mounted on a moving platform; he had, in short, 'done' America in much the same way as North Americans then and since 'do' Europe to-day. The total impression he carried away did not make him less of a patriot.

As his bachelor years rolled by he continued to travel. He was an almost annual visitor to Norway and Italy. In Norway he roughed it and fished. In Rome he mingled with the sophisticated international set. In Norway he had met and talked with Ibsen, and thereafter attended the Norwegian's plays regularly as they reached the London stage. The Italian visit brought him into contact with Mark Twain who found his company congenial and at one stage tried to promote some of Corbett's literary work in America, without success. 'Imagine', Corbett wrote, 'my living to take him about Rome as a real innocent abroad'. The two wandered amongst the ancient scenes and frequently stopped to talk, seated on 'a ruined column'. 'It is extraordinary how some experience of his old wild life in the West will illustrate a classical episode and I feel as if I were seeing Rome under a light that makes it as fresh as it was the first time I saw it'.

A visit to Algeria in 1890 was a variant to this routine. Julian's brother Frank still suffered from tuberculosis and his doctors recommended sun. They found it on the southern shores of the Mediterranean and for a few months travelled constantly. They had ample opportunity to observe the French colonizer and Arab colonized at first hand. The Arabs, who lavished princely entertainment on their guests, they regarded as remote, nevertheless individualistic and full of character. The admiration appears to have been mutual. The Corbetts found the French, on the other hand, 'not quite gentlemen', friendly, helpful, but uninteresting. It was a bracing time for Frank, and a useful point of comparison with his Indian and North American experiences for Julian.

At home his circle of friends included the Macmillans and others such as Hallam Tennyson, Mary Cholmondley, Rudyard Kipling, Hilaire Belloc, Arthur Conan Doyle, Henry Newbolt, Mrs J.R. Green and the historian S.R. Gardiner.

After turning his back on the law and painting Julian started writing. The Macmillans encouraged this aspiration, and he wrote a number of novels: *The Fall of Asgard* (1886) a Norse heroic tale; *Kopethua the XIII* (1889) a political story concerning the court of an imaginary island off the coast of Africa; and *A Business in Great Waters* (1894) a story of naval support for the French revolutionary rising in the Vendée. The most important of these, however, was *For God and Gold* (1887) which described piracy and policy in Elizabethan England. None of these novels achieved a signal success. Reviewers generally agreed that 'his sentences were worth reading', but they marked his tendency to fall between the two objects of writing credible history on the one hand, the creating believable characters in the historical situation on the other. It was also noted that serious discussion of events was often curiously mixed with the sort of 'broadsword bashing' that one would expect to find in action stories for boys. The criticisms seem, in retrospect, to have been perceptive and just. His incipient and real sense of history prevented him from delineating either great heroic figures or ordinary mortals in sympathetic terms. Even later when he acquired the talent for making political viewpoints and military plans understandable to any educated and attentive reader he could not suffuse his historical personalities with flesh and blood. Lord Nelson himself finally eluded him — not as a naval genius but as a man.

What then is the connection between these diverse novels and the mature naval historian who emerged by 1897? It is not too difficult to trace. *For God and Gold* had led Corbett to look for the real reasons behind the sea activities of Francis Drake. He did not investigate precise documentary history for that but, by a process of wide literary reading, acquired what might be called an empathy for the period and his political effects were more sophisticated, if less easily achieved, than those Kingsley had displayed in *Westward Ho* and

J.A. Froude in *The Elizabethan Seamen*. When in 1889 Macmillan asked him to produce a volume on George Monck, Duke of Albemarle for their 'Brief Lives' series, he consented. The volume is still worth reading and both author and publisher were impressed by the impact the book achieved with an economy of words. Pressed by the publisher he made cuts widely, without complaint, and yet kept the main lineaments plain. Not an easy achievement for any historian. Perhaps he was saved from folly by his lack of formal academic training in the discipline. Consequently he and his publishers easily agreed on terms for a 'Brief Lives' volume on Drake.

When completed this book was easily as good a production as *Monk*. However, more was known about Drake and so Corbett brought the wrath of the historians' trade union upon himself. Sweeping generalizations were not permitted to pass. How frustrating! For Corbett himself had come to understand, as his researches had progressed in the British Museum, that Froude had not said the last word, and he possessed a good deal more evidence than he allowed to appear for reasons of space.

So the question remained — what was he attempting to accomplish? Corbett was not a little disconcerted and embittered towards his critics. Almost at that moment his mother died. His pattern of life at forty-five was disrupted and he looked for a new path. He began to court Rosa Alexander, the shy and socially retiring daughter of the family's old Manchester friends. He gave the historical novel one more try — (*A Business in Great Waters*) — and when the public reaction was clearly negative this challenge to write a more significant work on Drake stood out in an unambigious way. Furthermore, the Navy Records Society had just been founded as a scholarly but self-conscious reaction against foreign naval growth and challenge. Miss Alexander encouraged him in history, and so he began to write *Drake and the Tudor Navy*.[1] When it was published it was at once acknowledged as a towering historical success. Doubts were ended. At the age of fifty he had forged a career; an amateur who had written a professional work that none of his contemporaries could match. Based on archival sources and in a detailed way that no one had previously attempted, he had enlarged at once the Elizabethan world, the perceived importance of the beginnings of English sea power, and his own reputation.

Drake and The Tudor Navy was followed, swiftly, by *The Successors*

---

1   2 vols. (London, Longmans, 1898).

of Drake,[1] a book that tidied up the loose ends of Elizabethan naval warfare. In fact the three volumes constitute a trilogy and ought to be read together. What made these books so formidable and obviously magisterial? It had been noted that Corbett could not convincingly delineate characters. That defect was not overcome. On the positive side was the fact that he consciously based his descriptions of naval growth on State papers and those that were available to him in private hands. Yet John Knox Laughton, the famous Greenwich mathematics professor, who became professor of history at King's College, University of London, and J.P. Oppenheim, also used such sources. It is important to note that the doyen of these naval writers, A.T. Mahan, the American, only came to the careful use of documentary and manuscript sources as his career developed. Corbett combined the virtues of the Laughton and Mahan approaches. From Mahan he learned, not meticulous use of detailed sources, but the salient fact that to pursue the minutiae of naval activity without a constant reference to the main purposes that generated that activity, was to wilfully distort historical perspective. *Drake and The Tudor Navy* had plenty of action description in it, but those exhilarating events were firmly subordinated to the controlling theme of developing maritime and even State policy. Every powerful writer on maritime history since that time has recognized the importance of this approach.

There is no written evidence to confirm that this approach came from Mahan who had first applied it in masterful fashion to British sea affairs, but it is wise to suggest that it did. More probably it was a product of Corbett's association with S.R. Gardiner, who followed such a practice in his seventeenth century studies, and who constantly stimulated and encouraged Corbett in his work. However, to this dedication to original sources and subordination technique Corbett brought two further qualities; imagination and a flexible and accurate narrative prose style.

Many writers of eminence have dilated on the use of the imagination by persons of genius. Corbett's imaginative abilities may not have included the ability to humanize his characters — this is true of many capable writers and formidable thinkers, Coleridge and Disraeli among them. But they could bring great ideas and historical trends, as they perceived them, before the minds of more ordinary mortals in vivid and cohesive fashion. Corbett possessed this talent, or capacity, to a high degree. He understood the way in which great projects conceived in the brains of planners of high ability acquired almost a

[1] London, 1900.

will of their own when launched on the sea of seemingly discordant movements. But it was his special quality that he could be the prose poet of British sea nationalism, for he understood, or claimed, that the best conceptual minds of statesmen and high naval personalities were those which attuned themselves, through a combination of instinct and study, to the traditions and possibilities of the State they served. This meant for him that, so tuned, such ideas were essentially limited in purpose when applied to warfare, and ultimately defensive in effect. Writers today, looking back on the phenomenon of the British Sea Empire often perceive it in terms of 'make her mightier yet'. Corbett saw it first in terms of a protective mechanism guaranteeing British security, and second, of a force to prevent Europe from falling under the control of one country with unlimited ambitions or objectives. The controlling factor for Corbett was that he never saw England's active sea traditions and responses as breaking the restrictive bonds that the developing traditions imposed, clearly and sensibly, on national or naval planners. He surveyed, from the palmy days of the Empire 'on which the sun never set', the historical beginnings of Britian at sea, with imaginative eyes that made it, by the very restrictions imposed by its traditional nature, a force for moderation, balance, peace and, ultimately, civilized values. Such was the strength and power of his imagination that he could subdue the ebb and flow of warfare into the mould of limited State policy, and cement this conception in the readers' mind by showing how humble an instrument sea power was when it came to winning wars. Yet he demonstrated that naval effects were important. He often did this by showing how apparently small occurrences, like the sailing of a small body of troops, a despatch lost at sea, or the vagaries of the weather, could frustrate any grand *offensive* designs. This was made possible by a command of language that marshalled tradition with changing cause and effect, with a lawyer's expertise. If his evidence was original so his effects were often contrived (as R.C. Anderson orally pointed out to me in a forcible way). His literary talents were equal to the purposes of his wonderfully subtle mind; a mind that none of his contemporaries matched in print on the subject he chose to make his own.

Before going on to delineate the special way in which Corbett saw sea power work, a viewpoint firmly and irrevocably worked out in his Drake studies, it is necessary to comment on his lack of economic preoccupation. Unlike Sir John Colomb, and even Mahan, he worked out his strategic-historical constructs not in ignorance of, but without frequent reference to, trade and commerce. He understood their existence yet never emphasized such factors. It may be that his own economic security — for he was comfortably off if not rich by the standards of the time — made him disdainful of trade activity. He wrote disparagingly of the 'adoration of the cash box' with the easy superiority of the comfortably off. It is merely a question of emphasis, to be sure, but the emphasis is important for Corbett's books deftly married warfare to high State policy in a way that made it all look heroic, pristine, attractive and perhaps somewhat unreal from our end of the twentieth century.

Finally, the strength of the Drake books, as well as all of his subsequent writings, was based not only on Corbett's perception of the central position that must be given to State policy but also on a clear understanding of the fact that military means were limited by tradition and geography. The fact was that without careful welding of army and navy capabilities Britain's power to effect anything would be seriously restricted. This is a most important point in view of the sensible work that Michael Howard has produced to illustrate England's real position in terms of twentieth century actualities.[1] Howard hardly mentions Corbett, and in terms of short term influence he is right to ignore him. But Corbett's purpose was to influence Britain's overall military stance no matter how much or little he succeeded, and his views were developed in his first books — not completely, but in fundamentals. It is impossible to say whether he was a devotee of army-navy co-operation before he wrote the Drake books. The question is interesting only because, as has been indicated, he was not above attempting to contrive his efforts before his researches were complete. Be that as it may, the lesson that he allowed to emerge from these early books was, that if armies were not adequate to, and tailored for, war work based on fleet-connected possibilities, and if fleets were not sensitive to real army potential, then British policy was, either way, based on unrealistic strategic thought. This was because his mind was turned to defensive purposes and limited effects for reasons already explained. This is a vital point. For, just at the moment that Sir George Clark and J.R. Thursfield[2] began to advocate service co-operation, the Drake book appeared from the hand of a man with no apparent axe to grind and no official or academic position to maintain. It clearly provided weighty historical evidence and impressive historical judgements for the position Clarke and Thursfield had put forward.

Thus, when Julian Corbett had finished his first scholarly history, he had come to his more important conclusion about British strategy,

1 Michael Howard, *The Continental Commitment* (London, 1972).

2 George Clarke and James Thursfield, *The Navy and the Nation* (London, 1976 r 7).

past and present. It was that the Army and Navy were mutually dependent, not mutually exclusive, arms of Britain's military power. Adherents to the so-called Blue Water School often wrote as though an army was a luxury to which a sea power granted an occasional indulgence to exist and operate. Pro-army men often wrote as though a navy was a luxury in an age of great-power continental politics based on army strengths. Corbett, of course, was a sea historian but he was not a sea power fanatic in any exclusivist sense. Always his pen was used on the side of balance, and moderated by references to historical precedents. He never made the classic mistake of those sea or land apologists who confused the aims of one service with the national policy of the State. His books were about statesmen striving to achieve national objectives, who used the services to achieve these aims, and who kept service purposes subordinate to those of the Nation. His opinion was not that there were too many soldiers, or not enough ships, but that the historical arguments for a blending of the services to achieve national purposes were improperly understood. His real enemies were indifference, ignorance and 'tunnel vision' in both services, and amongst their political masters. He did not write in a way that naval officers always understood or appreciated. He never wrote with the ultimate purpose of putting only one service dog in the policy kennel.

The subsequent delineation of Corbett's career will reveal how impossible it was for a man, with no position of personal power to sustain him, to decisively influence the plans of powerful men who could feed good copy to their press supporters, and reward their service supporters with promotion and passage along the path of the British honours system. Corbett was not immune to the blandishments of the powerful, nor ultimately from the rewards of the system, but he remained true to his original basic tenets and wrote important books, even official histories, without giving up his intellectual integrity. Ironically, his long term reward was to be acclaimed by the historians who, as a breed, he had scorned for such a long time; and to be largely ignored by the Service to which he had dedicated his intellectual abilities.

3

NEW BOY AT THE ADMIRALTY

Before beginning to describe Corbett's connection with the Royal Navy in the Dreadnought era it is important to grasp that what influence he possessed was based on his book production. From the point of view of his relationship to other historical writing, that has been discussed in my *Education of a Navy*.[1] The use of his historical writings to provide some sea power principles in the post Dreadnought Age is described in the next chapter. His publication achievement was staggering — he wrote or edited eleven volumes between 1895 and 1914. Thus it is vital to comprehend that the pages following describe activity that was carried on in addition to, and parallel with, continuous work at serious scholarship. For most people such historical production would only have been possible by following an exacting schedule; one that permitted little else. Corbett managed to find time, as will be seen, for much else.

In describing this activity no attempt has been made to dwell particularly on Corbett's private life. In any case, sufficient evidence does not exist for that, nor can one see that it would be desirable or instructive to probe into family affairs. But the pattern of his life did change when he became a serious historian, and married. Generally speaking his private life was serene. His children, Elizabeth and Richard, held him in great affection. Because of his wife's dislike of formal social activity, the family tended to live quietly. Small intimate dinner parties were the general rule for the Corbetts in London, and they spent a good part of each year in their much loved Sussex countryside — most often at Stopham Farm, near Pulborough. Elizabeth had a tonsilectomy in 1905, one of the first in England. Richard's chief difficulty was a great hatred of leaving home for public school, and the separations due to the rigours of British educational customs were endured but not liked by Corbett himself. Julian sometimes overworked, and was then ordered on rest cures in the country by his doctors. He did not perform well under secular mental stress and at times of crisis this tendency sometimes caused him to retire, temporarily, to his room.

The family enjoyed the pleasures of London, and were more playgoers than music addicts. Ibsen, Shaw, and Conan Doyle drew them out. Modern music did not attract them. Like most Londoners they

[1] D.M. Schurman, *The Education of a Navy* (London, 1965), pp. 147-84.

took the pomp and circumstance affairs of their city as a way of life. Incidentally, Corbett became a friend of Elgar's during the musician's declining years. In London the family lived in easy circumstances at number three, Hans Crescent, in Knightsbridge. There Corbett worked and kept his books. There Elizabeth and her friend Peggy Sichel were privately educated together. There the family remained from the time of the sale of Imber Court in 1900 until after Corbett died in 1922.

The nature of his work dictated that Corbett spent a good deal of time at home in his study. Most of the printed references necessary to his research he purchased. In the case of documentary materials, he made frequent sorties to the Public Records Office, the British Museum, the Library of the Royal United Services Institution and the Admiralty Library. As he became more involved in the writing of official history, and after the beginning of World War I, he spent more time at the home of the Committee of Imperial Defence (2 Whitehall Gardens), where he received and sorted the documents on which his history was based. Work at home then, punctuated by visits to places where he could find documents and men to discuss them with was the regular pattern of his life. He was a member of the Council of the Navy Records Society, a member of the Coefficients Society (a dining society composed of men interested primarily in the social condition of England). After 1913, he was a member of the Athenaeum and lunched there frequently. All of this was punctuated by visits at least twice a year to the War Course at Portsmouth.

Of all the people Corbett worked with the most interesting and helpful was Admiral Edmond Slade, whom he met when Slade was a Captain at the War Course, Portsmouth. Also important was W.G. Perrin, the Admiralty Librarian who gave him sound counsel and was a foil for Corbett's energetic mind. His association with O.T. Tuck[1] at the CID was of long standing, and his co-operation with Maurice Hankey[2] was to stand him in good stead when war allowed Hankey to wield extraordinary power from important secretarial positions. As the Official History progressed he was helped much by Lt. Col. E.Y. Daniel, R.M., of the CID who was first his associate in connection with the Russo-Japanese War, and also by Edith Keate who was a pleasant and unique combination of family friend and research assistant. These were the people, institutions, and boundaries within which Julian Corbett lived his semi-public life.

---

1   Instructor Commander O.T. Tuck, R.N.
2   Hankey worked at the C.I.D. and became its secretary in 1913.

Corbett's interest was naturally tuned to the modern Royal Navy because of his interest in its past. But there was more to it than that. Aside from his pleasure in the company of men of power, the Senior Naval Officers, he was impelled to involvement by his romantic temperament. It is easy to see how the romantic approach to ships and seamen so vividly displayed in Corbett's early books could naturally be expected to expand whenever he was brought into close contact with modern steel monsters of the deep, and with the glamorous and slightly mysterious men who manned and commanded them. To his (then) fiancée, Edith Alexander he laid bare the thrill of patriotic exaltation that was created by his visit to the fleet during the Jubilee Review of 1897.[1] That mammoth Review had been calculated to impress, and Corbett easily caught the congenial mood. He saw 'rows and rows of quiet tremendous monsters — twenty-five miles of them'. He watched them break out their flags and fire Royal Salutes. 'All was so smart and uniform and terribly strong — deadly'. It sent shivers up and down his spine.

It was not his first Review. But he had not fully realized, during the festivities of 1887, what a 'great and powerful fleet it was. It is quite different from then. Ten years ago it seemed a mass of ships got together anyhow for the occasion — now it was all new and homogeneous and business-like, as though, if the *Renown* had given the signal, they would have all gone off in a moment, just as they decked themselves out with flags, and knocked the bottom out of the ends of the earth. It made me more glad than ever that I was writing about the sea'. When the Royal Yacht came to anchor 'the whole twenty-five miles cheered together and my spine crept again . . . I can never forget it all. No one knew what our Navy was and the foreigners they say have all gone away sadder and wiser men'. This romantic, deep feeling of reverence that Corbett felt for the naval service never completely left him thereafter, it only needed a practical opportunity so that adulation could be transformed into service. What *is* surprising is that when the time came he was able to subdue his romantic instincts sufficiently to act as a prudent, judicious, scholarly critic or advocate — as various occasions demanded.

Membership in the new Navy Records Society also drew Corbett close to men preoccupied with the modern navy. But two things happened in 1900 that speeded the *rapprochement*. The first was Longmans' publication of his second serious book, *The Successors of Drake*. Whereas his earlier work had striven to explain the organic ties that bound the growth of sea power to strategy, this new volume had

1   Corbett to E.R. Alexander 2.VII.97; CP/B9.

a more direct, practical, message concerning the actual proportions of military force to be used by Great Britain in war. This book convinced him that the lack of decisive English success in the sixteenth century was directly traceable not to the stupidity of Queen Elizabeth's strategic policy nor even to the manner in which sea-power was deployed, but rather to the lack of a proper army, and army organization, to exploit naval opportunities. This clear conclusion was later noticed by Professor Laughton, the naval historian, who wrote, in support of Corbett,[1] that 'in the case of an insular power a navy can ward off attacks and prevent invasions, but it cannot unaided achieve more than negative results. The moral is one which some extreme advocates of the so-called "Blue-Water" school would do well to take into consideration'. In the United States too the argument for close interdependence of army and navy in any great war was noticed.[2]

At the beginning of an age in which the army and navy were to rival one another strenuously in their strivings for the largest share of the national budget, this kind of conclusion was bound to attract attention, even if it did not convert the heads of the rival departments to Corbett's ideas. Corbett shared his viewpoint with Major G.S. Clarke, later Lord Sydenham of Coombe, whose strong advocacy of joint service planning and whose attempt to change it was eventually responsible for his resignation as Secretary of the Committee of Imperial Defence in 1907.[3]

At the same moment that his book came out Corbett acquired another platform from which to expound his view. In September 1900 the first issue of the *Monthly Review* was published, and Corbett's friend of four years' standing, Henry Newbolt, was its editor. The *Monthly Review* was a periodical that undertook to dilate upon Great Britain's responsibilities as a great power. Nevertheless, the political bias of the paper was Liberal. It was not preoccupied with social questions at home except when they appeared to affect the prestige of the country in the world; it professed the ideas of Lord Rosebery, not those of Lloyd George. Its contributors included such literary figures as Sir Arthur Quiller-Couch, W.B.

1 *Edinburgh Review*, July 1904, p. 160.

2 Review by W.F. Tilton, *American Historical Review*, April 1901, p. 555.

3 Sir George Clarke had most seriously irritated the Admiralty by making comments on the Navy's strength in comparison to foreign navies. The Admiralty felt that this sort of judgement was outside Clarke's province as defined by his appointment. But the Admiralty Board also issued the judgement that 'he is a retired soldier, and entirely without knowledge of the fighting requirements of the Fleet . . . ', *Private and Secret* 'Statement regarding Admiralty responsibility for the strength of the Navy'. July 1906. PRO. CAB. 421/1 and Adm 1/3095.

Yeats and Rudyard Kipling: politicians such as Lord Rosebery, R.B. Haldane, and Alfred Milner. It involved military writers such as Spencer Wilkinson, Captain Carlyon Bellairs R.N., J.C.R. Colomb, Lt. Col. Maude, H.W. Wilson and Corbett. Its message was Liberal-Imperial, but Newbolt found room for intelligent Canadian dissenters from Imperial fever such as Goldwin Smith and Henri Bourassa. Newbolt himself had a considerable reputation as a poet although his professional background, like Corbett's, was the law. Between 1900 and 1904, Newbolt's years at the *Review,* the contact between Corbett and the editor was close and frequent. Their letters display an ardent patriotic fervour coupled with a sense of boyish adventure that bubbled like champagne. Only their preoccupations, the German menace, military unpreparedness, and the Imperial 'mission' betrayed the sense of insecurity lurking behind the bright citadel of national power at that time.

On 19 September 1900, Edith Corbett, on holiday with her husband in the north of England wrote in her *Diary* 'Murray's new magazine *The Monthly Review* published Julian's contribution "The Paradox of Empire", gave it first place'. It was the first of many articles. It was unsigned. Corbett was, of course, a Liberal, and actively supported his brother Charles, who stood frequently, (and in 1906 successfully), as a parliamentary candidate for East Grinstead. In international affairs the menace of the Germans, whom he regarded as the most barbaric of European peoples,[1] impressed on him the need for strengthening British power. At home he desired to help remove dissension amongst Liberals over the question of Imperialism. This long-standing division of opinion had been widened by the shock of the Boer War. Corbett wished, as he put it, 'to see us out of the Little England slough'.[2] Newbolt shared this view. The result was 'The Little Englander', in which Corbett attempted to seduce the holders of that philosophy into the Imperialist camp by publicly commending their virtues, and praising their conviction that 'empire, like charity, begins at home'.[3] That is to say, the critical spirit that distinguished those who shied away from Imperial enthusiasm had its uses. However, Corbett felt it necessary to force anti-Imperialists to face the fact that the Empire did exist, and to advocate that they should 'join hands with their old comrades and try to make the best of it. No one denies that it is a burden, but

1 Their main international attitudes were, in Corbett's view, coloured by envy and jealousy. CP/B3 31. VIII. 1900 to Newbolt. Corbett to Newbolt, 31. VIII. 1900; CP/B3.

2 *Ibid.* 19.VII.1900 to Newbolt. Corbett to Newbolt. 19.VII. 1900.

3 *Monthly Review* January 1901, p. 18.

it is a burden we have to bear and a burden we can lightly bear, if every capable man will put his shoulder under it, and not shrink from the task, however repellent he may feel it to be'. Furthermore they 'must try to feel the inspiration . . . not till then can there be any hope that liberalism can live again to do for the Empire what it has done for the Nation'.

The message was clear, clever, and nervous. It was his opinion that foreigners considered Englishmen to be in a state of recoil and unease after the Boer War. The reverse was the case, asserted Corbett. England had never felt so strong in a military sense. Indeed it was 'ready to take on any army with our recent experience giving us a great advantage'.[1] This was a somewhat extravagant assessment of the experience of the British army in South Africa.

He next examined a more purely naval problem. During 1902, Corbett wrote three articles for the *Monthly Review* entitled 'Education in the Navy'. On Christmas Day of the same year, the Second Sea Lord, Admiral Sir John Fisher, published his 'New Scheme' for naval education.[2] The connection between these facts is traceable, if not close.

Corbett did not initiate discussion on this subject. Everyone in the naval hierarchy and many publicists thought the existing system faulty. The problem was to formulate clear principles on which reform could be built. Captain Carlyon Bellairs and Admiral E.R. Fremantle had both written on this subject in the *Monthly Review* to attempt to secure some action. Both of them had intelligent criticisms to make of the existing system. Both wished to get education out of the hands of the academic and civilian men at Greenwich and back into the hands of proper seafaring men, with emphasis on practical training as opposed to theoretical knowledge.[3] Bellairs's viewpoint was characterized by a tendency to approve of maintaining the custom of separating the Executive and Engineering officers through the various stages of their training despite an instinctive dislike of too much educational preoccupation with training for the material side of the naval profession. In fact, they both saw clearly the disadvantages of having service thought dominated by equipment. Their approach, however, had the

---

1 Corbett to Newbolt 1.X.01; CP/B3.

2 Fisher's Paper was issued by Lord Selborne. (CD 1385).

3 C. Bellairs, 'The War Training of Naval Officers' *Monthly Review,* October 1900; E.R. Fremantle, 'Training of Naval Officers', *Monthly Review,* 1901, C. Bellairs, 'The Navy at School', *ibid.* July-September 1901, October – December 1901 and April-June 1902.

great disadvantage of being instinctive and mainly based on a romantic traditionalism. Modern problems demanded modern solutions, and not just the flexing of traditional muscles. How did the problem look to the men in power at the Admiralty?

When Sir John Fisher became Second Sea Lord, the agitation for educational reform quickened[1] The views of Bellairs and Fremantle and of James R. Thursfield, the Naval Correspondent of *The Times*, attracted the most attention outside the Admiralty. Inside the service, and with official encouragement, others were at work. These included Commander Herbert W. Richmond[2] Admiral Sir William M. Henderson[3] and Rear Admiral Arthur Moore, who had been Fourth Sea Lord until 1901. Fisher seems to have particularly drawn ideas from Moore and Thursfield.[4] Richmond and Henderson were in an intermediate position, attempting to press their views on Moore and Fisher, all within the service. There seems to have been no direct contact between Fisher and Corbett in this regard, but Richmond and Henderson both fed information to Corbett so that he could write powerful articles to whip up public opinion. The intent was to arouse a demand for official action.

Bellairs and Fremantle looked backward to the old days, and shunned the engineers. Richmond and Henderson were more concerned that attempting to combine seamen's duties and school instruction afloat should cease. They agreed that the Public School system did not train officer cadets up to the Navy's standard for entry at age fourteen and a half, but disagreed on whether the Navy's school instructional task should be performed best at a special, (or naval) public school, or at one of the existing public schools in the country[5]

1   See Schurman *Education of a Navy,* pp. 169-70 which briefly comments on Richmond's influence.

2   Richmond, who later commanded battleships and fleets, was an intellectual with strong intelligent views and a passion for service reform. He eventually became a professor at Cambridge, and finally Master of Downing College. He never became First Sea Lord. For his career see A.J. Marder *Portrait of an Admiral* (London, 1952); Schurman, *Education of a Navy,* pp. 110-16; Robin Highman *The Military Intellectuals in Britain 1918-39* (Rutgers U. Press, 1962); pp. 31-5.

3   Henderson was another reformer interested in education who became the First Editor of *The Naval Review,* see C.C. Lloyd. 'Royal Naval Colleges at Portsmouth and Greenwich', *Mariner's Mirror,* May 1966, p. 154.

4   Moore's part comes out clearly in Richmond's correspondence. See NMM. RIC/14/2: Fisher acknowledged Thursfield's ideas on 21 July 1902. See Fisher to Thursfield, A.J. Marder, *Fear God and Dread Nought* 2 vols. (London, 1952), pp. 254-5.

5   Richmond to Henderson 7.VII.02; NMM. RIC/14/2.

Henderson doubted the usefulness of taking boys into the service before they were sixteen.[1]

Richmond consistently and forcibly advocated the principle of 'get 'em young' so dear to the heart of the old salt, and which Fisher finally managed to get enshrined in the 'New Scheme'. Looking back on this amicable argument from the vantage point of the present day, it is impossible not to be impressed with Richmond's intelligent appreciation of the fact that it takes careful planning, a settled environment, and a certain length of time to educate a boy properly on fundamentals.[2] On the other hand, Henderson's view that training was the important thing had something to recommend it. Although circumstances forced the Navy to attempt to educate its own at elementary levels, he could never convince himself that service education for a boy between the ages of twelve and sixteen was likely to be of advantage to either the naval office or the naval service in the long run.[3] One thinks that they were both right. Richmond's argument was based on the quantity of instruction that had to be packed into a few short years; finished Lieutenants were needed at age twenty-two and a half and, consequently time was too compressed to do everything. But Henderson's contention that practical training and responsibility go together and are contingent on maturity has a sound ring to-day, when it is more generally accepted. At the time, however, Fisher, Lord Selborne the First Lord, and Corbett were most impressed by Richmond's arguments and there can be no doubt but that his was the decisive voice in much of the 'New Scheme' that was eventually announced on Christmas Day 1902.[4]

Corbett's first article, written in March 1902, was intended to stir public indignation against the inefficient naval education system in existence at that moment. It condemned the evils of combining formal education with sea training on ships, and clearly bears the marks of Richmond's mind. Nevertheless, Corbett argued the case against conducting naval education in the iron ship age as if the products were intended to be used on wooden vessels. With great force, and despite

1   Henderson to Corbett. encl. in Corbett to Richmond 9.VI.02; NMM RIC/14/2.

2   Richmond to Henderson 7.VI.02; NMM. RIC/14/2.

3   Henderson to Richmond 26.XII.02, NMM. RIC/14/2. Although Richmond himself wrote out a long list of complaints against the final version in a letter to Corbett dated 31.XII.02; NMM. RIC/14/2.

4   For 'The Scheme' see (CD 1385) In July, Corbett had written to Newbolt (9.VII.02) to say that Selborne was impressed but that Fisher was too busy to devote proper attention to the problem. NMM. RIC/14/2.

the fact that he had found it difficult, as a civilian, to acquire expert knowledge on a service matter, he put forward a clear logical argument.

A second powerful article appeared in April, and again Richmond's influence could be seen, as Corbett argued in favour of using time properly, and of gaining as much of it as possible by 'getting 'em young'. Corbett's own contribution was to set before the public a priority system to assist in making judgements. It was his way of approaching problems, and it was this, almost reflex action on his part, that distinguished his writings from those of most of his contemporaries – he could put a searchlight in the public reader's eye. Also he improved on Richmond's preoccupation with a shortage of time by directly attacking the unhelpful public schools where 'games were cultivated at the cost of half its boys wits'. Corbett advocated a course of basic instruction on shore for very young boys, conducted by or on behalf of the Navy, to be followed by long periods of sea time where practical skills might be learnt, along with a smattering of naval history, strategy and tactics. The young man's sea time should be broken by periods of leave on shore to allow for the release of animal spirits, and then, when all the practical training was complete, the Greenwich course, run like a war college, and dealing with the higher aspects of the naval profession, should be undergone. The ultimate aim was not to provide a complete higher naval education for each Lieutenant, but, rather, to provide a basic education on which the best of the young officers would continue to build more knowledge in the future.

Corbett's final article on this subject presented a clear historical picture of the fate of various schemes aimed at securing basic reform in the naval education system since 1870. Investigating committees on naval education appear to have been almost as recurrent as Admiralty Board personnel changes, but nothing ever happened as a result of their work. Actually, all of the investigating men, and bodies, had agreed on the need not to confuse practical sea training with general education, and all had come to grief in that 'graveyard of endeavour' – Whitehall. Remorselessly, therefore, Corbett set out the case against atrophy at the top – on the Board and amongst the politicians. He concluded with the assertion that the Second Sea Lord, at the moment Fisher, had too much work to do to enable him to deal with the problem. This was, strategically speaking, the most important article of the three. The spring-time agitation whipped up by Thursfield and himself seemed to have attracted a certain amount of attention,[1] and the authorities

---

1   Fisher to Thursfield 26.XIII.02; Marder *Fear God*, I, p. 268.

then seemed to be cooling. Corbett's article, therefore, struck just the right note at the right time, and officialdom, returning from holiday, was faced in late September with a challenge that it was difficult to ignore. Fisher wrote to Thursfield in December that the education scheme had top priority, indeed it had become important enough to stake his career upon. He also wrote to Newbolt to say that the *Monthly Review* had been a powerful influence in getting the thing done.[1] It was all very satisfactory, and a triumph for Fisher's methods of using publicity, Richmond's and Thursfield's basic thought, and Corbett's sense of timing and skill as a writer. But the controlling mind was Fisher's.

The year 1902 also saw the beginning of Corbett's long and intimate association with the Naval War Course. The War Course was first formally set up, as such, in 1900 under the direction of Captain W.J. May. Actually it had its origins in the history and strategy lectures given by John Knox Laughton at Greenwich before he left to go to King's College, London. After Laughton departed a series of six lectures a year on Naval Tactics was delivered by Vice Admiral P.H. Colomb, between 1887 and 1895. Colomb's influence with naval authorities was lessened by his propensity to public discussion of naval subjects in the press.[2] From 1895-1900 May took over these lectures until the more ambitious course was set up in the latter year. The model for the new departure was the American War College, which had been set up, in the teeth of American conservative opposition and political apathy, by Admiral Stephen Luce and Captain A.T. Mahan a little more than a decade previously. In the case of the Royal Navy the American idea was 'altered to suit the different conditions under which the work was to be carried out'.[3] The original course was of eight months duration, and was designed to include study in Strategy, Tactics, Naval History, and International Law as basic courses, supplemented by Navigation, Compass Adjustment, Meteorology, and Foreign Languages. In practice, however, it was not found satisfactory to combine the technical and broader courses, so the additional group was eventually dropped and the officers concentrated on 'the study of the Art of War', i.e. the 'basic' courses.

The War College also resembled the American pattern in the way it

---

1 Corbett to Newbolt 3.III.03; CP/B3.

2 See C.C. Lloyd 'The Naval War Colleges at Portsmouth and Greenwich', p. 153; and Schurman *Education of a Navy,* pp. 35, 38.

3 The early history of the War College was set out in a *Memorandum* by the then Director Captain Edmond Slade, and sent to Corbett, 20.V.06; CP/B13.

was treated by the authorities. It was starved for funds. Indeed, up until 1903 May had no assistance at all.[1] 'Since the subsidiary subjects were still being taught, and no work relating to the War Course proper was done in the afternoons it was still possible for him to keep up with it'. Under these conditions it is not so surprising that May died, suddenly, in the spring of 1904.

This overworked, brilliant, and undervalued founder of the War Course wrote to Corbett in August 1902, asking him to give a series of four to eight lectures at Greenwich.[2] There would, wrote May, be between fifteen and twenty senior officers in each course, some of whom 'are already fairly well read, others are not'. Corbett could choose his subject 'within reason', but the Director preferred that the lectures should 'treat more particularly of either the tactics or strategy of the period as apart from other considerations'. Furthermore the subject ought 'to be so modern that some lessons applicable to present day warfare should be deductable from it'.[3] Indeed May made it clear that what he most hoped for from Corbett was a proper attention to strategy, presented in such a way that naval officers could appreciate that 'expediency and strategy are not always in accord'.[4] Corbett's future strategic productions make it clear that he never forgot this sound advice. May ended his initial guidance with a wise admonition. Generally speaking, he held, 'the faults failures and decadence of nations and their commanders are insufficiently considered', so that difficulties 'likely to meet one in the present day are minimized'.

Twelve years later, addressing the annual meeting of the Historical Association, Corbett acknowledged his debt to May, stating that he had found it 'difficult to know how to handle the subject', but that 'Admiral May cleared the path by instructions that the leading line to be taken should be this: "the deflection of strategy by politics" '.[5]

May was not the only one who advised Corbett on these lectures.

---

1   In that year Captain Howell Jones RMA was appointed assistant, *ibid.*

2   May was not undervalued by Fisher, however. The latter had it in mind to make May Director of Naval Intelligence. See Marder, *Fear God*, I, pp. 229, 248, 264-5. It was a promotion to move from the War Course to the Admiralty, but when it occurred such an officer exchanged exacting work, for a position of little work and less power.

3   May to Corbett 14.VIII.02; CP/B13.

4   May to Corbett 22.VIII.02; CP/B13.

5   J.S. Corbett 'The Teaching of Naval and Military History', *History,* April 1916.

The basic strategic framework itself had been suggested by Sir George Clarke, the first Secretary of the Committee of Imperial Defence.[1]

Working in the basic pattern and ideas germinated by these two men Corbett transformed them with his genius not only into his lectures to the War Course in 1902-3, but also into the Ford Lectures, delivered at Oxford in 1903, and finally into *England in the Mediterranean* which was published by Longmans in 1904. The work was a sort of continuation of the Drake study and reconciled the development of British Mediterranean strategy between 1603 and 1714.[2] The shaft struck the target at which it was aimed. It was praised for 'showing that the presence of British warships in the Mediterranean exercised an indirect influence which far outweighed their actual achievements'.[3] Again, 'his canvas has been, it may be thought, unduly narrowed by the conditions under which he wrote; but, even so, the limitation has made his picture clearer, brighter, more intense'.[4] In short the happy result was that Corbett was able to instruct both the navy and the nation — as Sir George Clarke had hoped.

The first direct contact between the most dynamic executive officer the Royal Navy produced in the twentieth century, and its most distinguished historian and theoretician occurred in 1903. It was occasioned by the vitriolic and intemperate criticism of the new education scheme that marked the spring of that year, when Fisher went as Commander in Chief to Portsmouth. Initially the intermediary was Newbolt,[5] but by May Fisher was sending Corbett material to use for an article supporting the new scheme against its opponents, and especially those whom he classed as 'prehistoric' (such as Admirals Fitzgerald and Vesey Hamilton) who were 'trying to make mischief'.[6]

Corbett's resulting article 'Lord Selborne's Critics' appeared in the July issue of the *Monthly Review*. It was a forthright attack on those who were active in attempting to secure the reversion of Engineer officers to the status of second class officers. It encouraged the more responsible and moderate opponents of the New Scheme to see that, as

1   J.S. Corbett *England in the Mediterranean* 2 vols. (London, 1904), I, p.viii.

2   For a short digest see Schurman, *Education of a Navy*, pp. 160-3.

3   Review 'England in the Mediterranean', *The Quarterly Review*, July 1906, p. 6.

4   Review 'England in the Mediterranean' *Edinburgh Review* July 1905, p. 129.

5   Fisher wrote of 'Your excellent Mr. Corbett', Fisher to Newbolt 2.IV.03, CP/B12.

6   Fisher to Corbett 3 and 5. V.03; CP/B12.

it worked out, it would embrace changes that were bound to come, that it had some real merits, and that it deserved careful trial, since in practical operation rough edges would be knocked off. 'Do not throw grit in the works', advised Corbett, 'rather, reach for the oil can'. Fisher was personally singled out for praise and his virtues much canvassed. Fisher, and not through any sense of false modesty, objected to being named, realizing that this would only make his enemies more unreasonable in their attacks on him. Apart from that it was 'conceived in the exact right vein to meet the present situation', and Corbett deserved 'a lion's share in what bye and bye will be the whole country's gratitude'.[1] The country was to take its time about that.

From then onward Corbett maintained contact with Fisher until the latter's death. An unkind critic might say that from this moment, the time when he entered the 'fishpond' as Fisher's supporters were called, Corbett shed his capacity for independent thought, and became a mere producing puppet. As the nature of the relationship between the two men unfolds in these pages the wrong-headedness of such a criticism will become evident. It is put forward here in part to anticipate objections, but also as an excuse for a brief comment on Fisher himself.

The figure that emerges from the placid pages of Admiral Bacon's *Life,* and that literally jumps from the collection of letters edited by Arthur Marder, *Fear God and Dread Nought* is entrancing, repulsive, bewitching, and bewildering by turns. To acknowledge that one is confronted by a volatile genius, however, is quite another thing than to claim an understanding of the main thrust of that genius, and from passing final judgement on Fisher's effectiveness. Marder's and Bacon's defended judgements, that he was both necessary to his time, and generally right in his reactions to it, are still considered to be open to question by some critics. The general conclusion in favour of Fisher are not challenged in this book. However, in looking at Fisher's developing relationship with other men of real ability, and operating under the mantle of general agreement with Marder's defence of Fisher, it is still possible to show Fisher as a man for his times, but not by any means a man for all seasons. To be aware of some of the warts that mar the portrait is to see it as more human; and above all to bring out the services of other men to the development of the Royal Navy, men without whom Fisher might have been much less successful than he was. The quality of such support was by no means negligible.

Having said that, it is necessary to stress that however brilliant the

1   Fisher to Corbett 6.VIII.03; Marder, *Fear God* I, p. 274.

satellites, Fisher was the sun around which they revolved. His illumination, touch, position and need allowed them to relieve the darkness in their different ways. Corbett was one of these men. Intellectually he was Fisher's superior, yet his position was less, for his life and work, at the time, touched fewer people. Fisher's interest in Corbett transformed Corbett's life, the reverse is not true. Yet Julian Stafford Corbett was not a fixed satellite. The words 'public servant', which apply to so many permanent government employees, just suit, in the best sense, this talented individual whose real master was the Royal Navy — which for a time, *was* John Fisher.

While he was at Portsmouth, Fisher kept in touch with Corbett, and supplied him with information designed to show where the most serious naval deficiences were and to indicate the main lines along which reforms were to occur. For instance, Fisher passed on rough notes for the lectures he had delivered to the Fleet during his Mediterranean command. Current documents concerning naval policy also passed between the two men. This kind of material impressed Corbett, and indeed helped to make him into a steady supporter of Fisher's main reforming works. But it is also clear that even at this early date Corbett was disturbed by evidence of the Admiral's over-preoccupation with the material side of things, and he wrote to Fisher, who replied, impressed in turn, agreeing that it would not be the newest ships, the biggest guns, or the latest torpedoes that would win the next war. It would be 'the best men! preach that gospel!'[1]

Thus it may be seen that Corbett was valuable to Fisher in a number of ways. He could offer concrete support in propagandizing Fisher's ideas with the general public concerning such matters as the Education 'New Scheme', and later on the Dreadnought policy. As we shall see, he was able to help frustrate the conscriptionists when an invasion scare was used to disrupt naval planning. But there was more to the association than that. For his part Fisher, in the main, recognized a man who could appreciate the over-all importance of the reforms being forced on the navy, and who did not allow disagreement over some points of detail to obscure this general vision. He was also awake to the fact that material problems tended to over-bear the intellectual side of war policy, so that he was able to appreciate Corbett's views, even when he felt it unwise or impolitic to act on them. It was good that a man of Corbett's integrity should force Fisher to return to such problems again and again. It would be unfair to Fisher to suggest that he did not appreciate this emphasis of Corbett's, he was simply faced with

1   Fisher to Corbett 28.II.03; CP/B12.

establishing priorities for action. A First Sea Lord's priorities had to be dictated by circumstances rather than counsels of perfection. Corbett, on his side, appreciated both Fisher's genius, and the opportunity for serving the navy that support for Fisher made possible. It is also clear that the historian enjoyed the pleasure of basking in the attentions of men who ran the Navy. But with all this (and he had the usual human susceptibility to flattery) he kept giving Fisher unwelcome advice when necessary, the most important of which was the view that material in the hands of planners and activists of limited intelligence was almost useless. All in all it was an important and fruitful relationship.

The Naval manoeuvres of 1903 provided the first occasion for Corbett to apply his knowledge of strategy and tactics to the movements of a modern battle fleet. The invitation to accompany a section of the fleet as a *Times* special correspondent came from James Thursfield. It is likely that Fisher had something to do with the historian's being given this assignment.[1] In any event Corbett's special abilities and activities were well known in the service. Even in 1902 he had recorded that 'I feel I shall soon be offered the command of a squadron if this goes on'. [2]   Anyhow this task represented a new departure for him, and Thursfield was very considerate, helpful and meticulous in his pre-sailing briefings[3]   The plan of the manoeuvres, briefly, was that the fleet of country X had superiority to one section of the fleet of B country (B2) and had the latter bottled up in Lagos harbour. The other fleet of B country (B1) was to come south from Ireland to attempt a junction with the blockaded squadron so as to create, in turn, a B fleet combined superiority of four lineships over X fleet. In the actual manoeuvre the B fleets did unite without X forcing either to separate action, but subsequently a battle took place as a result of which the umpires awarded the decision to X fleet. Corbett wrote his copy from HMS *Empress of India* flying Vice-Admiral Poe's flag in Admiral Sir Arthur Wilson's B1 squadron.

Two pictures of Corbett emerge clearly. The first is that of the devout worshipper at last arrived in holy places. 'It was', he wrote to Newbolt while still breathing the incense, 'the most gorgeous time I ever had. The battle of the Azores was enough to make a journalist sing. A bard would have filled the skies with music. You ought to have

---

1   Fisher to Corbett 12.VIII.03; CP/B12 and Thursfield to Corbett 22.VI.03 CP/B4.

2   Corbett to Newbolt 23.VIII.02; CP/B3.

3   Thursfield to Corbett 17,19,24.VIII.03; CP/B4.

been there. But it was not only the battle. It was everything. My opinion of the Navy has risen to the highest. Indeed I wonder what on earth ever made me find fault with it'. The spirit of the sailors was wonderful and might well be emulated by the army, he thought. Perhaps it was the result of Fisher's reforming activity, or as Corbett called it the 'Jack-fish spirit'.[1] To his wife he wrote happily of attentive sailors, mysterious junctions at sea, and able silent admirals like Arthur Wilson who 'makes the impression of a simple quiet grey bearded man full of quiet confidence. He is the man you know that the whole service considers the finest fleet commander we have'.[2] Those remarks about Wilson were penned before it was known that the B fleets, under his command, had lost the exercise.

The other two fleets (B2 and X) were covered by Thursfield and John B. Capper, the principal assistant Editor of *The Times,* respectively. When the judges decided in favour of X fleet their decision was supported by Capper, even as Thursfield and Corbett in the B fleets dissented from this verdict. It is relevant to note that Thursfield and Corbett were supplied before sailing with private information by Prince Louis of Battenburg, that B fleet was meant to represent Britain and X fleet the enemy,[3] while Capper, as late as December, long after the manoeuvres, was under the impression that X represented Britain 'in the minds of the framers of the scheme'.[4] It is, perhaps, going too far to suggest that the hospitality of the various host Admirals seduced and divided the minds of the *Times* reporters, one from another, but clearly they were not completely disinterested.

Be that as it may *The Times* queried the results of the judges in November.[5] After Capper and Thursfield had had a collision over it the Admiralty published a laconic *Report,* and Thursfield wrote to Corbett to explain how the newspaper solved the problem. 'The leader which will appear in *The Times* will be in some measure a compromise between our respective views, but on all essential points I hope I have held my own. When we came to close quarters my fire was too heavy for Capper'.[6] The Admiralty eventually issued a Report[7] of the manoeuvres in which they refrained from expressing an

1   Corbett to Newbolt 20.VIII.03; CP/B3.
2   Corbett to E.R.C. (wife) 15.VIII.03; CP/B10.
3   Thursfield to Corbett 17.VII.03; CP/B4.
4   Capper to Corbett 4.XII.03; CP/B4.
5   *The Times* 20.XI.03.
6   9.XI.03; CP/B4.
7   (CMD 1824) 1903.

opinion of the judges' assessment, and finally Corbett attempted to sum it all up in the December issue of the *Monthly Review*.[1]

The battle that took place in the exercise involved X, a smaller force with superior speed (Admiral Sir Compton Domvile) and B, a larger force under Wilson. Domvile had the speed to avoid an action, but when Wilson stretched out his van to prevent, as he thought, an attempt by X to escape to port, Domvile saw a chance for a concentrated attack on that van and assumed the offensive. Corbett noted first of all that the 'superior speed, power, and homogeneity' of X fleet was 'a condition which, of course, could not exist in actual war'. He noted the tendency of the B ships to concentrate their fire on one of the enemy, allowing the others in the line to go relatively free. This concentration, he thought, which accounted for B not being given credit for more sinkings, would not happen in war, where one could see this happening and correct the fault. Finally he emphasized the *strategic* superiority of Wilson in that he had enticed Domvile to attack by exposing his van, and that Wilson, even granting the umpire's conclusions on ships sunk, had still not lost 'command of the sea'. Corbett went on to show that command of the sea was a relative term, embracing three separate states: total content, local control, and special or temporary control. Domvile had only achieved the last of these and that type of command was not sufficient to allow him to pass an army or a convoy over the sea in the area.

No doubt the 'command of the sea' was a useful concept to explain to the Admirals. Corbett's other points, however, were less weighty. If one looks ahead to Jutland it can be seen that the real fight and the 1903 mock action had similarities. There a smaller force was enticed into an attack, and the German ships did possess solid virtues not matched by their British opponents. Corbett's conclusion, in support of Wilson, was of the sort that encourages complacency. Secondly, his remark that visual sighting would not permit over-concentration of the line on one enemy ship was not borne out by the Battle Cruiser action at Jutland. He underestimated the difficulties involved in arranging for changes of target, in action, without proper pre-arrangement. Corbett's argument about whether Wilson's proffered van was a misfortune due to a misreading of enemy intentions, or a stroke of strategic genius, is debatable. Actually he had based his assessment on post-battle discussion with his Admiral. Taking it all-in-all it is impossible not to feel sympathy for Capper who dissented but was technically incapable of making his views prevail against the combined naval knowledge of Corbett and Thursfield.

1   *Monthly Review*, December 1903, p. 87.

Nevertheless, Corbett was a beginner at this work, and he did produce a readable article, the conclusions of which would be debated. In this he rendered the navy a real service, as Thursfield said of the Admiralty *Report* on the manoeuvres, that it was 'illogical, incoherent, and puzzle-headed if not wrong-headed'.[1]

Up to this point Corbett's main function as publicist and, indeed, as a writer of a special kind of history, was to assist in getting up public support for the Fisher-Selborne Naval Education Scheme, and to write history that pointed up the vital connection between the exercise of sea power and national strategy — the latter mainly for the purpose of educating professional sailors. He now moved into a more controversial, if not entirely unexplored, arena of activity.

It will be remembered that the main, and, perhaps unexpected conclusion to emerge from the *Successors of Drake* was that a powerful navy, if not supported by a strong army, was not a sufficient war weapon for England. Co-operation between balanced forces was essential to success. This opinion that Corbett had derived from a study of the past, he now applied to the present. Service co-operation was important. He did not hold this opinion in isolation. It had been expressed by Sir George Clarke and J.R. Thursfield in the *The Navy and the Nation*, published before the Boer War.[2] Thus when Clarke came to the C.I.D. as its Secretary, he came to it determined to make his office important, and he wished to bring the two services together to plan for war in the traditional or sea-oriented way.[3] It was natural that Clarke and Corbett should, at the time, gravitate together. They both agreed, as Corbett wrote to Newbolt, that 'all our mistakes are due to

---

1　Thursfield to Corbett, 9.XI.03; CP/B4.

2　In 1897.

3　Professor N.H. Gibbs has argued that British Tradition strategy in the past was as much continental oriented as it was ocean oriented. This seems to me to be a useful viewpoint as far as it goes — but it tends to be an either — or argument. Sea power was surely only one component of a double-barrelled strategy. If one avoids the Seven Years' War, which is often regarded as a special case, and looks at Marlborough, who was certainly continentally oriented, his great virtue as a war leader was that he, like William III, kept the possibility of the interaction of the two services constantly in mind. Indeed Marlborough brought about the Mediterranean strategy of his war by planning carefully with the two services continually in mind. Wellington, in turn had no doubt of his reliance on sea-power — the achievement of Sir John Moore had taught him the need for that — and his lines and movements were the results of a deep understanding of combined operations advantages, limitations and possibilities. Both the continental and the oceanic approaches were valid, and traditional, but they were not conceived in isolation from one another. See Norman Gibbs 'British Strategic Doctrine' M. Howard, ed., *The Theory and Practice of War* (London 1965), pp. 187-194.

neglecting to treat Naval and Military strategy as one'.[1] But Clarke was frustrated even in 1904. He seemed 'sad over his ticket — despairing of getting anything done unless people like ourselves can get up a public opinion'.[2]

Clarke failed. His failure was no doubt partly traceable to a defect in temperament that disposed him to be impatient of the realities of his secretarial position. He was a natural dictator, not a natural silent planner and manipulator. The failure was also in no small measure due to the suspicious, unco-operative nature of Sir John Fisher, who insisted on treating naval war planning as a purely Admiralty function, and whose attitude to soldiers was a curious blend of contempt and fear. Finally it was caused by the fact that in 1905 plans for combined operations were made by sailors, and rejected by planners at the War Office. Whether the C.I.D. was a useful place to force co-operation between the army and navy could, and can, be argued. Nevertheless the Admiralty was not prepared to let either the army, or the C.I.D., have a voice in determining Admiralty policy — if it could be prevented.

This tentative approach to Combined Operations (or military-naval strategy) in 1905, and its ultimate rejection, was to have serious ramifications on national defence thinking right up to and including the First World War. In the spring of 1905 on the death of Admiral May, Captain Edmond Slade became Director of the War Course. Both Slade and Captain Ottley, the then Director of Naval Intelligence, were involved in pressing on the War Office the view that amphibious projects would be of great value in the case of a Franco-British War with Germany — and Corbett was informed of their views, indeed he may have inspired them.

It was a crucial time. British defence planners were just beginning to adjust to the change in defence posture made necessary by the political *rapprochment* with France that had been the headline news of 1904, although it is difficult to know how much Admiralty knew of the details of the army conversations. Fisher talked to the French Naval Attaché in the autumn of 1905, and in January 1906 he objected to being called on by the Army to ferry 100,000 men to France in case of war with Germany.[3]

1   Corbett to Newbolt 15.IV.04; CP/B3.

2   Corbett to Newbolt 17.V.04; CP/B3.

3   See Marder *From the Dreadnought to Scapa Flow* Vol. 1 (London, 1961) pp. 116-19.

It is possible that Fisher would never have been amenable to a war strategy that envisaged the sending of *any* men to the continent. His views were not noted for moderation. On the other hand, as Marder points out,[1] the autumn of 1905 saw the definite rejection, by a minor Committee at the War Office, of Fisher's project for landing 120,000 men on the German Baltic Coast. This idea was to attract Fisher for many years to come. It is true that it was specifically Fisher's Baltic scheme that the War Office rejected. But their real objection was to the principle of such a sea-borne plan for the Army. Thus the seeds were planted against any scheme of co-operation that would limit the numbers of men which could be sent to France. It was in 1905 then, not 1911 or later, that the clear trend towards the commitment of the British Army to a continental war stems.[2] The Baltic scheme has survived amongst his foes, as an illustration of Fisher's unsound strategic thinking. It served for such a purpose, but that was not the whole story.

To return to Corbett in 1905. In July Ottley was writing to him about the dearth of strategic ideas amongst naval officers. He emphasized the need for Corbett's collaboration in furthering the strategic education of members of the Naval War Course. Furthermore, he stated that Slade was 'in close and constant touch with the Admiralty and is fully competent to give you the sort of assistance you require'.[3] A few days later Ottley was writing to Corbett on the value of throwing an expedition ashore on the German Coast. 'No other attitude', he thought, 'would be worthy of our traditions or would be acceptable to the French'. These ideas were circulating in July. In December, after the War Office had turned thumbs down on the Baltic scheme, Slade was writing to Corbett that he and Ottley were trying to get attention paid to a plan to keep 10-15,000 men at sea in an attempt to throw German strategy into confusion at the beginning of a war, and he especially referred to the deadly nature of a British assault from Antwerp, should the Germans violate Belgian neutrality. He was impressed with the probable effect of such a move against the German flank. It was likely to immobilize large numbers of German soldiers. Slade added a P.S. which stated 'I may say the army objects'.[4] A few days later he stated that the basis for the War Office objection was that

---

1   *Ibid.*, p. 386.

2   A point that emerged in conversation connected with the research of Dr. N.H. Summerton, and Dr. Nicholas d'Ombrian.

3   Ottley to Corbett 1.VIII.05; NMM. RIC/9/1.

4   Slade to Corbett 16.XII.05; NMM. RIC/9/1.

the Baltic Sea operations of 1854 had no influence on the Crimean War.
He intended to study the problem further.[1]

These few letters linking Slade, Ottley and Corbett are important.
First they give real evidence that strategic thought in naval circles did
not exist in quantity. Second they show that *some* naval planners
were at work, but that they were not in a sufficiently powerful position
to completely capture the head of the Admiralty, let alone the War
Office. Indeed, it would be hard to guess whether Fisher, from that
time on, was more afraid of independent thought at the War Office or
at the Admiralty. Third, it shows that serious all-round consideration
of a combined operations strategy never occurred. Finally, and equally
important was the fact that when Corbett had turned to Ottley for
help with ideas for strategic lectures at the War Course he had pleaded
'the really tremendous press of routine duties', that kept the D.N.I.
from his proper function of war planning, and had literally passed over
war planning to the War Course – that meant to Slade and Corbett.
Thus between that time and Fisher's fall, what co-operative independent thought occurred concerning war plans took place at the War
Course, so that Corbett and Slade, plus those they instructed and took
into their confidence, were the 'General Staff' of the Admiralty, so
far as it had one. It was from them that Fisher drew much of this
information when finally the row with Beresford forced him to put
some plans on paper. No doubt it suited Fisher to keep Ottley busy
enough with 'routine duties' so that this situation would persist;
at any rate it accorded well with his mounting desire to keep the
threads of naval strategy in his own hands. As far as Corbett was
concerned it gave him the idea that he could influence policy; and
the appearance, but not the reality, of power.

Opinion may differ concerning the value to the service and the
nation of having this planning going on at such a distance from the
Admiralty and at the War Course in Greenwich, but the fact that it
existed at all was due to Corbett's initiative and Fisher's response to it.
In May 1905, Corbett wrote to Fisher to complain that such Admiralty
Papers as he had seen were notable for the 'amateurish rubbish' that
posed for strategic thought in them.[2] This complaint about the state of
service knowledge on strategy was welcomed by Fisher. The result was
two meetings, one with Ottley, and then one with Fisher himself,[3] that

---

1   Slade to Corbett 26.XII.05; NMM. RIC/9/1.

2   Draft reply to a letter from Fisher to Corbett 22.V.05; CP/B12.   Fisher
replied the same day.

3   Fisher to Corbett 24.V.05; CP/B12.

led to Corbett being asked to undertake specifically strategic lectures to the War Course, which he agreed to do.[1] From that time onward, therefore, Fisher did have strategic advisers to draw upon.

Corbett's new appointment, then, as *strategic* lecturer to the War Course was much more important than it appeared to be at first sight, and certainly he undertook it in no light-hearted manner. His own strategic and tactical notions were grounded on a deep and growing knowledge of Britain's naval past, involving the handling and appreciation of original historic records and documents. The audiences he had to teach based *their* views on professional practice as they understood it. What historical knowledge they possessed was usually based on a cursory reading of Mahan who, in his early and most popular works, did not work from original sources. Thus, merely from the teaching point of view Corbett was faced with the almost insurmountable task of teaching strategy, and the history it was based on, at the same time. He had, as well, to entertain or be ignored. In October he wrote wearily to Newbolt 'my strategy lectures are very uphill work. I had no idea when I undertook it how difficult it was to present theory in a digestable form to the unused organs of Naval officers'.[2]

Indeed the whole problem that Corbett faced is unconsciously reflected in the book he was then writing: *England in the Seven Years' War*.[3] He began it at the same time as he began the strategy lectures, and no doubt the book eventually grew out of these lectures. He had intended to write a book on strategy, a sort of strategic commentary, but close inspection always revealed that strategy actually turned on minute details. This generally led to the discovery that other writers had got their facts wrong so that soon one was writing both facts and commentary. Indeed, 'I already see the public critics pronouncing mine (i.e. his book) absolutely unreadable for excess of matter and of technicalities',[4] and he also complained of the difficulty of 'always trying to paint the picture as well as tell the story'.[5] These were the words of a man who had a real audience in mind, and who was

---

1 Fisher to Corbett 6.VI.05; CP/B12.

2 Corbett to Newbolt 22.X.05; CP/B3.

3 (London, 1907) Discussed in Schurman, *Education of a Navy*, pp. 163-9. Since writing those words I have come more to the conclusion that Corbett allowed the history to be much influenced by the (then) present day needs of naval education.

4 Corbett to Newbolt 12.IX.06; CP/B3.

5 Corbett to Newbolt 22.IX.06; CP/B3.

grappling with real problems of communication while he was writing.

His fears were well-grounded. The one word that best characterized the reaction of his audiences was 'suspicious'. Years later an assessment of Corbett's impact was written up in good practical fashion by one who was there, who defined his attitude by reference to the first two verses of Job XII:

'No doubt but ye are the people, and wisdom shall die with you'.
'But I have understanding as well as you: I am not inferior to you: yea, who knoweth not such things as these?'

When this declaration of equality is coupled with the following comment, the resistance of the audience at the course can be properly gauged. The writer stated that 'he was most dangerous when most suave, and his oft repeated 'Gentleman, dealing with a subject on which you are far more competent to form an opinion than I am . . . ' was a sure and certain sign that he was going to advance ideas quite contrary to those generally accepted'. The pre-war professional sailor was somewhat disinclined to passively accept instruction from a landsman, whether he could down him in argument or not.[1] In retrospect the writer was prepared to say that Corbett's legal training and mind was shown in 'his preference for getting the better of the enemy in some other way than coming to blows'. And that 'despite all lip service and fine phrases, his teaching did not preach that to destroy or neutralize the enemy's armed force was the primary military aim leading to a military decision'. Since this idea was given currency by Lord Sydenham in the House of Lords in 1917, and after the war became a common assertion, it is not easy to tell whether this judgement represented the anonymous writer's mind in 1905, 1906, or 1931. Clearly, however, naval officers were terribly suspicious of scholarly erudition. Nevertheless the *Naval Review* writer thought that Corbett's reputation as an historian and strategist, as opposed to his reputation as a naval tactician, would stand. Corbett was given full credit for making his lectures homely and hence interesting, and for 'going to the root of things for information'.

This picture of Corbett is not easy to grasp at first glance for it is certain that he was witty, sensible, and forthright, as well as being erudite. But the quotation from Job is revealing since it lights up an aspect of Corbett's mind that is important to notice. Writers who wish to take their wares to the general public, or to people untrained in the

---

1   Anon. 'Some notes on the Early Days of the Royal Naval War College', *The Naval Review,* May 1931, pp. 242-3.

exercise of scholarly concentration, must enlist the active sympathy of their readers. One way of doing this is to delineate the character or personality of historical people in terms which make them life-like. Corbett almost totally lacked this ability. It will be remembered that the reason for his failure as a novelist was concerned, not with poor writing style nor the inability to devise reasonable plots, but because the people in his books were merely foils for argument, and not convincing in themselves. Even in describing his trips to India and America his references to people were to types rather than to individuals; they came out in his sketches, not in his prose. There can be no doubt but that this approach characterized his serious history. Drake and Marlborough live as symbolic figures 'plugged in' to the story of developing British sea strategy. Even Nelson is presented as a strategic or tactical instrument to inspect. Only with 'honest George Monk' did he come close to making a character live.

Men in the real world, such as the War Course audience, not being learned in the scholarly sense, saw command problems in a somewhat personal light. They were men of the world whose foils were other people. If they had read Southey or Mahan on Nelson they no doubt looked for the human qualities, and leadership reactions resulting from those qualities, and drew conclusions. They might draw strategic nonsense from this exercise, but from the command point of view they found support, inspiration and guidance. It is likely that such men subsconsciously resented being instructed subtly about historical personages whom they thought they understood. It is difficult not to suggest that this may have been a correct assumption on their part. In any event, it was at the human level that the divorce between teacher and taught occurred at the War Course. Also it probably explains why so many of Corbett's brilliant books did not become best sellers. Corbett's son-in-law, Brian Tunstall, saw this instinctively when he began to write, and when Tunstall studied the earl of Chatham it was the mind and personality that he investigated first.[1] History has patterns, but it is about men. Corbett could not render this distinction in detail.

At the end of 1905 the War Course moved from Greenwich to Devonport, and it shifted again in the spring of 1906 to Portsmouth where it remained, except for occasional lectures given at Chatham and Devonport. By this time Corbett and Slade, who continually encouraged, criticized and helped each other, felt that they were beginning to penetrate the massive reserve of their audiences. This

---

[1] Brian Tunstall, *William Pitt, Earl of Chatham*, (London, 1938).

optimism may have owed something to their new environment where they had 'every modern convenience'.[1] More likely, as Slade suggested, the officers were getting into some sympathy with Corbett's developing strategic approach.[2] Indeed Corbett himself thought he was 'getting the Admirals' blood up', as they were more and more adopting his strategic ideas in getting up material for the war games that formed a part of the curriculum.[3] In fact, at the beginning of 1906 he was able to report that the Admirals were treating him 'in a deferential way'[4] and were complimenting him afterwards 'which has never happened before'.[5] It was all very exhilarating, and he was conscious of the fact that 'we are fast becoming something like a General Staff'.[6]

The problem of a naval staff, however, was not to be solved so easily. At the end of 1905, Corbett had brought it to the fore when he reminded the First Sea Lord that even a strategically oriented War Course was not a sufficient substitute for a proper Admiralty Staff organization. To this Fisher replied: 'I do not see my way as yet to dis-associate the First Sea Lord from the present way of doing the business but there is force in your remark (*not written but implied*) that an effete First Sea Lord would be the *very* devil. I will think more of it'.[7] No immediate action resulted. In the spring of 1906, however, Fisher was writing to Corbett that he wanted to interest him in a 'scheme for the extension of the Naval War College at Portsmouth. I hope to fascinate you'.[8] Corbett promptly replied: 'You will find no difficulty in interesting me in your scheme of extending the War College. My mouth waters already'. He went on to say that nothing, not even plans for combined training seemed to 'offer more for the future of the Service'. For three years 'I devoted all my energies to it', and Slade had been doing an 'admirable job' and it was time he had more help. He went on, cleverly, 'For another and different reason I rejoice at what you tell me. It is this. Those who are the strongest and most serious opposition to you — so far as I understand them — will find, if you carry this new idea through, the main strength of their current switched off. It is your supposed neglect of what you are now

1   Corbett to Newbolt 31.I.06; CP/B3.

2   Corbett to E.R.C. 15.III.06; CP/B10.

3   Corbett to E.R.C. 17.I.06; CP/B10.

4   Corbett to E.R.C. 29.I.06; CP/B10.

5   Corbett to E.R.C. 6.III.06; CP/B10.

6   Corbett to Newbolt 31.I.06; CP/B3.

7   Fisher to Corbett 22.XII.06; B12.

8   Fisher to Corbett 12.V.06; see Marder *Fear God* II, p. 81n; also CP/B12.

devoting yourself to that is their strongest attack'.[1]   Thus it was undoubtedly with Fisher's concurrence that Slade and Corbett prepared two articles for *The Times* (published 5 and 9 June 1906) dealing with the past, present and future of the War College.

Slade provided Corbett with a basic history of the college and with comments on its development from his point of view.[2]   When Slade took over in 1904, the numbers attending were increased, and the institutional time was shortened to four months.   This was 'more or less of a cram' but some balance had been achieved by dropping subsidiary technical subjects and concentrating on the War Course proper.   In 1905, when ships in the Home Ports were put into Commission, Greenwich was abandoned, and it was first intended to rotate the course at three month intervals from Chatham, to Devonport and then Sheerness.   A beginning was made at Devonport in November 1905.   This was found to be unsatisfactory, and it was then decided to hold the regular course, henceforth, at Portsmouth, and provide *ad hoc* lectures at the other ports when possible.   In 1904, Slade had gone even further, assisted by the interest of Prince Louis of Battenburg, and worked out exchanges with The Army Staff College at Camberley. The first Camberley men attended in 1905.   'This had the important effect in that it brought about the Joint Naval and Military Tour in which we join forces with the officers studying at the Staff College for a week each spring to go somewhere on the coast and thus study the problem of combined operations'.   This brought together forty or fifty officers with a concrete problem to discuss and 'the result is very considerable modification of previously conceived ideas, and a much broader view of the whole subject on the part of everybody concerned'. It is important to note that the War Office turned thumbs down on this sort of strategy, just at the moment when this particular practical experiment was a fledgeling.   When he considered the future develop-ment of the War Course, Slade was emphatic that it was important not to emulate the Germans or any one else, and certainly 'not to Teach anybody their work', but merely to assist the First Sea Lord 'by establishing a board of officers whose function it is to thrash out systematically all sorts of war problems, quite independently, and unhampered by the routine work of an Admiralty department such as the N.I.D.'   The Director of the War Course would need to be kept abreast of the latest information and would therefore work very closely with the N.I.D. but with a little expansion could do the work

1   Corbett to Fisher 13.V.06; see Marder, *Fear God* II, pp. 81-2; also CP/B12.
2   Slade to Corbett 20.V.06; CP/B13.

'without interfering with anyone else'. It was obvious that Slade worried about being accused of empire-building. Such caution was necessary in those days.

The work, Slade felt, would divide itself into two parts. The whole course would be asked to study and pronounce on modern problems, but the cases used were to be hypothetical. War problems as they actually existed, however, would be dealt with by only the Director and Staff, for reasons of secrecy. Considering that some of the course participants might outrank the Director, this second part involved the possibility of annoying a hierarchically conscious group of men. How much Corbett knew about the real problems is by no means clear. In 1906 his knowledge of *secret* planning was probably quite limited, though the importance of secrecy is always advanced by insecure planners to ward off intelligent comments by outsiders.

Corbett sent *The Times* articles based on Slade's paper. The first emphasized that the War Course had shown its value at the annual manoeuvres. Naval Officers had been encouraged to think of proper advice to give their superiors in war and to think constructively about war planning, as well as to discipline themselves to carry out orders in the traditional way. It was pointed out that co-operation with the army was developing, as was the war planning technique derived from the introduction of War Games that had occurred when the Course moved to Devonport and to Portsmouth. The War Games gave a sense of interest, reality, and urgency to the whole thing.

The second article emphasized that the War Course and the N.I.D. were complementary, not conflicting establishments. Corbett argued strongly that the experiment, which had begun at Portsmouth, should be allowed to follow its own natural development and grow, in time, into a great naval university. Really, the burden of both articles was that the War Course had originally developed despite the lack of strong Admiralty encouragement. If that encouragement were now increased, then the War College would develop naturally along intrinsic lines without involved planning and intricate organization. He even suggested that the War Course might be a good place for preparing information reports for the C.I.D. In conclusion Corbett claimed that the Admiralty was certain to obtain public support for just such a development as he and Slade advocated.

Fisher was delighted. The article had obviously given him something for nothing. Ottley, the D.N.I., was reassured that he would not become redundant. The Admiralty preserved its sphinxlike expression and allowed Corbett and Slade to continue perambulating their compound, but under close spy glass observation from the First Sea Lord. At the same time, although Fisher was wary of allowing strategic planning to slip from his grasp, he was aware of the problem and again returned to it in October 1906 in a letter to the First Lord. He spoke of the development of the War College at Portsmouth as 'a very pressing matter' and admitted that 'I do feel personally guilty in not having pushed it', and, further, that he was open to attack along that avenue but, fortunately, his opponents had not grasped this fact. Fisher could only afford so many enemies at a time in the service and great support for the Portsmouth work might have alienated Ottley, who was not nearly as calm about possible trespassing on his territory as he had appeared to be in the spring.[1]

Meanwhile Corbett and Slade were having their difficulties with the course itself. They needed a more satisfactory method for giving strategic instruction. It was not easy to teach the basis of strategy, and strategy itself, at the same time. This sort of thinking was the genesis of 'Notes on Strategy', which later became notorious as 'The Green Pamphlet', which Corbett wrote up, in consultation with Slade, in November 1906.

Since this document was to be used for the most telling attacks on Julian Corbett's work in the future it is worth some comment and description, based on an attempt to discover what Corbett and Slade were attempting at the time, rather than what others many years later, and in retrospect, accused them of wishing to do.

It has been made sufficiently clear that Slade and Corbett found the task of teaching strategy difficult, due to general service ignorance of strategic terms and definitions. It is not easy for an admiral or a captain to admit that the rules of thumb that they have generally taken for strategic laws are, in fact, neither logically nor historically true. This is not to assert that all of Corbett's and Slade's conclusions on the subject were infallible pronouncements, but it is to assert that they had studied the problems involved from logical and historical points of view, and that they were prepared to defend them on the basis of logic and historical proof. They were both better equipped mentally than their 'students' for this kind of argument. They generally prevailed in argument, which explains both why their ideas dominated the War Course and why they were often disliked and mistrusted by their audiences. Furthermore it explains why the counter-attack, when it came, fell on the civilian, Corbett, and not on Slade.

1 Fisher to Tweedmouth 16.X.06; Marder, *Fear God* II, p. 101.

At the base of the Corbett-Slade position stood the figure of that formidable German thinker, Carl von Clausewitz. Slade was a linguist, and much of his instruction to the course was based on a study of the German wars of the 1860s, and he had undoubtedly read Clausewitz. Perhaps he introduced Corbett to Clausewitz. At any rate, as we have seen, Corbett wrote *England in the Seven Years' War*, in connection with his War Course work, and nothing could be clearer than the fact that Clausewitzian thought informs this book, and yet there is no hint of it in *England in the Mediterranean*.[1]

The Green Pamphlet was entitled 'Strategic Terms and Definitions used in Lectures on Naval History'.[2] While Corbett was the author Slade was undoubtedly consulted at every turn. First of all it was laid down that naval strategy was not an isolated separate branch of knowledge but a part of the art of war taken as a whole, and that war is a form of political intercourse that begins at the point where force is introduced to gain the ends of foreign politics. This introduction set the tone for the whole work which was permeated with the idea that the gyrations of fleets, at the command of Admirals, were not ends in themselves.

Strategy divided itself into two main types: major strategy that was worked out with reference to the purpose of the war as a whole, embracing diplomatic and trading considerations; and minor strategy that had to do with planning specific operations, which might be mainly naval, mainly military (army), or even combined, when the two services would interweave for a specific purpose.

Next, it was the nature of the selected objectives that determined the *posture* adopted in the war — defensive or offensive. When the object was negative, that is if the purpose was to deny some possession or claim of the enemy's to him, then the strategy was defensive. When, on the other hand, the object was positive, aiming at the acquisition or assertion of something at the enemy's expense, then the strategy was offensive. The offensive, which, as a rule, leads most quickly to a final decision, was generally adopted by the stronger power. At this point the strengths and weaknesses of each posture were duly set out.

Another section described the 'General Characteristics of the Defensive'. In general it was true that the only charms of the defensive lay in its value for disguising offensive plans. Otherwise defensive war was a second best policy that ought to be discarded as soon as

1   See Schurman, *Education of a Navy*, pp. 164-5.

2   CP/B6.

circumstances and strength permitted. Clever use of the defensive, however, would enable offensive attacks to be made in areas and situations, sometimes minor ones, that were unfavourable to enemy success.

In addition to defensive operation *per se* it was possible as well to conduct 'offensive operations with a defensive intention'. Both counter attacks, (against an exposed enemy offensive) and diversions, (which were intended to confuse enemy offensive strategy and movements) fell into this category. The authors did not neglect to note that successful diversions ought to draw off more enemy force than they themselves comprised, and that the suddenness and mobility requisite to success in this kind of war 'are most highly developed in combined operations'.

It was claimed that wars could be regarded as either limited or unlimited, according to the appetites or objectives of the protagonists. Theatres of wars and theatres of operations were defined. Referring specifically to the situation where the object was to give command of a particular sea area it was noted that the enemy's 'fleet will usually be the objective'.

Then followed a definition of 'lines of operation' and 'lines of communication'. The latter lay at the very heart of naval strategy, and comprised supply lines, running from base to theatre of operations; lines of lateral communication, being the communication between various operations theatres; and lines of retreat, which were merely lines of supply in reverse. 'Maritime Strategy', they wrote, 'has never been regarded as hingeing on communications, but (in fact) probably it does so even more than 'Land Strategy', as will appear from a consideration of maritime communications, and the extent to which they are the main preoccupation of naval operations'. Put another way, 'problems of Naval Strategy can be reduced to terms of 'passage and communication' and this is probably the best method of solving them. For communications govern both commerce movement and oversea expeditions, and the disruption of an enemy's communications or the securing of one's own links with allies determined the flow of trade, and furthered or hindered military operations ashore. It was again emphasized that 'the above is the best working "Definition of Naval Strategy" as emphasizing its intimate connection with the diplomatic, financial and military aspects of major strategy'.[1]

---

[1] This idea was not new and was first put forward, in its modern setting, by J.C.R. Colomb, see his *The Protection of Our Commerce and Distribution of Our Naval Forces Considered* (London, 1867).

There can be no doubt but that the emphasis of the writers, up to this point, was on the proposition that sea power was not an end in itself. Thus combat was not emphasized. This attitude undoubtedly arose from their experience, in teaching, that officers tended to leap to the conclusion that combat settled all things automatically. From this position it was only a step to the ridiculous conclusion that combat was an end in itself. This strong argument attempted to force their listeners to the probably unwelcome conclusion that naval strategy was neither simple, nor axiomatic, nor final.

This reasoning led the writers to consideration of one of the most seductive and yet imprecise popular conceptions of Naval Strategy — 'command of the sea'. First, they asserted that there could be no such thing in peacetime. In war, when command could be asserted it was by no means a self-evident blanket term. On the one hand general command might be asserted, which meant that the enemy could not seriously disrupt one's own communications and that he could not effectively maintain his own — and this referred to trade and diplomatic posture as well as to military operations. On the other hand, local command referred to this situation existing in one or more theatres of operation, and not in the over-all situation. In both of these cases command could be temporary, or permanent, the latter situation applying when the enemy's sea power ceased to be a possible determining factor in either the war as a whole or in the temporary situation.

Command of the sea was not therefore a clear blanket term, for general, local, or temporary command could not only be held by one power, or by its enemy, but it could also be in dispute. This was a very important point because this 'is the normal condition, at least in the early stages of a war, and frequently all through it'. They pointed out that it was clearly to the advantage of 'a preponderating Navy to end the state of dispute by seeking a decision'. In the same way it could be to the advantage of a weaker navy to avoid it. This point was made but not greatly emphasized, for the point that the authors wished to make most clear was that general command of the sea was '*not essential to all oversea expeditions*'.

This led directly to a conclusion that, if taken out of context, could be taken to mean that battle should not be sought. They stated; 'under certain conditions, therefore, it may not be the primary function of the fleet to seek out the enemy's fleet and destroy it, because general command may be in dispute, while local command may be with us, and political or military considerations may demand of us an operation for which such local command is sufficient, and which cannot be delayed until we have obtained a complete decision. . . .' 'From the above it will appear that 'command of the sea' is too loose an expression for strategical discussion. For practical purposes should be substituted 'control of passage and communication'. Thus a proposed operation would draw from the planner not 'have we got command of the sea' but can we 'secure the necessary lines of communications from obstruction by the enemy?' The point cannot be over-emphasized.

Thus while general control could only be obtained by a decisive fleet action, local and temporary control might be secured merely by a partially successful defensive action, by forcing the enemy to concentrate elsewhere, or by merely marking or containing the enemy's sea force bearing on a particular area.

With respect to blockade the obvious but often neglected point was made that while close blockade had as its purpose the preventing of the enemy from putting to sea at all, an open or 'observation blockade' had as its object the enticing or forcing of an enemy fleet to sea in order to secure the opportunity for a decisive engagement leading 'towards general control'.

Finally it was re-emphasized that all naval strategy ultimately turned on the nature of sea communications. Ashore, the communications of opposing forces tend to run in opposite directions to one another. At sea they could be parallel or identical, and indeed frequently are. 'This peculiarity is the controlling influence of maritime warfare'. It was the lack of appreciation of this fact that led to confusion of thought when the strategic principles governing land warfare were applied unthinkingly to sea warfare. At sea, fleets must control common lines of communication. This gave rise, in the past, to the maxim that the proper place for a fleet was off the enemy's coast, which was generally, but not universally true. Furthermore in modern conditions it would be almost impossible.

The usual maxim was that 'the primary object of the fleet is to seek out the enemy's fleet and destroy it'. The true maxim was 'the primary object of the fleet is to secure communications, and if the enemy's fleet is in a position to render them unsafe it must be put out of action. The enemy's fleet usually is in this position but not always'. That is to say, in nine times out of ten the 'seek out and destroy' maxim 'is sound and applicable' — but it was the sitting on the enemy's lines of communication that 'nine times out of ten' generally brought the enemy out to offer decisive action. It was, after all, better to force the enemy to fight on your terms and in your selected area than the reverse, and certainly the enemy was not always impelled to give you battle when you wanted it. Both of these factors tended to modify the 'seeking out the enemy's fleet' doctrine. For if his enemy did not wish to come out and fight, this predisposition could only be changed by forcing him to do so, regardless of his wishes.

This then, was 'The Green Pamphlet'. It was a document aimed at the marriage of naval with national strategy, and at impressing naval officers that a purely naval strategy based on traditional rules of thumb could not be applied successfully to every situation that faced a nation and a navy in war. In its careful explanation of the lines of communication theory it bore evidence of the fact that this line of reasoning was not part of the general strategic thinking of most naval officers of the time. Finally, the care given to the explanation regarding the 'seek out and destroy' theory provides eloquent testimony to the resistance of naval audiences to modifications of a theory heretofore thought to be the naval equivalent of a summary of the Ten Commandments.

'The Green Pamphlet' was issued again in 1909. Lord Sydenham of Coombe later referred to it as being 'somewhat heavily revised . . . but without apparent improvement'. Actually the second edition did not alter Corbett's fundamental viewpoint.[1] One paragraph, stating that in some circumstances 'seek out and destroy' was not the most useful strategy, was omitted, and one sentence — to wit 'it is to the advantage of the preponderating navy to end the state of dispute by seeking a decision' was placed in italics thus giving it a prominence that Corbett may easily have originally intended. In general, the pamphlet was lengthened, notes were absorbed into the text for clarity, and the 'blockade' sections were expanded to include a mention of the influence of modern weaponry in close blockade. From Lord Sydenham's point of view the changes did not amount to much. Despite criticism, then, neither the naval officers at the War Course nor the Admiralty subsequently forced Corbett to do violence to his strongly held views.

Corbett's views were attacked after his death. An example was 'Sea Heresies', published in the *Naval Review,* May 1931.[2] It would not be profitable to go into these arguments in detail, for the charge is always the same, i.e. that Corbett by playing down the importance of big-battle victory undermined the confidence of naval officers in the traditional approach, and thus taught, 'heresy'. Clearly, since we have

1 'Sea Heresies',*Naval Review,* May 1931. p. 266. Lord Sydenham was doubtless the author.

2 *Ibid.* pp. 223-47.

examined Corbett's arguments in detail it can be seen that sea battle is given high priority; indeed it is only subject to the qualification that it is not *always* a desirable end in itself. The question is not one of rightness of argument, but of emphasis. Consequently, whatever the rightness of Corbett's overall argument, there can be no doubt that subtle reasoning was not easily assimilated either by audiences at the War Courses or by readers of his *Principles* book, that advanced the same arguments.[1] Like Clausewitz, Corbett is not read as much as he is quoted. Why did he not convince strategic thinkers? There can be no doubt that Corbett's lectures engendered a feeling of unease amongst some naval officers. In the general frustration at the lack of a clear cut naval fighting victory during the First War it was natural that this feeling of 'unease' should grow — especially as Corbett was the official historian of the First World War, and therefore in a position to influence future warfare by his teaching. So far as Corbett failed to make his naval audiences, and others, understand his arguments, he was an unsatisfactory instructor and hence, as Lord Sydenham later suggested, a not wholly benign influence. Whether it was, or is, possible to continually reduce the subtleties of naval strategy to quarterdeck cliché is another matter. Put another way, the question boils down to this: were Corbett's arguments too complicated for Naval officers to grasp, or was his presentation inadequate? What we know is that communication between lecturer and audience was not complete.

Ironically, if the quarrel with 'The Green Pamphlet' was occasioned by a misunderstanding of emphasis caused by oversubtlety, the original purpose of the work had been precisely to secure understanding — not to obscure it. Because naval officers appeared to be incapable of drawing sound strategic conclusions from complicated historical evidence 'The Pamphlet' was intended to supply a clear guide, to simplify the process: to provide a common approach to problems, allowing lecturer and audience to work together in harmony. A common pedagogic solution to teaching in different stages of development is to provide either a common body of factual knowledge, or a common philosophical framework to secure rapport between teacher and taught. It has its dangers. Reginald Custance, Flag Captain to Sir Charles Beresford, the Commander in Chief of the Channel Fleet, was shown the 'Pamphlet' by Slade. His reaction was that it provided an excuse for officers 'going no deeper than learning the terms and definitions by heart'.[2] Slade admitted the objection, but claimed that it must bow to the need to 'fix the terminology, as the looseness with

1 *Some Principles of Maritime Strategy,* (London, 1911).
2 Slade to Corbett 2.XII.06; CP/B13.

which men talked about strategy was one of the great hindrances to the proper appreciation of what it meant'. Custance's view was sound, but he under-estimated the strategic naiveté of the War Course audience and did not understand the instructional problem this involved.

However, there was a deeper design behind the 'Pamphlet', Corbett and Slade were not merely attempting to instruct with clarity: they were attempting to convert. Corbett's historical work, and Slade's critical study of continental strategic doctrine had led them to quarrel with Mahan's doctrines. Mahan reinforced what the service had generally held to be the traditional wisdom of the age of Nelson — especially what they conceived to be the paramount importance of large scale sea fights. The War Course instructors challenged this. Custance was a firm disciple of Mahan and resented the new approach. Furthermore, since Slade and Corbett were preaching new ideas they were assumed to be Fisher innovators — perhaps Fisher-inspired. Slade knew that Custance felt this.[1] Corbett's correspondence reveals that there was, in fact, much foundation for the suspicions that linked strategic innovations with Fisher discipleship.

Consider the case of Captain Doveton Sturdee. Sturdee was Chief-of-Staff to Admiral Charles Beresford, around whom opposition to Fisher tended to form in 1907, not entirely without Beresford's encouragement. Professor Marder states that Sturdee was an able man who ought to have modified Beresford's views, and might have, had he, too, not disliked Fisher.[2] Corbett and Slade were aware that Sturdee was in a position of importance, and they tried to capture his interest. Corbett wrote:

> 'the work here (Portsmouth) has been more interesting and important than ever, owing to the presence of Capt. Sturdee and another Capt. Gamble. They are two of the coming men in the service who are in the opposite camp — the Beresford camp. I tell Slade it is a comedy we are playing called 'Captain Sturdee's Conversion'.[3] He, as I think I told you, is Chief of Staff of the Channel Fleet and Beresford's *eminence gris.* If we got him we get the whole service that has not been with us, and we are getting him. It is most entertaining to see how he and Gamble have come to see what a lot they can learn here. Besides preparing my lectures very carefully and expressly to talk with them I have to engage Slade in long discussions with them and it takes all our brains . . . now I must get to my last clinching lecture for Sturdee tomorrow.[4]

1 *Ibid.*

2 Marder, *From the Dreadnought,* 1, p. 91.

3 The allusion is to G.B. Shaw's play *Captain Brassbound's Conversion.*

4 Corbett to E.R.C. 14.III.07; CP/B10. for Marder's opinion of Sturdee see his

Captain Sturdee was not converted. Corbett's and Slade's activities did nothing to reduce the tension between Beresford and Fisher. What they did was discredit their own teaching of strategy by their conversion tactics. Hence the Pamphlet was suspect by anti-Fisherites and by others who found the arguments too subtle. One cannot win everything at once using the weapon of intelligence. That they thought it was worth a try, however, is understandable.

The honest response of blunt sea-officers has been explained. The ultimate reaction of Coombe (Lord Sydenham) is not so easily explicable. It developed in the immediate post-Jutland period, when there was some uneasiness about the fact that the German High Seas Fleet had not been annihilated. In the September 1916 issue of *The London Magazine* Winston Churchill defended the main lines of post-1914 strategy as it applied to the North Sea. Sir Reginald Custance then took the matter up in a letter to *The Times*.[1] He quoted Churchill as saying that 'without a battle we have all the most victorious of battles could give us'. No doubt Churchill was using his special knowledge, having been First Lord until well on in 1915, to clam the general public; to explain that the blockade of Germany was still in relentless effect, despite the apparent indecisiveness of Jutland. Custance used the occasion to quote from 'The Green Pamphlet' portions that did not stress the need for decision by battle. He did not name Corbett or the 'Pamphlet' but he clearly held Corbett's doctrine responsible for having taught the navy to look for victory without hard fighting in the mass. A few days later 'N.O.' pointed out that Custance's explanation was unfair because of what it left out, and named Corbett as the object of Custance's attack.[2] Then, suddenly, on 15 November, Sydenham rose in the House of Lords to call the doctrine described by Custance heretical.

Corbett wrote at once to Sydenham to point out that the latter had seen 'The Green Pamphlet' before it was printed, years ago.[3] Sydenham had then written, Corbett informed him, that 'I think this is perfectly admirable and is exactly what is required as the basis on which to build'; and again 'I am particularly pleased with the treatment of Command of The Sea as I have for sometime tried to inculcate the doctrine that is really a matter of control of maritime communication'. Sydenham who had now labelled this theory 'dangerous heresy',

From the Dreadnought I, pp. 407-8.

1   Published on 9.X.16.

2   Published on 27.X.16.

3   Corbett to Sydenham 30.XI.16; CP/B7.

replied that he could not be expected to remember one state document written years before, and he apoligized to Corbett.[1] The historian replied that the question was not one of his own reputation; rather, he argued, it was a matter for national concern that Sydenham had founded an attack on strategic behaviour on a partial quotation from a secret document. In response to Sydenham's comment that he was really attacking Churchill, and the naval conduct of the war, Corbett wrote, 'I must add that I cannot at all agree that "our handling of the Navy generally had been deplorable", or that the "strategy in the North Sea" has been in principle other than that which you say you would have adopted'. Therefore Corbett requested that Sydenham make his real views known to the public.[2] Silence ensued until Corbett was dead and Sydenham then felt free to attack him in the *Naval Review*.

It is not necessary to defend Corbett's view, any more than it would be useful to comment on Lord Sydenham's shifting viewpoint. The foregoing description, however, shows that Corbett's views were easy to misrepresent or misunderstand. It also shows how little defence any writer has when he writes 'secret' documents. Furthermore, it illustrates the fact that quite intelligent service and ex-service thinkers held the opinion (or appeared to hold the opinion) that the Grand Fleet sought, by doctrine, to avoid battle, and the High Seas Fleet to seek it. It is quite remarkable that intelligent professionals could hold such views, and the episode serves as a commentary on what passed for naval thought generally at the time. On the other hand it may merely serve as a commentary on the vanities of men sidelined from the onrush of important events during a Great War. It is not without interest that they were Fisher's enemies.

The correspondence also reveals some of the frustration Corbett must have felt when he looked at the result of his work at the War Course. He wrote in 1916, that, 'the task of lecturing on strategy was imposed upon me, much against my will, by the Admiralty'.[3] Probably if one substituted the words 'against my instinct and better judgement' one would be closer to the truth. For this disclaimer does not accurately reflect the excitement felt by Slade and Corbett in 1906 when they set out blithely to convert the service to their views. The fact Corbett was reluctant to face was that they failed. That is why Sydenham was happy to support Custance — or at least it is one of the reasons.

1   Sydenham to Corbett 1.XII.16; CP/B7.

2   Corbett to Sydenham 2.XII.16; CP/B7.

3   Corbett to Sydenham 30.XI.16; CP/B7.

4

HISTORICAL WRITINGS AND THE SYNDICATE OF DISCONTENT

It has been seen that Sir George Clarke's encouragement and the War Course lectures came together in Corbett's mind and gave rise to *England in The Mediterranean*,[1] which covered the wide period from 1603 to 1715. As an historical production it was based on a greater spread of evidence than any other book written by Corbett, and from the point of view of detailed historical description it was the least satisfactory. The fragile constructs that were created to illustrate his strategic points in the early chapters have annoyed many readers. Nevertheless, the book had a message. In Mahan-like fashion Corbett took one leading idea from his previous book and applied it with imagination to a broad survey of history. He claimed that small numbers of ships, directed intelligently, could achieve ends out of all proportion to their offensive fighting strength. Selecting his examples he showed how the growing understanding of how to apply sea power gave England a voice in the councils of Europe, and how, once even a fragile Mediterranean squadron was established, pressure could be exerted against the southern flank of Europe in a way that crucially affected the military dispositions of continental powers. It was in this book that he portrayed the genesis of the Royal Navy's Mediterranean presence that occurred during the reigns of King William III and Queen Anne. Subsequent histories have altered the details of this picture but Corbett was the first to grasp the significance of the strategic events of that period. Mahan was not the only one who could translate War College lectures into print.

England in the Seven Years' War,[2] a more closely-knit and more scholarly production than its predecessor, also owed something to Corbett's War College work, written, as it was, between 1905 and 1907. In it he described both the military and the naval aspects of this most maritime of Britain's wars, and it reinforced what he had learned when studying Drake and Marlborough. He read Clausewitz with admiration. It must be emphasized that he had no quarrel with the way warfare was explained by the great German military thinker, nor for the way land warfare was practised by that indomitable soldier Frederick the Great. His conclusion was not that land war, as

---

1   Julian S. Corbett, *England in the Mediterranean*, 2 vols. (London, 1904).
2   Julian S. Corbett, *England in the Seven Years War*, 2 vols. (London, 1907).

understood by those imposing figures, was inferior to British maritime war practice, but that the dictates of geography and politics made it different. It confirmed him in the previously acquired viewpoint that the study of British past practice was more instructive for the development of British strategic principles than was the study of German, Spanish, or French warfare. It was his view that British and German military and naval activity in the Alliance complemented rather than rivalled each other in the Seven Years' War.

Despite the fact that this war produced the *annus mirabilis,* 1759, and that it involved the beginnings of empire in India, plus the conquest of Canada, Corbett did not over-value the effects of armies and navies operating along a sea axis. The real-estate benefits were fortuitous, in his judgement. But he carefully showed that the best support for Prussia came, not from Pitt imitating Frederick and carrying out extended army operations on the European land mass, but by Britain exercising the strengths that the sea provided for operations along the littoral of Europe, and in the colonies, to *complement* the activities of Frederick. Nowhere did he state that armies for the Continent were wrong, only that if they did not draw off to themselves disproportionate numbers of the enemy they were not being as effectively used as they might. At the base of it all lay the conviction, traceable to the Armada, that the British did not have the army potential to intervene decisively on the Continent so long as the Navy required army support to preserve national security or safety from invasion. *England in the Seven Years War*, then, was not a paean of praise to the so-called 'Blue Water School' but rather an illustration of the advantages of using national forces in balance.

From the point of view of the development of Corbett's strategic ideas this book heavily fortified what he had learned in his Drake studies, broadened his appreciations and increased his knowledge. From a study of the campaigns in North America, and especially from his careful consideration of James Wolfe, he was able to write clearly about the detailed, practical, and theoretical foundations of sound combined operations. From his consideration of French threats to invade England, and the naval responses to them, he was able to formulate general rules for insular security and, in particular, to define the difference in commitment involved in an invasion as opposed to a raid — a raid involved a maximum of 10,000 men, in his view.

Looking back it seems clear that some of Corbett's pronouncements, especially his comments on the value of diversions as a contribution to a continental alliance were over-strained. Certainly he would have understood such criticism. When he described British raids, such as

Rochefort (1757), he clearly described the actual operational failures; he never claimed that the British ran an infallible system in war. But even such tactical failures enabled him to illustrate what thoughtful planning could produce in the way of strategic effect if the Army and Navy were used together in intelligent conjunction.

The strength of the book as a strictly historical piece of work lay in the way in which Corbett firmly subordinated the detailed descriptions of all movements and actions to the overall planning of the statesmen — or to Lord Chatham. Much of his description of the events of the Seven Years' War has been superseded by subsequent, more specialist studies. By the same token Corbett's book remains unique. He wove cause and effect, national policy, and the imaginative war direction of Chatham into an intricate fabric that still flashes its brilliance. Every historian is superseded in the fullness of time. Corbett's achievement in this sometimes obscure, sometimes illuminating, sometimes maddening history, still stands as a historical work of art.

Corbett's writing on tactics and signals, which will be discussed in context in the chapter dealing with the Battle of Trafalgar, *The Campaign of Trafalgar*[1] and *Some Principles of Maritime Strategy*[2] were his last two non-official books. The *Principles* Book was simply the 'Green Pamphlet' writ large, carefully supported by arresting historical examples; a powerful compilation of his accumulated knowledge and one that is probably consulted more often than the historical works on which it is built.

Aside from its tactical exposition *The Campaign of Trafalgar* constitutes a careful description of strategic cause and effect. It pointed up the necessity for service co-operation, showed the dispositions necessary to frustrate invasion of the United Kingdom, and carefully played down the ultimate effect of sea power in defeating Napoleon. The book was designed to show that sea power was the limited but effective arm of British state policy. The defensive potential based on carefully disposed sea power, was enormous; its total effects on continental events important but always peripheral. The argument was not new but the method was detailed and apt for its particular purpose, which was to instruct naval officers. Corbett had in mind those engaged on lonely commands in detached and often smaller craft, and he wished to show them how their activities related to the

---

1   Julian S. Corbett, *The Campaign of Trafalgar*, 2 vols. (London, 1910).

2   Julian S. Corbett, *Some Principles of Maritime Strategy* (London, 1911).

whole pattern of changing dispositions. He described in detail the shifting situation in 1805, as British ships moved to secure national purposes, containing but not dominated by Napoleon's threat of invasion. It was a professional answer to objections that his work was too ethereal for more pragmatic minds to appreciate. It brought together his unrivalled knowledge of the strengths and weaknesses of sea power.

Taken together, Corbett's historical works reveal the genesis and development of a British strategy of sea power, and they were based firmly on a study of state papers and other primary sources. When writing of the sixteenth century he once almost involuntarily exclaimed that nobody understood the Elizabethan age who did not appreciate the combination of 'shame and disaster through which it marched to its successes'. That is the key to his views on sea power. Having studied its fragile beginnings he was acutely aware of its continuing weaknesses as well as of the peculiar nature of its strengths, and he demonstrated that knowledge in his descriptions of Britain's growing competence in the art of applying its sea power. What he tried to combat in the Dreadnought era was what he considered to be simplistic naval history, or addiction to rules often devised for armies in 'continental' situations. In this sense Corbett's work was didactic and it is clear that from the time when he completed *Drake and The Tudor Navy* he consciously chose his material and shaped his chapters to achieve the effects he required.

Corbett worked for a navy when exciting, reforming ideas were in the air, despite the fact that the motivating force behind these ideas, Sir John Fisher, was not universally loved. From late 1906 onward, opposition to Fisher began to harden and achieve focus. Since Corbett's public usefulness was profoundly influenced by this change it is necessary both to describe it, and to comment on how Fisher reacted to it.

Professor Marder has summed up the 'Syndicate of Discontent', as Fisher referred to his critics, as a group of men who did not agree in their attitude to Fisher's individual programmes, but who 'in general . . . profoundly distrusted Fisher and all his works'.[1] One man deserves special attention. Until Lord Charles Beresford took over as Chieftain of the Unhappy in 1907, the leader was Admiral Sir Reginald Custance:

1 A.J. Marder, *From the Dreadnought to Scapa Flow*, vol. I (London, 1961), p. 77.

Barfleur as he was known by pen name. Custance was well read in naval history. He had brains, tenacity of purpose, a wide circle of friends, and professional courage to the point of foolhardiness. He had intelligent criticisms to make, and which needed to be made, of recent reforms. Nevertheless, at base, there was a feeling of profound distrust, not to say hatred of Sir John Fisher. The consequent harm that followed from Custance's obsession is incalculable. Others disliked Fisher at certain points and levels. Custance was total in his opposition and he was unrelenting in its application.

Fisher himself was always inclined to account for opposition on the personal level. In Custance's case he thought it was due to some plain speaking between them in 1901, when Custance was Director of Naval Intelligence.[1] Certainly it is true, and Fisher did not know this at the time, that Custance referred to the genesis of the New Education Scheme thus: 'It is an immense misfortune that the moulding of it has fallen into the hands of such a superficial mind as that of Fisher.'[2] The odd phraseology not-withstanding, this reveals Custance's steady opinion of Fisher; an opinion that lay behind all his relentless criticism of the details of Admiralty policies between 1904 and 1909.

In 1905, when Fisher was First Sea Lord, Custance was on half-pay. Although he still wished for employment, he publicly attacked the 'new scheme' and Admiralty building policies. To Sir Gerard Noel, then C. in C., the China Squadron, he wrote of his efforts to persuade officers to exert pressure to 'moderate the pace' of Admiralty reforms.[3] He thought Fisher had no settled convictions, so that it would be easy to force him to change his mind. 'It is', he wrote, 'not at all our duty to accept the decisions of the authorities when we perfectly well know that they are those of one man who has not understood his business and is doing an immense amount of harm'.[4] There were, therefore, no holds barred, and he intended to point out 'everything which seems to be wrong . . . we shall get him [Fisher] out of Whitehall before his five years expire if we only persist in exposing his methods and errors. Single-handed it is hard work, but I hope that in time others will join in the hunt'.[5] Altogether there is clear evidence in

1 A.J. Marder, *Fear God and Dreadnought*, vol. I (London, 1952), p. 155.

2 Custance to Noel 30.VI.03, NMM NOE/R/A. Admiral Sir Gerald Noel was Admiral Superintendent of Naval Reserves 1900-03. He was later C-in-C China Squadron.

3 Custance to Noel. 21.VIII.05; NMM NOE/4/A.

4 Custance to Noel. 31.VIII.05; NMM NOE/4/A.

5 *Ibid.*

Custance's correspondence with Noel that the former acted as stimulator and clearing house for anti-Fisher plots. He organized a meeting between Noel and the Prince of Wales, and tried to influence King Edward through Noel as well. Custance advised Noel that his best line of attack was to emphasize Fisher's 'innate impulsive instability which will certainly come more prominently into action in time of stress and danger' – a viewpoint which he felt Noel shared.[1]

By this time, Admiral Sir Cyprian Bridge had joined the plotters. He was specifically opposed to Admiralty building policy.[2] Then in the autumn of 1906, Admiral Lord Charles Beresford began to emerge as an open anti-Fisherite, although his animus probably developed independently until he and Custance came together in the Channel Fleet (as C. in C. and Second in Command respectively) in the second half of 1906.[3]

When the active appointment came to him Custance was surprised – as well he might have been. He decided to pass off Fisher's lack of vindictiveness, that opened the door again from what he had every right to expect was the end of his naval career, as 'a great sacrifice in keeping *publicly* silent while afloat'.[4] He managed to subdue his scruples. Just previously he had written to Sir John Colomb, the Imperial Defence expert,[5] that he desired not so much Admiralty reform in particular spheres, but rather the undermining of the authority and power of Sir John Fisher – the author of wrong Admiralty policies.[6]

Professor Marder has brilliantly discussed the manner in which the 'Syndicate of Discontent' operated, and said much about the way in which it affected Fisher's mind, spirit and reactions. It is probable as well that his extra sensitivity to attack had something to do with the fact that by 1906-7 he realized that the army had taken up a strategic stance that did not admit of any other naval share than that of

---

1 Custance to Noel. 16.VI.06; NMM NOE/4/A.

2 Bridge to Noel. 14.VI.06; NMM NOE/5. 'I have never been a pessimist about the Navy till of late, and I am certainly one now'. Admiral Sir Cyprian Bridge, Director of Naval Intelligence 1889-94, C-in-C China 1901. This writer had had very considerable sea-going experience.

3 'I wonder whether Beresford knows what has happened'. Custance to Bridge 15.VI.06; NMM NOE/4/A. These two were helped by Captain Doveton Sturdee, Beresford's Chief of Staff who hated Fisher.

4 My italics. Custance to Noel. 1.IX.06; *Private*. NMM NOE/4/A.

5 See Schurman, *Education of a Navy*, pp. 16-35.

6 Custance to Colomb. 22.XI.06; NMM Colomb Papers.

protector and ferry service for troops destined to fight in France. In other words, Fisher thought not only that his idea of the Navy as the determinant of British strategic policy, might be impossible to sustain, but that the Navy's very competence to do its own job (protect Imperial commerce and the British heartland against invasion) might be seriously challenged by ambitious army thinkers.[1] This made the threat to his position appear even more deadly to him. One can thus understand that Custance's position in all this was strong and central, and how much the basic disagreement hinged on a personal mistrust that almost reached the level of a vendetta.

What did Corbett think of all this? He knew Custance, and understood the animus that the latter showed for Fisher. He also knew that all aspects of the Fisher reforms were not perfect. Indeed Corbett's *Diary* reveals that Custance continued to dine at the Corbett's home from time to time even in 1908. He probably saw in Custance a lack of balance, attributable to the fact that Fisher would allow no separate planning apparatus to grow up with power on its own. As we have seen, in his June 1906 articles in *The Times*, he had advocated a development along those lines and had informed Fisher that to decentralize war planning, and organize it properly, could help to draw the teeth of most of his opposition.

Fisher, for his part, was concerned with getting on with his work, as he saw it. He was prepared to devise expedients to weaken his critics, but he was not prepared to seriously decentralize planning activity in the face of opposition that he regarded as sinister, coming as it did from different levels and sources simultaneously. The handling of so called 'War Plans' of 1906-7 was a good example of this method in action.

Realizing that he was vulnerable to critics if called upon to produce war plans, Fisher decided to use the War Course as Corbett had suggested. The actual plans were drawn up by a small group chaired by Captain Ballard. The Committee's secretary was Captain Maurice Hankey, R.M.A. The Committee was instructed by Fisher to work closely with Slade at the War Course and there can be no doubt that the latter influenced the formulation of the plans and provided material from the War Course war games.[2] Corbett probably did not see all of

---

1   The point could be developed but it appears clear from reading unpublished MSS by Dr. Nicholas d'Ombrian and Dr. Neil Summerton. This subject has been discussed with both these scholars and we have had mutually beneficial exchanges of viewpoint.

2   There is a covering letter from Slade attached to the copy of the *Plans* as finally drawn up. For *Plans* and material see PRO Adm. 116/1043B.

this 'secret' material that covered fleet deployment, but he was certainly asked by Fisher to write up the general strategical principles on which the plans were to be developed — 'to add most materially' to their 'educational value'.[1] The two men met privately to discuss the nature of Corbett's contribution. What was wanted was to bring the whole service into harmony on the question. 'I can only repeat you will be doing the Navy a lasting service by giving us in the proposed Preface an epitome of the Art of Naval War'.[2] Corbett was enjoined to take his time — 'it's going to live', and be known as 'the Bible of the War Course'. Fisher promised to show it to the King. The document, entitled 'Some Principles of Naval Warfare' was in Fisher's hands by 14 April 1907.[3]

Fisher's enthusiasm for Corbett at that moment was based on his recently published pro-Fisher article 'Recent Attacks on the Admiralty' which will be discussed later. He obviously wished to flatter an ally with such a powerful pen. But the Ballard Committee had been sitting since 1906 and there is no evidence that Slade or Ballard ever told Corbett exactly what the War Plans were to look like. 'Divide and rule' was in operation. Indeed, while Fisher was flattering Corbett with such effusions as those noted above, Slade and Ballard were attempting to get him to introduce questioning notes into 'Some Principles of Naval Warfare'. Skilfully, Fisher had followed Corbett's advice. He used the War Course to concoct plans about which he probably cared little except that they should exist, and that they should seem to keep his allies busy. Everybody's self-importance would be pandered to, and a document duly produced for pigeon-holing, and for a wider readership if attacks on the lack of war planning became irresistable.

What Corbett thought about being caught in this cross-fire between Fisher and Slade can only be estimated. That he was taken in by Fisher is highly unlikely. He produced a paper to satisfy everybody and worthy of the obscure fate in store for it. He robbed his own 'Green Pamphlet' to put the importance of 'big battle' in perspective. Then he praised the *Dreadnought* type, dilating on the supreme virtue of speed. He admitted, however, that the cost of the type prohibited vast numbers being produced. This problem would be solved by the production of battle cruisers, or intermediate ship types. He defended

---

1   Fisher to Corbett. 9.III.07, see Marder, *Fear God*, II, p. 120.

2   Fisher to Corbett. 17.III.07; CP/B12.

3   For the document see P.R.O. Adm. 116/1043B. It is sometimes referred to as the 'Preface' to the War Plans, and sometimes as the 'Introduction'. What is quoted is the real title.

the *Dreadnought* on other grounds as well. Slade at once saw that Corbett was using a general paper to support Fisher. He wrote, forthrightly, that the work was good, but 'all special pleading should be carefully avoided, or anything like special pleading, and it seems taken as such . . .'[1] He also defended the battle cruiser, another Fisher hobby-horse, but he used the occasion skillfully to include an argument for more small cruisers, the provision of which Fisher appeared to have neglected. Slade had written at the end of March, 'I am very glad that you are going for his cruiser policy. Ballard and I are sending him a paper on the same subject pointing out the necessity of providing proper cruisers for the fleet. Coming from two *independent sources* I hope it will have some effect . . . I hope you will put your arguments forward very forcibly'.[2] Arguments set out to please everyone could hardly have had great force.

The reason why Corbett argued as he did had much to do with his unenviable assignment. However, he did read the Admiralty a disguised lesson on the importance of battle cruisers based on a sane theory of communication. Cruisers, the eyes of the fleet before and during an engagement, and the work horses of commerce regulation in war, had an important function. But could one denude the battle fleet to build cruisers, or slow down cruiser building to produce more battle ships? Surely it was impossible to be strong everywhere. Corbett saw the need for priorities. His solution was to support a battle cruiser that could serve as 'Jack of all trades': a commerce watching workhorse, the 'eyes of the fleet', and worthy company for a line of battle ships in a fleet action. Hybrids are not generally successful inventions, and the value of battle cruisers can certainly be challenged from an absolute functional point of view. But, aside from submarines, Fisher foresaw the war that actually was fought between 1914 and 1918. If his budget limitations would not allow the Navy to be strong everywhere he was forced to compromise. Whether Fisher needed to be read a lesson on the value of cruisers is doubtful. As usual when forced to choose in impossible circumstances he wanted strong allies: not strategic teachers. Corbett no doubt knew this and his strong desire for anonymity (respected in the event) was perhaps a wise precaution.

When Admiral Sir Arthur Wilson added his comments to those 'Plans' in May 1907, he noted with regard to Corbett's work, that 'it

---

1 Slade to Corbett. 22.IV.07; CP/B12. Slade was obviously under the delusion that the *Plans* would be duly circulated to the Board and to Fleet Commanders.

2 My italics. Slade to Corbett. 30.III.07; CP/B13.

does not require any remarks as it only deals with general principles'. Some such fitting comment might be applied to the whole cynical exercise. The real plans, (and certainly Fisher was contemplating a strategic shift to the North Sea) were buried deep in the First Sea Lord's cranium. Beresford and Custance were right if they thought Fisher distrusted them too much to tell them what he really thought. They were wrong if they thought that this strange production known as 'War Plans' represented either the cast or the range of Fisher's mind. One must ask the question: if Fisher had told the strategic truth, would his Channel commanders have been more concerned to use the information to attack Fisher or to protect Britain's secret designs from becoming the property of the Germans? Cynicism has its uses, as no doubt Corbett understood.

Corbett gave good evidence of the fact that the moment for inter-service trust in war planning had not yet arrived when he wrote 'Recent Attacks on the Admiralty' for *The Nineteenth Century*, published in February 1907. Fisher provided Corbett with the necessary information, but the method was Corbett's own. Fisher thought it the most useful propaganda paper Corbett ever wrote. He was right. Instinctively understanding what has been described above about Custance and Co., Corbett wrote so that the reader was forced to choose between the desperate piecemeal attitudes of the critics, and what Fisher was actually doing at the Admiralty. He affected mild outrage at the irresponsible immoderation of attacks on the Admiralty. He argued that one should not assume a total lack of brainpower amongst senior naval officers. He contrasted the stately movement of Admiralty decision making, from phase to phase, with the inconsistent and/or irresponsible commentators who seemed in many cases to have separate axes to grind. After all, to answer the attacks in public would be to violate the need for military and naval secrecy so necessary to the formulation of efficacious and responsible planning. The argument was strong, and for Fisher it was a godsend. Nevertheless, it was crude, for such arguments lead to the conclusion that secrecy is patriotic and criticism close to treason. The fact is that in all societies there are moments when complete trust is necessary, but they are not frequent, indeed must not be if either efficiency or liberty are to survive. Corbett did distinguish between responsible and irresponsible criticism. Responsible criticism was criticism put forward only when an overwhelming *prima facie* case was evident, so that Parliament would appear justified in assuming that 'the trust they have given has been misplaced'. Where was this evidence? Corbett had clearly appealed over the heads of the naval specialists to general readers open to broad rational argument: to men with no axes to grind.

He defended the *Dreadnought*. It was not pleasant to make decisions for mere size. But Great Britain was not alone in forcing the naval pace. When a size limit was reached beyond the point of tactical and strategic harmony then no doubt the Admiralty would change the trend. Until that time, they had to meet challenges. It might be that some theorists were right; but being a theorist was no guarantee of rightness. There were other arguments for the *Dreadnought*. This subject has been much canvassed.

Custance was always saying that Fisher was a materialist who did not favour study of the art of war. Corbett challenged that view. Perhaps he really thought that Fisher had been captured by War Course ideas. In retrospect it appears that Custance was wrong in thinking Fisher had not considered the problem, but that he was right in pointing out an imbalance. Indeed, it is most likely that Corbett wrote as he did because of worry over Custance's point, and that he wished to encourage Fisher to move to meet it. Mercifully, the whole naval problem was not revealed to him as it was to Fisher.

There was nothing half-hearted about this writing. Fisher got exactly what he wanted with no quibblings or qualifications attached. It was 'just the thing to meet the present distress as St. Paul would say'.[1] His gratitude increased as important people, the Prince of Wales, among others, commented favourably on the article.[2] The combination of erudition and calculated support was irresistible. What staggers the retrospective student is the fact that Corbett realized what he was doing. He knew how dangerous it was for a man to mix propaganda and scholarship under the shadow of the power structure and, with one further exception, he resisted the attempt to do it again. Corbett chose his moment. He allowed himself to be used for what appeared to be a creditable reason; but he did not fool himself by what he did. Fisher may well have been right; that one article may have saved Sir John at the Admiralty: not an unimportant effect for a literary man to have achieved.

The one further exception occurred in March 1907. At the R.U.S.I. Corbett directly joined issue with Custance and the anti-speed (and hence anti-size) battleship advocates.[3] He tried to show that there was something to be said for the Admiralty concentration on speed in

1   Fisher to Corbett. 15.I.07; CP/B12.

2   Fisher to Corbett. 4.II.07; CP/B12.

3   Julian Corbett. 'The Strategical Value of Speed in Battle-Ships', *RUSI Journal*, July 1907. The paper was delivered on 6 March.

preference to radius of action, and in many ways he covered the same ground as he had in his War Plans 'Introduction'. There was, however, an important difference, in that he did not base this argument on a general theory of communications as he had done hitherto. What he did try to do, was to suggest that controversial subjects such as this one were best dealt with by an attempt to assess all the relevant arguments for and against a particular course of action rather than simply marshal arguments in support of a favoured policy. He tried to introduce his hearers into the basic logic of debate, and although he gave due credit to the opponents of the pro-speed school for initiating discussion on this important subject and claimed his main desire was to ventilate it, he had hard words for the selective use of historical and other kinds of argument used to prove a preselected point of view. It was certainly clear to his audience that it was Custance whom he was attempting to educate.[1]   Also, Corbett emphatically disagreed with Mahan on questions of speed and size. But again, it is doubtful how much of this lesson on the art of naval controversy impressed his audience. The Chairman revealed the same sort of mind with regard to the talk as Admiral Wilson had in reference to the 'Introduction' to the War Plans. He said, after the audience largely declined to cross verbal swords with Corbett, 'we have heard a very instructive lecture from the philosophical and historical point of view, and it is not easy for us to criticize it or speak about it at short notice'. In other words, it was too much for them, but silence certainly did not mean consent.

Also in 1907, Corbett published an article on the 'Freedom of the Seas' as background British propaganda for The Hague Peace Conference.[2] This article does not bear directly on the subject of this chapter, although it was written with Fisher's blessing. That is to say, it was not controversial in the national, as opposed to the international, sense.

When he wrote in 1907, Corbett was attempting to moderate attacks on the Admiralty, attacks which were impossible for Fisher to answer in public both for reasons of protocol and security. The continuing problem was that specific attacks, say against either the *Dreadnought* type or against fleet dispositions, were presented by Fisher's enemies

1   In the discussion when the paper was read, Admiral Bowden Smith specifically referred to 'Barfleur', which was Custance's *nom de plume,* and Corbett made it clear by an interjection that it was indeed 'Barfleur' whom he meant. See *ibid.* pp. 833-4.

2   See 'Capture of Private Property at Sea', *The Nineteenth Century,* June 1907. Separately reprinted in Admiral A.T. Mahan's edited *Some Neglected Aspects of War* (Boston, 1907).

as being motivated by the fact that no real war plans existed. In 1908, the critics shifted their attack to Whitehall, and within the confines of the public service and government circles. Again Fisher called upon Corbett, this time to write in defence of the 'all big gun type', i.e. specifically the 13.5 gun. He needed assistance, since he was facing army criticisms regarding invasion possibilities. Beresford men were attacking his construction and war planning policies, and from the politicians he was finding a reluctance to meet the Naval estimates as the Admiralty Board put them forward. Corbett, however, was in general agreement with Fisher's construction policy anyway and so he consented to help. He probably never knew just how much Sir John needed that help. He produced a Cabinet paper, begun on 11 March, in a couple of days.[1]

This piece of writing was undoubtedly effective, since Corbett was next asked to assist Commander F.C. Dreyer, the Director of Naval Operations, to prepare a similar paper to educate people within the service along the same lines. Actually Corbett was to supervise Dreyer's work. According to Fisher, Dreyer had the brain of a Newton, to which Corbett was to play Demosthenes, since only one in a hundred could understand this Newton.[2] Poor Dreyer! He had a reputation in the service for having a swelled head. Corbett found him intelligent and sound regarding his facts, but 'like most of them cannot easily distinguish detail from principles'.[3] Finally, Corbett was forced to take over and write the paper himself, as Dreyer kept writing about the overwhelming evidence in favour of the *Dreadnought* type (with which Corbett agreed), but writing as if he were simply attempting to convince an Admiralty Board, and not writing a state paper. Corbett informed him that serious arguments against the type had to be logically refuted and not merely denounced.[4] The naval historian enjoyed this work. He called it 'licking into shape the confused memoranda of the experts'.[5]

As we have seen, the lack of an effective War Planning body was linked to the lack of trust in the service chain of command. Previous to the Dreyer episode, Fisher had asked Corbett's opinion as to whether

---

1 Corbett *Diary*. General entry 1907-8, RCP. This piece of evidence seems to prove the assertion that Corbett wrote his general entry well into the spring of 1908.

2 Fisher to Corbett. 10.III.08; CP/B12.

3 Corbett *Diary*. 14.III.08; RCP.

4 *Ibid*. 4.LV.08; RCP.

5 *Ibid*. General entry, 1907-08; RCP.

Lord Charles Beresford should be called in to give evidence before the Invasion Sub-Committee of the Committee of Imperial Defence[1] Corbett said no. He argued for the superiority of the Board of Admiralty over the various area command officers, owing to the Board's ultimate responsibility for the course of events in wartime. 'That responsibility rested with Admiralty or, ultimately, with the Cabinet'. There were historical exceptions to this rule, but the exceptions were specified as such when instructions to area commanders were sent out. Corbett wrote in that way 'in the view of what seemed to me their (Admiralty's) inadequate handling of the position Lord C. Beresford was trying to arrogate to himself'.[2] Actually, Fisher had already made the power structure clear to Lord Charles, so Corbett's ideas, although congenial to him were not decisive in any way — as Corbett attempted to claim.[3] But when Fisher wrote to the Foreign Secretary in January 1908,[4] to complain of a tendency to treat the Admiralty and its commanders as equal to each other, the First Sea Lord used Corbett's historical arguments to bolster his claims. The historian had given something of value, not for propaganda, but because he believed it to be sound advice based on historical precedent.

Most of the pull Corbett had with Fisher ceased in the spring of 1908, as the Invasion inquiry drew to a close. Much of the evidence Corbett recorded to support his claim to have influenced Fisher on naval affairs is contained in a general entry, written for a *Diary* that began in 1908. It was in the form of an introduction which in particular covered the events of late 1907. Whether this was written in late 1907, or in the spring of 1908 is uncertain; probably the latter for it is clear that he knew his days of frequent consultation were over. It is ironic that he began to keep a *Diary* outlining his contact with naval affairs just at the moment when his real influence with Fisher began to wane. Also it is interesting and perhaps significant to note that Slade, recently translated from the War Course to be Director of Naval Intelligence, began his *Diary* at the same time. Nothing is more certain than that they began to lose influence together and at the same time. Eventually Slade was banished to the East Indies; Corbett was excluded from the corridors of power. Why?

To speak of Corbett's own position first. He had, really, nothing to

1   Fisher to Corbett. 4.XII.07; CP/B12.
2   Corbett *Diary*. General entry, 1907-8; RCP.
3   See Fisher to Corbett. 4.XII.07, Marder, *Fear God*, II, p. 153.
4   Fisher to Grey. 23.I.08. Marder, *Fear God*, II, p. 155.

offer Fisher but his brains. He had no influence due to rank or position
similar to that of such a person as Lord Esher who was omnipresent at
Court. Fisher wrote pointedly in the spring of 1909 stating that more
articles like that in the *XIX Century* of 1907 would be useful.[1] Corbett
just as pointedly replied that the article had made him only one friend,
(Fisher) and mentioned the interruptions such propaganda caused in
'the spade work which wants doing so badly for the Service and for
which the labourers are so few'.[2] This letter was written almost a year
after he had begun to lose the confidence of his 'one friend'. The value
of propaganda outstripped that of long term history in the First Sea
Lord's mind.

It is likely that Corbett was quite well aware of the fact that he was
not moving Fisher's mind or even arousing his interest. This will appear
even more clearly as a result of his involvement in the invasion
investigation. That he knew the whole reason for this turn of events
is very unlikely. On the other hand, to dismiss Corbett's strong reply
to the First Sea Lord's request for propaganda on the grounds that his
historical work was more important, as mere justification for a loss of
prestige, would be wrong. He was a historian and he knew that his
strength lay in that work. He knew that Sir John wished to use him for
propaganda because of his professional prowess. He believed that it was
his duty to help educate the navy, strategically and tactically and when
faced with the choice between being at the elbow of the powerful, on
sufferance, and working his long term plan, he had no real difficulty in
not only accepting but declaring for, his fate.

In Slade's case it is clear that, from the beginning, he wished to be
regarded as a bridge between Fisher and the best of the minds of the
First Sea Lord's opponents. Slade understood a good deal about the
necessities of the Navy. He pushed for the creation of a naval War
Staff, he wished Fisher would modify his views concerning the
involvement of the Army leaders in strategy that was partly naval, and
he attempted to moderate Fisher's views on the Beresford group. His
Diary makes all of these things clear, even as it makes it clear that
Fisher appeared to be behaving irrationally, or at least like a cornered
animal. What Slade did not grasp was that Fisher's frustrations were
real and that they were based, not just on mere personal spite, but on
the realities of his position due to general political considerations. A
few examples will suffice to show that Slade did not possess the whole

1   Fisher to Corbett. CP/B12. 3.IV.09.
2   Corbett to Fisher. 4.IV.09; CP/B12.

truth, and will reveal how Corbett could get a warped picture from contact with the Director of Naval Intelligence.

With respect to the value of combined operations, it is clear that Fisher objected to the Invasion inquiry because the Army was proposing a separate role for itself independent of the Navy. Slade and Corbett pressed continually for combined operations planning. Fisher had recognized this as early as 1905. By 1908 he was attempting to preserve the Navy's freedom of action. Yet Slade noted complacently on the first of February of that year that 'Sir J(ohn) agreed that the best form of defence would be to send an army to sea. It would paralyze all German initiative and would tie up a large portion of their forces to the sea coast'.[1] Slade thought that he had a convert. He was two years out of date.

The War Plans problem was clearly related to Beresford. Slade asked Fisher for permission to see Beresford. At the lunch, to which Fisher reluctantly agreed, Beresford alternated between conciliation and threats.[2] Seven days later Slade recorded that Fisher said he would not discuss war plans with Admirals afloat because 'C [harles] B [eresford] was unreliable from a security point of view'. But Slade suggested that they 'might discuss *a* plan with C.B. and let him *think* it was the real one. J.F. agreed'. Again Slade was a year out of date. As we have seen, Fisher had thought of that in 1906.

Fisher of course shifted in his personal response to Beresford. Slade felt free to criticize these shifts.[3] Clearly the reason why he did not sack Beresford at once was political. Yet Slade complained that Fisher himself spent most of his time lobbying the politicians.[4] By 13 November, when Fisher was most desperate, Slade wrote; 'The real fact is that his [Fisher's] whole energies are now given up to intriguing with the politicians and not to working out war problems'. With friends like that who needed enemies. The more charitable truth is that Slade was incapable of seeing that the light of pure reason (from a naval officer's point of view) would not prevail in the milieu of the time. For the same reason his plans for a Naval War Staff which fill

---

1   Slade *Diary*. NMM. Later on he wrote happily of a small committee set up to draw up a handbook on the subject. See *Diary*, 29.III.08.

2   Slade *Diary*, 6.I.08.

3   For instance, Fisher sent a rude message to Beresford regarding a request of the latter for submarines and mining vessels. He was 'now frightened at what he has done . . . Sir J is not well and looks very old and worn to-day'. Slade *Diary*, 24.IV.08.

4   Slade *Diary*, 6.V.08, 20.V.08.

up pages of Slade's *Diary* were only paper proposals. He was intelligent but naive — not uncommon attributes of naval reformers within the service. Fisher was aware of his subordinate's limitations, so that he was bound to become progressively disenchanted with Slade.

Corbett was involved in this dangerous situation because of the opinions that he and Slade held in common about the need for a Naval Staff. He wanted the Staff and Sir John at the same time. Slade was prepared to be content with the former. Consequently Slade was a dangerous ally for a man with no position to keep him safe.

The Fishpond was losing its fish. Richmond claimed later in life that his advocacy of a Staff caused his break with Fisher.[1] There it was again: Naval Staff. Considering how little confidence intellectually arrogant men like Richmond, Corbett and Slade inspired in the general run of naval officers, it is surprising that they could not read Fisher's mind on the matter. Furthermore, the Staff idea had been put forward by Beresford as early as 1886! It was one of the hallmarks of the 'Syndicate of Discontent'.

It is hoped that the political reasons for the neglect of a Naval Staff, that graveyard of naval reformers, have been made clear. Since Corbett was a casualty, it may not be improper to say a few words on what was achieved and what was possible. First, Corbett and Slade did set up planning apparatus and a critical study approach at the War Course. Corbett's and Richmond's historically oriented thought assisted this process. That accomplishment held. It is impossible to claim more than that for them. From the point of view of realism they appear to have been a credulous lot.

Fisher, of course, introduced a Navy War Council not long before his fall in 1909. It had no power. Marder has written 'this modest reform was not a true naval staff'.[2] Richmond damned it with the words 'a most absurd bit of humbug'.[3] It was not an effective creation. Reforms are made by men, and in a hierarchical service naval officers, when they reached positions of power, habitually fenced off their vineyard and guarded it. How do you create a Naval War Staff of such men? What is requisite?

Vice-Admiral Kenneth Dewar has written that a War Staff ought not

1   Richmond gave this information orally to Arthur Marder in 1946. See Marder, *Portrait of An Admiral* (London, 1952), p. 367 n 1.

2   Marder, *From the Dreadnought*, I, pp. 247-8.

3   Marder, *Portrait of an Admiral*, p. 62.

to be composed of men with administrative functions to perform.[1] Mr. Churchill is usually given credit, and indeed gave himself credit, for forming a War Staff later on. But he knew the claim was hollow. He set up an organization and blamed its failure on the poor quality of its members, not, of course on himself. The confused Appendix A at the back of his book *The World Crisis* indicates that he did not thoroughly understand the problems.[2] Marder has written, charitably, that 'there was no serious effort made in Churchill's time to separate staff from administrative duties. The First Sea Lord, who was responsible for operations, continued to carry out a multitude of other duties. At any rate, war plans were no longer locked up in the brain of the First Lord'.[3] One is inclined to remark 'a pity'.

It can now be seen that there were two ways to institute War Plans. The first was to use the Corbett-Slade War Course method and nurture it *slowly* until it could be grafted onto the Admiralty power structure. We have seen why this ultimately failed — but it was reasonable, before 1908, because it took account of the need for the First Sea Lord to activate planning, and it took account of Fisher's problems in a realistic way.

To set up a complete scheme absolutely *de novo* could only be a paper exercise unless the formulators of war plans could be drawn into the operational arena by an executive officer who was willing to identify himself with such plans. In short, at some stage plans had to be integrated into the policy of the Admiralty Board — or its Chief Officer, and no amount of talk about the need for a separation of functions can disguise that fact. This is the pit, not uncongenial for one of such a self-confident cast of mind, into which Churchill fell in what was not his finest hour. Reflecting in the 1920s, his acute mind perceived the real problem well enough. Also he was right to comment on the lack of trained manpower available to him in 1912.

What needs to be pointed out is that Corbett saw all of this in 1906. Fisher saw it too. So did Slade. The vision smashed on the rock of circumstances that paper schemes could not conquer. Looking back it can be seen that the trio who fell out over this problem in 1908, saw what needed to be done. It took Churchill ten years to find this out. Knowing what we do now it is difficult to wish the Navy had got rid

1   K.G.B. Dewar, *The Navy from Within* (London, 1939), pp. 140-1.

2   W.S. Churchill, *The World Crisis,* 4 vols. (London, 1958), vol. IV. pp. 137ff., also vol. I. pp. 69-70.

3   Marder, *From the Dreadnought,* I, p. 266.

of Fisher before 1910. Such an event might well have had disastrous consequences when war came. Corbett and Slade must accept some share of the blame for pushing for the impossible in an impossible situation.

When, however, one looks at the whole range of criticism of Fisher that characterized the reaction of many of his contemporaries, criticism that still titillates the minds of some 'prehistoric' naval officers even today, one is amazed at the maturity of Corbett's overall response. From the first, he understood the general nature of Fisher's position, and its vulnerability. It was for this reason that he continually attempted to raise naval controversy above the level of personal axe-grinding. Like Fisher, he saw that perfection was not going to be attained in this fallible world in a time of national naval emergency, and he constantly strove for broad, balanced viewpoints rather than peep-show looks at perfection in details. Fisher's tragedy was that his 'never explain' mentality and his general view of the situation, kept him apart from any particularists who might have helped the service. While understanding Sir John, Corbett, somewhat like Slade, attempted to bridge that gap. It turned out to be not only impossible, but dangerous. Yet the fact that he made some headway in forging that communications link is well worth noting. It appears to have been, as well, a worthwhile ambition, if not a practical one.

The Invasion enquiry of 1907-08 provides further evidence of this gallant attempt of an outsider to box the compass.

5

INVASION 1907-8

During the year 1907-8 the Committee of Imperial Defence appointed an important Sub-Committee to study the possibility of a German invasion of the United Kingdom. Julian Corbett was involved in its deliberations.

The subject of a possible French invasion had been investigated by the C.I.D. in 1903. The result was that the then Prime Minister, Arthur Balfour, expressed the opinion that such a French invasion was not a reasonable war risk.[1] He also wrote a paper in which he expressed the idea that a raid (10,000 men or fewer) might succeed, but that it would involve an almost prohibitive risk.

Subsequently, after the Franco-British military conversations began, apprehension shifted to Germany. By 1907 the possibility of an invasion from that quarter was being canvassed. The most eminent of those concerned was Lord Roberts, who was also a promoter of the National Service League which advocated conscription for home service only. The conscription issue was not one that either political party was inclined to embrace, since it was more potentially a divisive rather than a rallying issue. The League, therefore needed more public support and attempts were made to promote it by questioning the Navy's capacity for defence against invasion. This is not to say that the Leaguers, or Lord Roberts, were not genuine in their fears. Yet, clearly, it would be difficult to justify the formation of a large home conscript army unless it had a direct threat to confront. If it could be demonstrated that an invasion was possible, despite naval preparations, the threat would be clear. So Lord Roberts raised the question in the House of Lords, asking whether or not a large enemy force could land in England at that moment. The First Lord, Tweedmouth, replied that the bulk of the Fleet was at present off Lagos on manoeuvres but added that the Government did not anticipate a mortal threat at a moment of profound European peace. Lord Roberts said that the Government was living in a fool's paradise, and he prepared to precipitate more official action. In June he called on Balfour, then Leader of the Opposition, who was regarded as a non-partisan defence expert, and presented him with 'Notes on Invasion' which, he claimed, contained

---

1 Extracts from the Memorandum on Invasion, by Mr. Balfour, when Prime Minister. RIC/9/1.

material that proved an invasion from Germany to be a realistic stroke of war. Balfour took the submission seriously and it was arranged that a high-powered Sub-Committee of the Committee of Imperial Defence would shortly sit to deal with the problem.[1]

The Navy, to whom this enquiry came as unwelcome news, was not, under Fisher's dynamic methods, exactly a 'band of brothers'. Also on the executive side it was preoccupied with problems of ship design and construction. In these circumstances naval budgets aroused controversy. All this is well-known and certainly kept Sir John Fisher, the driving centre of this sometimes unwilling dynamo, preoccupied with matters of more importance, to his mind, than invasion possibility.

Relations between the two services were not close. It has been seen that some naval and military men wished to increase the amount of overall joint planning that took place. They had some success in respect to colonial or peripheral thinking about small expeditions but had no influence on basic policy or main thrust activity. In the French conversations army personnel perceived a new role for their service and their minds were shifting to the continent. This new thinking was viewed with extreme distaste by Sir John Fisher. He could hardly expect that War Office officials would not take pleasure in his discomfiture. Army authorities had nothing to lose. This was a mercy for them since Haldane was in the process of creating the small regular army with which his reforms are associated. They needed a breathing space.

Fisher felt he had a great deal to lose. In the circumstances an attack on naval capability could only be interpreted by him as a direct attack on himself. He was faced with the natural disadvantage of an autocratic man in a democratic situation. He had reached the stage where his prestige, and that of the Service, were equally and inseparably vulnerable. While attempting to cajole the C.I.D. to drop the matter, he began to prepare his defence.

Despite the fact that Sir George Clarke was being dropped from the Secretary's post at the C.I.D. because Fisher had not supported his view of service co-operation, Clarke was an amphibian and he denigrated the idea of a German invasion in a letter to *The Times*.[2] Also, in 1907 when Ottley left the Naval Intelligence Department to take Clarke's post, Slade became Director of Naval Intelligence in his place. Fisher provided Slade with a copy of Lord Roberts's 'Notes on

1   *Invasions and Raids* (Secret Admiralty Print) pp. 30-7. NMM. RIC/9/1.

2   'Navalis' to *The Times* 5.X.07.

Invasion' and urged him to work up a response.[1] Slade did this and was designated as the chief Admiralty spokesman for the enquiry. As he did so it became apparent that a gap existed between Slade's and Fisher's thinking on how the Admiralty defence should be handled. It was Slade's view that in order to retain the good will of the War Office it should be admitted that (as he believed) a raid was possible, if risky.[2] Fisher maintained that nothing could get through the naval net — 'not even a dinghy'.[3] He stayed with the dinghy view throughout. As the date of the hearing approached, and Sir John was not capable of either quashing it or of making his dinghy view prevail amongst his service supporters, Corbett was brought in and informed that he was to write the Admiralty paper in rebuttal to the 'Notes'.

The Roberts case had been supported and somewhat publicized by Charles A. Court Repington, Military Correspondent of *The Times,* who used its columns to canvass the invasion danger.[4] Roberts had other allies such as Lord Lovat, the Cambridge medieval historian G.G. Coulton and L.S. Amery, the author of *The Times History of the War in South Africa*; but it was Repington who kept the issue before the public and who appeared as Roberts's chief technical expert at the hearings. The Admiralty people thought him the chief propelling force behind the whole attack, and he certainly played a prominent part. His motives are hard to determine. Certainly he was not content with mere Admiralty denials that invasion was possible. Fisher did not think Admiralty policy should be made available to the public. In fact, he trusted no one. He was open to attack on this matter, as we have seen, and very inclined to be sensitive about it.

Lord Esher wondered what Fisher had to hide. After all, a body set up by the Prime Minister, containing a galaxy of important men in public office, could hardly be called irresponsible, or equated with 'the public'.[5] But Repington was a newspaper man, ex-army but none the less, at that moment, a civilian. It is worth noting that Fisher,

---

1   Although when they replaced Clarke at the C.I.D. Slade was designated the new Director of Naval Intelligence, and he had probably been notified of the change by August. He wrote to Corbett the day after he signed his *memo* on the Notes to say that he had been made DNI. CP/B13.

2   Memorandum by Head of Naval War College. See Admiralty Secret Print *Invasion and Raids* 16.VIII.07; pp. 6-22 NMM. RIC/9/1.

3   Confidential memo by First Sea Lord. See Admiralty Secret Print, *Invasion and Raids,* pp. 1-5. NMM. RIC/9/1.

4   *The Times* 28.VIII.06.

5   Esher to Fisher 24.VIII.07; M.V. Brett, *Journals and Letters of Reginald, Viscount Esher* (London, 1934) p. 247.

while maintaining his right not to divulge detailed Admiralty war plans to the C.I.D., nonetheless turned to Corbett to support his case — and Corbett was certainly a civilian. It may well be asked therefore, how much of the naval war plans, such as they were, had Corbett seen? We have noted that it is unlikely that he saw the Ballard Report, despite the fact that he wrote the 'Preface' to it.[1] There appears to be no evidence that Fisher ever took Corbett entirely into his confidence, or let him see either the war plans — or what passed for them. It is possible that Fisher enlightened him orally. The precise purpose he was called in to effect, however, did not call for any knowledge that his scholarship and natural civilian intelligence had not already given him. It is impossible to be certain.

The Sub-Committee was chaired by the Chancellor of the Exchequer, H.H. Asquith, who became Prime Minister before the inquiry concluded. It also contained David Lloyd George, (President of the Board of Trade), Edward Grey, (Foreign Secretary), Lord Tweedmouth (First Lord of the Admiralty — succeeded by Reginald McKenna in April 1905), R.B. Haldane (Secretary of State for War), The Earl of Crewe (various Ministerial posts), Viscount Esher, Admiral Sir John Fisher, Captain Edmond Slade R.N., Generals Sir N. Lyttleton and Sir W.A. Nicholson (successively Chiefs of Imperial General Staff), General Sir John French (Director of Military Operations), and Captain Charles Ottley, R.N., (Secretary of the C.I.D., and to the Sub-Committee).[2] It was the sort of committee that could be expected to pronounce authoritatively on the matter it was called to consider, and one not likely to be overawed by Sir John Fisher.

It was while Corbett was completing the 'invasion' chapters in *England and the Seven Years War* that Roberts's agitation began to surface. It may have influenced that writing. In any event, Fisher had read the proofs of the book, and in September 1907 wrote to Corbett suggesting a public article on invasion since 'Repington and Co., will assuredly be at it again soon'. Corbett might help to induce 'the returning warmth of security and bliss by convincing the public that 40 million Pomeranian Grenadiers can't be landed in five minutes'. Fisher mentioned the *Notes on Invasion* in disparaging terms, and expressed the conviction that Repington was behind it all, the others

---

[1] *Ibid.*

[2] Secret Report of the Sub-Committee to reconsider the Question of Overseas Attack, 22.X.08. PRO. CAB38/14.

being merely 'like putty in Repington's hands'.[1]   Corbett refused,
claiming that too much propaganda from his pen would reduce his
influence, and hence defeat Fisher's object.

In the meantime, however, Slade, now installed as Director of Naval
Intelligence in London, had enlisted Corbett's help in preparing the
Admiralty case; to provide historical examples to contribute to the
Admiralty presentation.[2]   The result was that Corbett was soon
summoned by the First Sea Lord himself, and accepted as a partner in
full trust.[3]

'It began', Corbett wrote, 'by Fisher sending for me and telling me
he wanted to place the whole thing in our hands (Slade's and mine)'.
Fisher decreed that Corbett was to write the Admiralty Memorandum
in reply.[4]   That, of course, had to wait on the first official meeting of
the Sub-Committee, and in the meantime, Slade and Corbett busied
themselves going through a paper submitted by Repington involving
German planning in the 1860s. They plunged into Moltke, and found
that the great German strategist had been by no means converted to the
idea of oversea attack even against Denmark.[5]

In the meantime, Fisher was still doing his best to get the
investigation quashed at the political level by roundly claiming that it
was only the Admiralty that was concerned over the invasion problem.
He got no support for this move. Haldane referred to it as a 'silly
ground' to take up.[6] Esher, who had often championed Fisher's causes,
was equally firm. Actually, Esher had concluded that the Committee
of Imperial Defence needed to be won to Fisher's ideas, not treated
constantly as an enemy. Even a genius needs allies. The difference
between Esher and Fisher was one of temperament as well. For Esher
saw politics as a process of continual change and adjustment. For
Fisher, every challenge at that time appeared to be mortal, and he was
determined to kill the invasion challenge once and for all.

There was some reason for Fisher's viewpoint. Morley had been
offered the chairmanship of the Sub-Committee, and refused,[7] and

1   Fisher to Corbett quoted in Marder, *Fear God* vol. II, pp. 137-8.
2   Slade to Corbett. 28.X.07 and 25.XI.07; CP/B6.
3   Slade to Corbett 14.XI.07; CP/B6.
4   Slade to Corbett 18.XI.07; CP/B6.
5   Slade to Corbett 22.XI.07; CP/B6.
6   Haldane to Esher 23.VIII.07; Brett, *Journals,* pp. 246-7.
7   Esher to Prime Minister 17.X.07; Brett, *Journals* pp. 252-3.

the views of Asquith, who got the job, were not known. Furthermore, while Fisher was raging in frustration, Roberts was attempting to get Custance, Bridge, and the Prince of Wales, to give evidence against Fisher; in other words to publicly split the Navy over the invasion inquiry. More predictably, Beresford was attempting to get himself called as a hostile witness.[1] Hence, it was a trifle complacent for Esher to write: 'After all we are not putting the Admiralty or anyone on their defence. We are endeavouring to elicit the truth, and to draw sound inferences from ascertained facts'.[2] It was all right for Esher if 'truth' demolished Sir John; Esher had no official position to lose. Fisher might have been easier in his mind had he known that General Sir John French thought that the ground taken up by Roberts, for his 'decisive struggle', (i.e. the invasion danger) was 'absurd'.[3]

The inquiry opened on 27 November. That day and the next were taken up by Roberts and Repington reading prepared statements, the first of which stated Robert's general position regarding the possibility of invasion, and Repington's dealing in great detail with the enemy possibilities for success.[4]

Roberts said that he wanted an impartial inquiry based on new information, and he wished the starting point to be that of Balfour, whose 1905 memo had neglected the question of fleet actions and based his rejection of the proposition on points of detail. He also stressed that the Germans would take the initiative and strike with surprise on their side. His next point was that present naval dispositions were faulty *vis-à-vis* a North Sea attack. This moved him into the realm of Admiralty policy. He admitted that, while his convictions on this point were strong, his information was not authoritative and he requested enlightenment regarding Admiralty dispositions. Anyhow, the Germans would only fight a main fleet action if forced to do so, the plan being that when the convoy was ready to sail, or at sea, German naval units would attack British seaborne defences along the East Coast, carry out diversionary feints, blockade the straits of Dover for forty-eight hours, and deliver the invasion force to its destination seventy-four hours after the order to act had gone out in Germany. Roberts claimed that the German General Staff was not blind to the problems and merits of combined

1 Esher *Journal* 24.XI.07; Brett, *Journals,* p. 262.

2 Esher *Journal* 18.X.07; Brett, Journals p. 260.

3 Esher *Journal* 24.XI.07; Brett *Journals* p. 262.

4 *Secret Memorandum Read by Lord Roberts at the First Meeting of the Sub-Committee for Invasion,* 27 November, 1907; NMM RIC/9/1.

strategy, and that there was historical evidence for this. German planning would also be helped by the possible absence of both the British Army and the Royal Navy from the United Kingdom 'at any time'. It is an army, said Roberts, not a navy that constitutes a final guarantee against invasion, and the use of the word 'impossible' Roberts held, was 'encouraging lethargy' and preventing 'any serious consideration by the people of this country of any military problem'. After all fleets *could* miss one another, and since surprise methods worked on land he had no doubt but that they also would work at sea. Invasion was, he said in conclusion, becoming every day more probable.

Repington's paper purported to view the possibility step by step through the eyes of German Staff officers. He declared that the committee should not decide what points of detail were most important until they had heard all the evidence, and 'it may be that they will have some difficulty in deciding even then'.

Repington made a number of points regarding the adequacy of German ports, railways, etc., that, as we have seen, no one then or afterwards quarrelled with. Regarding the sea operation, he claimed that if the German Navy and the convoy sailed separately, it would, given some surprise, be necessary to blockade the Straits of Dover for forty-eight hours. If both fleet and convoy sailed together on the assumption that they would achieve complete surprise, then the time necessary for holding the Dover blockade would be reduced to seventeen hours. This Napoleonic concept, in 'a new form', would succeed since 'the present distribution of our Navy in home waters does not appear to give us an assurance of naval superiority in the North Sea' in the time required for a German invasion. Repington then went on to canvass the value of land forces as an invasion deterrent, cited people's awareness of this in 1588 and 1805 as proof of its being a traditional viewpoint, and also claimed that the withdrawal of the fleet to home waters was a sign of the decline of Empire brought on by small army forces in the United Kingdom. He also mentioned the possibility that the Germans might use Baltic Ports and further stated that Ireland appeared to him as a traditionally vulnerable area. He postulated an invading force of between 70,000 and 100,000 men.

On these two days of meetings, Esher's comments were that Roberts's 'peroration' was 'very well done' and that Repington's collation of evidence was 'impressive'. Fisher was full of wrath and had to be told that only the C.I.D. stood between himself and a full inquiry into the state of the Navy. 'What', wrote Esher 'has he to conceal?'[1] However, the naval case had been carefully thought out. Slade, who had been working on the problem for months sounded a note of happy relief when he wrote to Corbett that the evidence had revealed 'nothing new'. It was the old story done over in detail; its ulterior purpose was to secure conscription. He was not worried about the witnesses who might be called, since they would deal with troop movements in Germany — a theme that the Navy did not intend to dispute.[2] Fisher was due to leave for a Sandringham visit for the weekend, and Slade called Corbett in to see him before Sir John left. The talk showed how Fisher was really thinking. Slade thanked Corbett for cheering Fisher up, as the First Sea Lord was down in the dumps; 'it is as much or more estimates than invasion which is weighing on his mind. He wants to make political capital with the Government and finds he cannot carry the Board with him'. To Corbett, Slade wrote revealingly, 'the more I think of this invasion business the more I am pleased that it should have come up, as we ought now to have a very good chance of showing that the Army and Navy are not separate forces, but only divisions of one force and should never be thought of as apart from each other'.[3]

Meanwhile, Fisher impressed on Corbett that his attempts to get the investigation stopped (which never ceased) were aimed at keeping Beresford at bay, since he was convinced that Lord Charles was Repington's ace of trumps. But if things went on and Roberts and Repington were cross-examined (as was proposed for 12 December), he asked Corbett's advice on the proper line to be taken up.[4] Corbett understood the point and its importance for the inquiry.[5] To call Beresford, he replied, would be to admit the right of the C.I.D. 'to review the naval strategy of the Board'. He felt that the function of the C.I.D. was 'to co-ordinate military and naval strategy, not to interfere with Admiralty responsibility for the details of naval strategy'; if it was not, then the Admiralty Board had sunk to a 'mere section of a great General Staff'. Whether or not this was its logical place was too important a matter for a sub-committee of the C.I.D. to decide — it was a matter of high Cabinet policy. Traditionally the Board had never

---

1   Esher *Journal* 27.XI.07 28.XI.07; Brett *Journals* p. 263.

2   Slade to Corbett 27.XI.07; CP/B6.

3   Slade to Corbett 1.12.07; CP/B6.

4   Fisher to Corbett 4.12.07; CP/B12.   Marder, *Fear God* vol. II, pp. 152-3.

5   Corbett to Fisher 4.12.07; CP/B12.   This letter is partially quoted by Marder in *Fear God*, vol. II, p. 153 n.

had its strategic functions abrogated by politicians in time of peace. The letter dealt with the 'no man's land' of C.I.D. purpose and function.[1] Corbett's purpose was to give Sir John understanding and to calm him down.

On 12 December the committee met again. The First Lord, Lord Tweedmouth, had decided that he would question Roberts. On this occasion the professional navy had to suffer for an excess of zeal on the part of its civil ruler. Even 'Sir J.' [ohn], wrote Slade, says 'his questions are too bloodthirsty' and asked him 'to moderate the tone down'.[2] Corbett helped Slade formulate questions — but unfortunately no one could do anything with Tweedmouth whose intentions were good, but whose judgment was bad, and who, by throwing sarcastic and indecorous remarks at Roberts, created a thoroughly bad impression.[3]

A weak First Lord was one of the prices paid for the dominance of the First Sea Lord. It was a thoroughly dangerous place to be weak and it proved to be costly.

Slade's report of the day's meeting was more explicit and gives some behind-the-scenes information. It is quoted in full.

> The seance today was a great success. First of all your memorandum was extremely well received. Mr. Haldane said to me that it was one of the most important state papers that he had ever seen. Several of the members said that they did not know what the naval side of the question was before. When I got to the C.I.D. room this morning I met Sir J. French on the stairs — and he said to me I 'see the pulverization has begun' — referring to your memorandum.
>
> We began by a discussion on procedure in the course of which Mr. Haldane again spoke of the memorandum. Then Lord Roberts and Col. Repington came in and Lord Tweedmouth asked questions of Lord Roberts. They both lost their tempers and began a very heated discussion. This wasted time and led to no result, and it was not until nearly 1 o'clock that we could really get to work on Repington. The War Office people took him in hand first and showed that his views were to say the least of it very optimistic. I began on him after lunch and had him for just over an hour. I got him to the stage of saying that he did not know and could not answer my questions. I have only got as far as placing the German Fleet — which has been reduced from everything that floats to the ships in active commission in the Channel to cover the transports. I am now worrying him about the escort to the transports, but I have not got very far with that. Lord Roberts who is allowed to be present says we cannot know where the troops are going to land — but that will be very easily disposed of. We do not meet again until the New Year, so we shall have plenty of time to work up a fresh

1 Slade to Corbett 6.XII.07; CP/B6.

2 Esher, *Journal* 13.XII.07; Brett *Journals*, p. 269.

3 Slade to Corbett 12.XII.07; CP/B6.

attack. They have put in a paper dealing with historical precedents which we will go over together when it is printed. P.S. Thanks for the book and corrected proof. I will send you a final copy when I get to the office tomorrow.[1]

Corbett's memorandum was a twenty-three page typewritten quarto essay.[2] It was based upon his personal knowledge of the patterns developed in the course of threatened invasions of England in the past; 1588, 1744, 1759, 1779 and that of Napoleon in 1805. In addition to his own researches he had been able to draw on 'a most able assistant' Captain P.H. Colomb,[3] and, for the 1805 period, on the work of the French military historian, Edouard Desbrière.

Corbett marshalled this formidable array of historical precedents to demonstrate just what the principles of British strategy against invasion had been in the past. The most important rule was that if an enemy invasion was launched, then the Royal Navy's target was not the battle fleet of the foe, but the troop transports. It was the fear of risking large numbers of vulnerable soldiers that accounted for the nervousness with which foreigners always regarded final commitment to such an enterprise. Either they felt compelled to combine their escorting forces in order to increase the chances of safe passage for the army, or they divided those escorts to attempt to defeat the British forces in detail, or to screen them from the transports. Either way if the British battle fleet maintained an interior position, and was sufficiently large for the task involved, the enemy battle fleet would be dealt with firmly, either as a mass or separately, when it exposed its selected formation. In the face of mass fleet superiority, battle might be declined in which case the enemy had to convoy and land an army in the face of an undefeated British battle fleet — a dangerous occupation. These conclusions were possible because the chief defence against invasion was not the battle fleet but the flotilla, protected by cruisers. The work of destruction would be done by these ships especially equipped for the task. British cruisers protecting the flotilla would call in enemy cruisers to protect enemy transports. Consequently, for Britain's safety it was necessary that she keep a sufficient force of cruisers in the North Sea to force the Germans to employ battle fleet units as supports to their cruisers. Then, they would be forced to give battle encumbered by escort duty. This, Corbett stated, was 'the weakest known operation of war'.

---

1   *Ibid.*

2   Memorandum: *In Reply* etc. CP/B6.

3   Corbett *Diary* 1907, Colomb was the son of Admiral P.H. Colomb the naval writer, who had died in 1899. RCP

These methods of dealing with an invasion (not a raid) operation were imperfectly understood, Corbett asserted, because non-British modern strategic thinkers accepted the doctrine that in all circumstances the golden rule in warfare was to attack the battle fleet of the enemy. This doctrine was, he asserted, tritely repeated and unthinkingly accepted by some strategic thinkers in Britain. This, also, was what Corbett meant when he referred to 'continentalist thinkers' and he included A.T. Mahan (though not by name) as a 'continentalist' in that sense. Mahan's writings certainly encouraged such ideas.

While conceding that modern means of transport on both land and sea gave an enemy greater facilities (i.e. port and rail modernization) wherewith to launch an invasion, Corbett explained that, on the other hand, the mine, torpedo, and submarine increased the dangers of such an enterprise. Put another way, he suggested that the defensive was enhanced more than the offensive in invasion circumstances especially if the defenders fell back on interior lines, as they had always done, whereas modern offensive preparations would be easily penetrated by modern intelligence and swift means of communication. Since the main opponents were postulated to be the Germans he was able to show, for instance, how much more difficult it would be for them than it had been for the French, or Spanish, since they were forced to concentrate in their one or two developed ports. For them such an elementary ruse as a diversion would be much more difficult.

But, it was not Corbett's purpose to give the impression that the Navy was a complete shield by itself. He did not believe this in any event. A powerful army was an essential part of any sane anti-invasion scenario. This required a system flexible enough to meet widely dispersed geographical emergencies so as to prevent an enemy from setting up a viable beachhead. This force should be large enough to ensure that without the enemy risking 70,000 to 100,000 men the undertaking would be foolhardy. For Corbett, while he might have maintained that a raid in force was an unlikely risk for a foe to take, never said that it could not be done. Thus it was the army's task to maximize the effort required by a foe, since the more intense the effort the more intense the strain on enemy decision-makers would be. It is a tendency in war that when an enterprise grows, the more the demand for absolute security for it also grows. The greater the risk the more the pressure will grow on the decision-makers to ask whether it passes the bounds of rational calculation. So it can be seen that an army was an essential part of the Nation's anti-invasion stance. It was not in Julian Corbett's view a task for sailors alone. He ventured the view that the Territorial Army as it stood was sufficient for the purpose, but he was hardly an expert on that subject.

It was the historical evidence that Corbett deployed, of course, that gave these views their febrile strength. But history was assisted by his rigorous confinement of the argument to the points at issue. The arrangement was set out with the skill of a trained lawyer. He reminded his readers that the Roberts Memorandum had referred precisely to a German attempt at invasion, not one lauched during the course of a recognized conflict, but a wholly preventative strike that would be undertaken, in secrecy, before formal war was declared. In these circumstances it was assumed that 'strained relations' or 'port troop concentrations' would not be observable to neutrals, or to the nationals of a shipping country like Great Britain. This kind of thing had never happened before and, Corbett held, was unlikely to happen. If this were put forward seriously as argument, he wrote, the Admiralty could only regard the enquiry 'as an academical exercise'. Opinions may vary on the question of whether a 'bolt from the blue' as it was then called was, or is, possible. Corbett thought such a suggestion 'academical' only because of the amount of secrecy required to make it possible, for such an enterprise would carry with it the seeds of its own destruction. Crews, troops, ships, warships, and planners, would need to be brought together for a 'once only' gathering and then, without practice, carry out one of the most difficult acts of sea warfare in a situation where the need for speed and secrecy would slowly give way to a desire for more men to ensure victory when they landed, and this, in turn, would call for more ships to guarantee their safe passage. As the operation thus mushroomed, the strain on enemy commanders' nerves became, or would become unbearable. This had inevitably happened in the past. Referring to the Germans' need to blockade the Straits of Dover for forty-eight hours, he claimed that no rational Admiral commanding would so put his head in the lion's mouth at the start of a war.

The argument was further bolstered by Corbett's insistance that only Germany was being considered by the Roberts Memorandum and with only Britain as the object — there was no mention of alliances. Corbett gave what he considered were practical measures that could be implemented, considering the hazards of a North Sea crossing. One, that a sufficient land force should exist at home to make the risk intense for the foe, and two, an improvement in the readiness of East Coast naval bases.

Corbett's historical examples were numerous. All claimed that surprise was almost impossible to achieve. They also demonstrated that the progression of events subsequent to the eventual piercing of the enemy's design, led logically to the increase of the army component and its escort, and it also led logically to the junction of the transports with *all* the escorts. One example will illustrate his method.

A projected invasion occurred in 1744, and Corbett, with Captain P.H. Colomb's help, described it in detail in a supporting paper.[1] No doubt it was thought to be a good example since it showed Britain's classic riposte operating in a bad situation. The predicament included a nervous and incompetent ministry, an octogenarian First Sea Lord in actual command in the Channel, internal problems at home (i.e. Jacobite restiveness), and a great dispersion of main fleet units overseas. It also clearly involved what the Roberts Memorandum stressed as a likely factor, viz., enemy planning, organization and assembly took place before the actual declaration of hostilities. It was the 'bolt from the blue situation'.

Briefly, the plan required the Admiral at Brest, de Roquefeuil, to either defeat the main British Home Fleet, stationed at Spithead, or draw it off to the west in the Channel while a secretly prepared force at Dunkirk crossed, unescorted, to land 8,000 to 15,000 men at Malden in Essex, where they would be poised, two days march from a *coup de main* on London. With regard to the Brest squadron, great care was taken to equip it (twenty-two of the Line) as if for a long voyage. This plan was set out in November 1743 in conditions of great secrecy. By 15 December the British had a cruiser watching Brest. The Dunkirk preparation did escape serious British attention, but the British were watching the French coast, and even if the troops had sailed in January there would have been three line ships plus local flotilla forces with which to confront these transports without escorts. Winter problems postponed the operation but as the winter wore on news of activity in Dunkirk filtered through. De Roquefeuil got to sea in early February. The stationed British cruiser (Captain Broderick) watched the movement to determine that the fleet was not bound for the Mediterranean or overseas. Broderick then reported to Spithead, and by mid-February the British Admiral, Sir John Norris, was collecting his forces at that port. From that time onward also, all spare troops in the United Kingdom, except for Scotland, were set in motion for the London area, so that by the time it was ready to sail the Dunkirk force would have had to face the possibility of force equal or superior to its own if it landed on the banks of the Thames, or in Essex.

Norris's problem was, where should he commit his force?

---

1 'Invasion 1744' CP/B6. This was a special paper, researched by Colomb and written by Corbett on that particular operation. It was attached to the memorandum.

Resolutely he made no move until he was certain of why the French ships were at sea. De Roquefeuil, for his part, was so impressed by the growing magnitude of his task, that he split his forces and sent one squadron east as an invasion cover. Norris, however, steadily gathering and filtering intelligence, including distracting and often incoherent reports from frightened ministers in London, finally decided that the French invasion convoy was assembling east of him. By this time the British knew about the extensive activity at the port of Dunki.k.

At the same moment (early March) as the French General, Maurice de Saxe, came to Dunkirk from Calais and began loading his transports, the British Admiral was off the Downs with seventeen ships of the line and a powerful cruiser and flotilla force. The French then faced an undefeated main fleet between themselves and their goal. Their separated forces rejoined. At that point it was not a sensible act of war to attempt to move transports and united escorts across the Channel in the face of an undefeated British fleet and flotilla waiting to attack them. A storm came up that temporarily dispersed all sea forces. The French returned one by one to Brest. Norris regrouped. The operation was cancelled. The French blamed the failure on a lack of promised Jacobite pilots, and the storm. Had there been no storm the British Admiral would almost certainly have attacked both French fleet and convoy against the shore.

In fact, once Norris realized that he had a possible invasion on his hands no amount of conflicting orders, enemy temptations, or desire for battle glory, would have forced him to forsake his objective — the enemy transports. He did not move his concentrated force until he knew where those transports were. When he was certain of their whereabouts he moved, once, and the game was over. This kind of example, one where every supposed card was in the enemy's hands, was very telling. It was never Corbett's claim that an invasion could not be successful, luck is a feature in war, but that the chances of failure, for reasons he had set out in this and his other examples, made commitment to such a scheme like a throw of the dice, and not the considered act of a military statesman. The fact was that in every historical precedent the enemy had refused to commit himself and to take the risk. The obstacles were not due to luck, but to the traditional practice of the Royal Navy. The 1744 illustration, as did the others, raised this defence to something more than speculation or special pleading.

Looking at all his historical examples Corbett was able to assert that in no case of this sort were enemy movements, or deceptions, successful in drawing away battle forces from the protection of cruiser and flotilla forces which were aimed at enemy troop transports. In 1779, when faced with a superior fleet concentration, the British fleet prudently refused action and no invasion force sailed from France. Furthermore, in no historical case had an enemy projecting an invasion of England left base with his troop transports, using the cover of stealth.

This document was, on any judgement, a powerful compilation. The reasons for this have very little to do with whether he was 'right' or 'wrong' in his assumptions, or in his ultimate verdict. The very powerful men he was attempting to instruct were all men who were knowledgeable about military affairs, and indeed keen students of military history. But although it is likely that the purely naval members had an instinctive feeling of sympathy for Corbett's general argument, none of them were capable of drawing together historical examples in such a way that they remained subordinate to, and yet illustrative of, the difficulties that the problems raised. He was able to keep their minds firmly focused on the Roberts and Repington claims which raised the real questions, and then to combat them. Corbett then asked, by inference, what kind of argument, apart from his historical argument, was of any use in a case like this? To be sure, new developments had come about but they could only change strategic concepts that already existed. He argued on the basis of his conviction that existing concepts were the product of history, and could be recognized in historical constructs.

Of course there are other kinds of strategic thought than that which is historically based. Corbett's favourite phrase for such non-historical thinkers was 'fragile web-spinners'. Such views did not make him universally popular. It was his strength that he grasped the strategic nettle at the point where British maritime history and national strategic planning met, as no one else had. He was thus bold to dismiss the ideas of the Roberts 'Notes . . .' writers in strong language. He was comfortable in discussing variations of sea strategy. He was accustomed to giving precise examples of such concepts as 'Command of the Sea' and he knew very well that the authors of the Roberts Memorandum were not. The very idea of invasion by stealth as proposed by the Memorandum meant invasion over 'an uncommanded sea'. What was that? An uncommanded sea meant, to him, a sea over which 'command was in dispute'. He anticipated that most of his readers thought of command of the sea as an absolute which one side or the other held, and that a battle was customarily thought to decide the issue. But suppose one side wanted to decide the issue and the other did not? How could command be secured in those circumstances? Those are difficult enough questions in retrospect. He was master of them then. He pointed out that Roberts and Repington displayed ignorance of the real attitude of the Navy towards invasion, of the elementary elements of strategy involved, of the methods that would be used to secure lines of passage at sea, of the meaning of the threefold division of a fleet into battleships, cruisers and flotillas, and, finally, of the reflex habits of the naval past.

The most remarkable tribute to this document is that those to whom it was presented used it to secure a harmonious result to their talks. It would be too much to claim that it converted the whole committee, but it impressed them. It brought the question of invasion out of the realms of misinformed speculation and provided it with a sound basis for discussion. Perhaps its hard-hitting quality stored up trouble for Corbett in the future. Perhaps it was not tuned properly to politics, or not partisan enough for a long-run effect. But 'twas enough, it served'. Be that as it may, in his composition Corbett's hard line indicated that he took Lord Roberts and his associates, and his non-naval friends seriously, and his skill was equal to the occasion even when he thought their appreciations wrong. The overall impression was strong.

Corbett's point of view was immediately taken up by the sailors and remained their bedrock defence. Not all supporters of the Admiralty swallowed it whole. Tweedmouth, as we have seen, wanted to state the extreme navy case, and to do this proposed cutting out all references to the army.[1] Then Sir John tried his hand at extremism. Slade stood firm. 'They [Fisher and Tweedmouth] were', he wrote, 'very anxious to go back to their contentions that the navy can guarantee that nothing comes across, and the army will never be used, but I don't want to put it in such a bold way. It will only get their backs up all round. We want them to see that they are required, and that they are contributing to the defence of the country, as long as they do not take too great a view of their relative importance to the whole question'.[2] Despite a further attempt at change by a nervous Fisher on 24 December,[3] and with the exception of a few verbal alterations, the thing stood. As Corbett wrote in his Journal, 'Lord Tweedmouth and Sir John kicked a good deal about what I said about the necessity for a home army. Slade insisted it must go in and it did. I think with good effect in bringing the two services together a little more'.

1 Slade to Corbett 20.XII.07; CP/B6.
2 Slade to Corbett 24.12.07; CP/B6.
3 Slade to Corbett 3.1.08; CP/B6.

The sailor and the historian had used their friendship and built up knowledge to good effect. Not only did they succeed in getting Corbett's view accepted as the Admiralty point of view, but Slade used the moment to persuade Fisher to produce more specific war plans, and to extend the use of the War College as a strategic sounding board.[1] However, this was high tide for the Director of Naval Intelligence. Fisher was worried lest the cleverness of Repington should overturn Slade, even as he himself did not like having his conclusions forced upon him from below.[2] Slade remained in the Fishpond for eight months more, but he was less fishy than he had been, and certainly the First Sea Lord remained nervous and unconvinced of his loyalty.

There were four meetings of the Sub-Committee between 22 January and 11 February. During that period the politicians dropped their attitude of impartiality and began to favour the Admiralty case. Asquith's grip seems to have been weak at first, and on 27 January he allowed the meeting to degenerate into a general discussion. In any event when Repington was questioned (by Slade) towards the end of the meeting he did not show up so well.[3] However, at the next meeting, Repington gave a long rambling discourse in lieu of explanation, finally bringing the Secretary of State for War himself into the lists against him.[4] By 11 February, the army was attempting to make up its mind as to what attitude to take since its representatives realized that the navy was likely not only to demolish Roberts's ideas, but to sweep the board with its case. They began to anticipate and object to a conclusion that was likely to limit the size of the army.[5] They too wanted to muzzle Roberts and Repington, but not to yield strategic priority to the navy.

Whereupon Slade moved swiftly. He found out that General Ewart was writing the final War Office paper, and, on investigation, found him to be 'quite in agreement with us'. Haldane was swinging over, and although the C.G.S., Nicholson, still remained an adamant opponent, Slade wrote on 15 February that 'I talked to him yesterday and I hope impressed him with the fact that we should never get on unless we

1   Slade to Corbett 4.12.08; CP/B6.

2   Slade to Corbett 11.1.08, CP/B6. See also Fisher to Corbett 31.1.08; CP/B12.

3   Slade to Corbett 4.2.08. Interesting because Fisher thought the only reason why the enquiry had gone forward was that Repington had 'made himself indispensible to Haldane'. See Fisher to Corbett 10.2.08; CP/B12.

4   Slade to Corbett 11.2.08; CP/B6.

5   Slade to Corbett 19.2.08; CP/B6.

settled on the principles first and the details afterwards'.[1]   Meanwhile Slade stonewalled the still restless and unconvinced Fisher.[2]

By 3 March, Slade entered into green pastures, as Asquith showed that he had a grip on the proceedings,[3] and at the same time made his basic criterion for judgement 'command of the sea'.[4]   By 12 March, it was clear that agreement was to prevail, and it was Corbett's arguments that had made it possible.   Corbett wrote in his Diary that Slade had told him that, not only had Admiral Sir William May said that Corbett's paper 'had lifted the whole controversy out of mere detail',[5] but also that Generals Nicholson and French had found it possible to accommodate themselves to agreement on the basis of Corbett's *Memorandum*.   The War Office and Admiralty, 'are now practically one on the question, but', he added ominously, 'JF sticks to his dinghy view'.[6]

Although the final Report was not issued until 22 October, the investigation was virtually concluded.   On the basis of the co-operation between Slade, Corbett and Ewart, Balfour was able to make what Esher called his 'masterly'[7] speech of conciliation on 29 May.

Directly rebuking Fisher, Balfour said he thought such investigations were greatly worthwhile.   He thought that the Admiralty ought not to discount a bolt from the blue, and that it should make sure by its dispositions that such a thing was impossible at any time.   He then went on to kindly but firmly disagree with Roberts and Repington and support the Admiralty contention.   It had the effect of bringing things to a conclusion; as Corbett said, it let Roberts and Repington 'down very easily'.[8]

The final paper, issued on 22 October 1908 supported the Admiralty case in general, but recommended that it not take anything for granted.   In a way, it represented a slight censure on Fisher.   The agreement on which the *Report* was made was reached in May.[9]

1   Slade to Corbett 19.2.08; CP/B13.
2   Esher Journal 3.3.08; Brett *Journals* vol. II, pp. 290-1.
3   Slade to Corbett. 3.3.08; CP/B13.
4   Corbett *Diary* 10.III.08; RCP.
5   *Ibid.* 12.III.08; RCP.
6   *Ibid.*
7   Esher Journal 29.V.08; Brett *Journals* VII, p. 316.
8   Corbett *Diary* 15.VI.08; RCP.
9   *Ibid.* 19.V.08; RCP.

That it went no further is a great tribute to Corbett, Slade, Ewart and French. This is made clear by three entries in Corbett's diary bearing on the inquiry made during May and June.

1. [Slade] told me J.F. was getting more and more outrageous and harder to control.[1]

2. 'Slade came for a yarn. Told me of invasion committee. Balfour reconciling speech — then Army Council's memo which they had read with result usual out burst from J.F. — didn't agree with a word of it and McKenna backing him up like little dog behind a big one. So all the fat in the fire again and more work for me, as an answer explaining him away must be prepared. Slade said all the ministers laughed at J.F.'[2]

3. Meet at 9:40 Charing X for 'Dreadnought' show. Travelled down with Haldane, Ottley, and Thursfield. Long talk on Army and Navy. Haldane said old quarrel as bad as ever. I protested and we all eventually agreed a solid community of opinion was being formed. It would be all right. He agreed but for men at the top meaning Fisher and Nicholson. Haldane told Corbett that he was convinced that the German General Staff considered the invasion idea impracticable. I said conscription would wreck any government. He agreed and said Balfour was of the same opinion'.[3]

It is clear from the above that the result of the invasion sub-committee's deliberations was to deny that invasion could take place in the way Roberts and Repington had thought possible. The Admiralty was spared what Fisher had feared, an investigation. To those results Corbett's memorandum had made a crucial contribution. But, at the top, as Haldane said, the tendencies to departmentalism and separate defence policy thinking in the two services remained firmly entrenched. Corbett's papers had not altered that, partly owing to political tendencies implicit in the French 'conversations', and partly due to the mutual suspicion that existed between the two power structures. It was also partly due to Fisher's personal methods. Fisher might be defended by reference to his other preoccupations, including worry over the estimates, and in-service bickering that kept him off balance at a time when there was intense pressure on him due to foreign naval developments. He was worried about maintaining his ship programme. What the invasion enquiry did not do was give him, and the Admiralty as it stood, a clear vote of confidence. That was what he wanted after he failed to get the enquiry quashed. In the final sessions he was driven to create scenes that struck responsible friends and opponents alike as ridiculous.

1   *Ibid* 29.V.08; RCP.

2   Corbett *Diary* 19.VI.08;RCP.

3   *Ibid*.

In these circumstances he wanted almost unquestioning and total support from Slade and Corbett. He did not get it. What they attempted was to provide what they thought he required, at the moment, for the good of the country or the Navy. Slade was posted to the East Indies. To Corbett he sent a beautifully bound book full of blank pages — clearly a call for propaganda. Corbett declined the apparent invitation.

6

QUEBEC, 1908

Apart from holidays with his family in the country Corbett's life during these years was closely bound in by naval history, lectures to the War College, and antiquarian pursuits. The outstanding exception to this routine occurred in 1908, when he was able to attend the commemoration of the founding of Quebec City. Distinguished British guests, of whom the most important were the Prince of Wales and Lord Roberts, and including such lesser figures as Halford MacKinder the geographer, and Corbett, were to take part. They were transported there by units of the Royal Navy. It was a month's holiday of an exciting and different kind.

His selection to make the trip was owing, in part, to the fact that his latest history, *England and the Seven Years' War*, had devoted a good deal of space to the 1759 siege and capture of the city, so that he could be considered an expert on one aspect of the military and naval life of Quebec City. Another, and more important reason was that the Director of Naval Intelligence wanted him to investigate aspects of Canadian defence planning. That is to say, Slade wanted Corbett to determine, quietly, what military (especially naval) contribution Canada was prepared to make to the defence of the Empire as a whole. The mission was not a straightforward one. Corbett was given no right to negotiate with responsible Canadian politicians; that is, he was simply to gather what information he could without either alarming Canadians or revealing British attitudes — since the attitude of the Admiralty especially was by no means clear or consistent. Put simply, The First Sea Lord and the rest of the Admiralty Board were not at one on questions of Imperial Defence.

Sir John Fisher had no confidence in Dominion assistance. His doctrine was clear: the Royal Navy would control and dispose of its own. Even with regard to Australia, where there was some disposition to contribute financing to naval defence Fisher was against stationing ships in Australian waters. This was not very surprising, but the First Sea Lord was even against sending ships there on visits.[1] With regard to Canada his views were even more forthright. 'He says he knows the Canadian', wrote Slade, 'and that they are an unpatriotic grasping

1   Slade *Diary* 7.V.08. Fisher refused to send ships to join with those of the United States on a special visit there. See also Slade *Diary* 1.VII.08 which described Admiralty as unfavourable to having an Australian naval force established and expressed preference for a subsidy. NMM.

people who only stick to us for the good that they can get out of us, and that we ought to do nothing whatsoever for them. . . . His policy would be an absolutely fatal one for this country to follow and it is sincerely to be hoped that the Cabinet will not have it'.[1]

This situation was complicated. It was being canvassed by the C.I.D. where the view held that a naval threat to the coastline of the United States would serve to divert a wartime American threat to the Canadian Frontier.[2] Fisher, who distrusted the C.I.D. almost as much as he did Canada, hoped to get the discussion of Canadian defence transferred from the C.I.D. to the Cabinet. He was supported in this view by John Morley, the Secretary of the State for India. But Sir Edward Grey, the Foreign Secretary, wanted the problems thrashed out in the C.I.D. before a Cabinet decision was taken:[3] In spite of Fisher's opposition,[4] Slade managed to convey to the C.I.D. his views that two divisions, one in Newfoundland and one in Jamaica, would 'hold' the Americans.[5] Corbett had been consulted by Slade and agreed that the two divisions would contain all that the 'Canadian militia could not handle'.[6] Meanwhile Haldane, the Secretary of State for War, wished the C.I.D. to work up a vast design to milk the Dominions of both men and money for ships.[7] It was this sort of thing to which Morley objected, holding that such a subject, being political, was a Cabinet matter. It was a great muddle. (Incidentally, Corbett informed Slade that, constitutionally speaking, Morley was right, but that was no reason for the various Secretaries of State not getting expert advice from knowledgeable soldiers and sailors, and the right place to get that advice was at the C.I.D.)[8]

Whatever one may think of the procedural question it is clear that Sir John held the view that Canada was both indefensible and niggardly in defence matters. Slade was sending Corbett to check up on these views. He was to discover whether there was any Canadian disposition to 'take the defence of her frontier in hand — and

1   NMM Slade *Diary* 9.V.08.

2   NMM Slade *Diary* 10.V.08.

3   NMM Slade *Diary* 14.V.08.

4   NMM Slade *Diary* 12.V.08.

5   Corbett *Diary* 15.V.08.

6   *Ibid.*

7   NMM Slade *Diary* 15.V.08.

8   This point, perhaps, has some bearing on Fisher's reluctance to speak at War Council meetings in 1915. It was a point that was not properly settled before World War I — if, indeed, it was generally understood.

[towards] starting a naval militia. She must make herself sufficiently strong on the Lakes to prevent [the] U.S. from rushing them. It must be done very carefully and slowly without ostentation and parade, but if it is efficiently carried out she [Canada] will add enormously to the strength of the Empire as a whole and assist the navy quite as much or more than if she went in for Battleships and Cruisers'.[1] No doubt Corbett went out to Canada disposed to Slade's viewpoint.

The Quebec Naval Force was under the command of Admiral Curzon-Howe, who was very attentive to Corbett, partly because Admiral W. Henderson had written commending him, and partly by virtue of the historian's own reputation.[2] The Squadron comprised two divisions: the battleships *Exmouth, Duncan* and the cruiser *Arrogant* in the first, and *Albermarle* and *Russell* with the cruiser *Venus* in the second. On board the *Russell* with Corbett was the distinguished geographer Halford J. MacKinder, whom Corbett already knew as a fellow member of the Coefficients dining club, and who was 'no end of a swell' in Tariff Reform circles ashore and 'a very nice fellow'.[3] Rear Admiral John Jellicoe was in the *Albermarle* and impressed Corbett and everyone else as 'perhaps the cleverest young flag officer in the service'.[4]

Corbett went as the guest of the Captain of the *Russell,* and he had been given the 'State' cabin. As an honorary member of the Ward Room he was made to feel quite at home, and he reciprocated the friendly kindness by lecturing the officers on the taking of Quebec, while MacKinder talked to the same audience on Canadian geography.[5] As a further gesture of appreciation, Corbett presented the Ward Room with a drawing of the Battle of Solebay.[6]

Moving through the shimmering seas the ships practised evolutions as they approached the Straits of Belleisle. Corbett was especially pleased with the effect as the two squadrons passed a giant glinting iceberg and manoeuvred so that nature's great ice palace passed close by the *Russell* in the centre of an echelon formation. He found the enthusiasm of the sailors infectious, and it was generally fading evening light above that forced him below where he improved what

1 NMM Slade *Diary* 1.VII.08.
2 Corbett *Diary* 4.VII.08.
3 Corbett to Edith Corbett (ERC) 4.VII.08; CP/B10.
4 Corbett to E.R.C. 5.VII.08; CP/B10.
5 Corbett *Diary* 12, 13.VII.08.
6 Corbett *Diary* 7.VIII.08.

extracurricular time was left by writing enthusiastic reports to his wife and reading Sir Gilbert Parker's book *In Old Quebec*.

The North Atlantic in July was colder than he had anticipated, but the weather warmed up as they entered the Gulf, and finally, on the 18th they took on the pilot at Father Point and began the ascent of the stately river. Every landmark had an historical connection for him. He was lucky in nature as well, for swift changes between mist, clear sun and thunderstorms as they sailed gave life to those kaleidoscopic visual marvels for which Champlain's river is famous. They went through the Traverse at the east end of the Island of Orleans at seventeen and a half knots on a carrying seven and a half knot tide providing a great contrast to Saunders's stake-boated procession in 1759, and literally shot in to the Basin with the old city rising behind it. Occasions like these bring out all a battleship captain's latent destroyerman's instincts. The big ships fairly surged up under the citadel and dropped their gigantic anchors with a flourish under the walls of the historic bastion.

One small mishap marred the beginnings. The fleet coal-carrier ran aground, a greater mishap than Saunders had suffered in wartime years ago, and this delayed the coaling for a few days. This was a matter of some annoyance since both the dressing and the entertainment of guests on board had to wait on the completion of that filthy task.

But there was much to be seen and done on shore. In particular, Corbett eagerly walked and sailed over the old campaigning ground. The water investigations were carried out with the help and interest of Admiral Kingsmill, who placed a boat at Corbett's disposal on several occasions, and in this way he visited both the Montmorency end of the battle area and the water route above the city where the final dispositions for the 1759 landings had been facilitated by the ships of Admiral Holmes's division. Corbett's first comments, beyond the fact that he made visits, were few. But he did mention that at Montmorency, the water in the river was now low enough that it was currently a much less formidable obstacle than it had once been. With regard to the land side of the campaign, he was helped and interested by Colonel William Wood, 'a nice refined manly scholar — a real historian and a real scholar',[1] who walked over much of the field with Corbett, Jellicoe, and Burrows, the son of the late Chichele Professor of War at Oxford. Corbett was particularly interested in Wolfe's Cove, and remarked that 'it does not look much from the fleet but when you get close you see

---

1   Corbett to E.R.C. 20.VII.08; CP/B/10.

the cliff is all loose shale — that is like a slope of sliding slate chips — most difficult to get a foothold in'.[1]

The ships had dropped anchor on Wednesday, 15 July, and although there was a continual round of sightseeing and entertainment, in which His Majesty's ships took their full share after the coaling, the official programme itself began with the arrival of His Royal Highness, the Prince of Wales, a week later. In the meantime, Corbett was presented to the Governor General. He also talked to that most eminent guest, his old opponent over the invasion affair, Lord Roberts of Kandahar. During a trip up the river, the historian and the famous soldier talked, not unnaturally, of the strategy and methods of combined operations. Corbett asked him about the command of such expeditions, and found that 'he takes [the] German view but I put its difficulties which worried him but did not alter his opinion'.[2] The old soldier pointed out that during the Afghan campaign he had insisted on and secured political as well as military control of affairs. Also, Corbett sought and obtained advice on 'many points on Wolfe's tactics that puzzled me' from Roberts.

After the politicians had arrived and the appropriate welcome had been given, and speeches made, the celebrations moved ahead swiftly. Thursday saw the arrival of a replica of Champlain's ship, followed by a fireworks display from Levis at night. The next day was very hot and featured a Grand Review of Canadian militia forces on the Plains of Abraham, which Corbett thought very badly arranged — the only thing that impressed him was the physique of the men. He turned his back on the State Ball in the evening to commune with his far away wife by letter.[3] But he was watching the next day as the Prince reviewed the fleet. It is noticeable that both the French and the United States Governments had fleet representatives there and yet Corbett wrote nothing about their part in the naval show except that on one occasion the *Russell* entertained officers from the *Admiral Geupratte* who became more congenial with the passage of time and wine, but who presented, according to Corbett, a most unseamanlike appearance. He noted that one officer wore a pince-nez which seemed incongruous in a sea warrior.[4]

The next day Corbett's enthusiasm for the sea had to take second

1   Corbett to E.R.C. 15.VII.08; CP B/10.
2   Corbett *Diary* 21.VII.08.
3   Corbett to E.R.C. 24.VII.08; CP B/10.
4   *Ibid.*

place to his admiration for the historical pageant executed on the Plains of Abraham. It is worth repeating in detail here:

> After lunch it was a case of top hat and frock coat again for the gala performance of the Pageant. I had an official seat again and saw it splendidly. My dear, I wish I could give you a faint idea of what it was like. To say it was the most beautiful thing I ever saw, except your dear self, seems but a faint indication of the elation it aroused in us all. Though the Prince had a great dinner in the evening at 8.15 and the pageant did not begin till 5.00 nothing could induce him to leave till it was all over and our Admiral went away ferocious because he had to get away to dress in his ship for the state dinner. I was invited too but H.R.H. or no H.R.H. I simply could not leave till the end. Winchester[1] was far surpassed. Not that the Pageant itself was much better, but the *mise en scène* was beyond description . . . .

> You must imagine first the grand stand on the grassy plains of Abraham where the battle was fought — some Two to Three Hundred feet above the river. The broad open piece of grassy plain was in front of it about as big as the fields between Imber and the road.[2] At the right front it sloped gradually to a wooded glen and beyond a glade stretched for half a mile until it was lost in the thickening woods. On the left and left front, the plain ended in bushes below which it falls abruptly to the river. So that the characters in the pageant would be concealed below the crest and emerge at the right moment as though coming up from the river where Wolfe landed. The background was broad still river with its cliffs on the other side and then the miles and miles of woodland dotted with villages stretching away to the dim blue of hills of the American frontier. Can you imagine what a setting it made in the evening sun; for it began at 5.00 and ended at 7.30 as the sun sank below the horizon bathing the last scenes in a flood of rosy light. There were between 3,000 and 4,000 performers, some hundreds of whom were real Indians who had begged to take part and they did it with vigour in their wild leather and feather costumes, fighting, war dancing and chanting. The first scene opens with a solitary Indian watching the river from beside his wigwam — then Jacques Cartier came climbing up the cliffs from the river attended by his crew and friendly Indians and he took possession of the country for Francis I. Then came his return to France and reception at Fontainbleau by Francis I the change of scene from the wilderness to the garden was very much applauded. Parties of blue jackets had been lent by the fleet. As Jacques Cartier disappeared below the crest they rushed heavy frames, garden vases, statuary etc. and in a minute the rough bushes were transformed into gorgeous Rhododendrums and the place given the look of a formal garden. Then at the high forest at the end of a glade half a mile away began to emerge from the trees the Royal hunting party, hundreds of gaily dressed men and women — and singing as the|y| came coming across the little valley — up again to the arena in loose groups, yet one informal procession just like a return from hunting to-day. With that lovely background of river and wilderness it was really a beautiful thing to see. So it went on as lit by the changing light of the half clouded evening as tho some skillful hand were playing the lime

---

1 Comparison with the Winchester Pageant in England.

2 Imber Court at Thames Ditton.

light. I cannot tell you all the scenes but they alternated with gorgeous court pageant in France and then simple counter-parts in the infant colony with Indians and trappers for lords and ladies. Then we had fights – Indian fights, but none between French and English. They dare not do that – besides the whole thing was meant . . . to heal old sores. So the last scene was the armies of Wolfe and Montcalm marching in shoulder to shoulder and doing a sort of trooping the colour to the English and French heroes of Canadian history on horseback in the centre and surrounded by the courts of Francois I and Henry IV and Louis XIII. Then when all was in order blue jackets formed behind all with the last glow of sunset at the back. They bore the arms of all the provinces and as the band played 'O Canada' they released a little cloud of white doves. It gave us all a thrill down the back and we cheered and cheered again.[1]

The dinner Corbett attended that night he had originally thought to be a mere 'consolation to the riff-raff of guests like myself who had not been to the other State dinners. But I found out to my joy it was *the* great function'. They began at 9.00 and it was nearly midnight when they rose. Speech after speech pledged eternal peace between the English and the French, the solidarity of the Empire, and loyalty to the Crown. The pageant had generated tremendous enthusiasm that found voice at the dinner table. Englishmen found it a poignant moment when de Villiers, the Chief Justice of South Africa, 'solemnly announced the message of loyalty from the Boers'. It was, wrote Corbett accurately, 'one long Imperial debauch'.

That night before he went back on board, Corbett was introduced to the Prince of Wales, and had an opportunity to congratulate the happy Governor General. Long after he returned to *Russell*, the historian, with his geographer friend MacKinder, paced the deck under the St. Lawrence moon, and pondered the secrets of Empire, rocked in its Canadian cradle.[2]

Aside from official functions and historical sight-seeing, Corbett was exposed, for the second time in his life, to the Canadian scene. What did he make of it? When he had first visited Canada in 1879, he had been enraptured by the scenic wonders of the Quebec-St. Lawrence area. In this scene, time brought no great changes. He fully appreciated the unique beauty of the area and once more responded to it. He had not met any people of importance, or indeed many people at all, on his first visit. This time he had a much greater opportunity. His response to it was a conditional one, and he remained, in a sense, sealed off from Canadian life. He obtained most of his information about the colony from his English contacts, and he listened with care to the views of the Governor General, Earl Grey, who honoured him

1   Corbett to E.R.C. 26.VII.08; CP B/10.

2   *Ibid.* Corbett left no record of the details of his conversations with Mackinder.

with confidences, and to the views of General Lake[1] and Admiral Kingsmill. All of these men were inclined to refer to the native born Canadians as 'they' and this applied with even greater force to the French speaking Canadians. He found in Colonel Wood, the historian, a less segregated figure, but their common interests made conversations cling to military history. He was entertained at a luncheon by Professor G.M. Wrong of the University of Toronto, and Sir Charles Fitzpatrick the Chief Justice. He also met the Canadian Prime Minister, Sir Wilfred Laurier, and his Conservative opponent Robert Borden, and heard them speak.

Chance seating at dinner placed him alongside a Mr. Mackenzie King whom the Governor-General thought 'the coming man'. He was, wrote Corbett, 'deputy minister of Labour a young clean-shaven man of thickset Canadian type', who told Corbett of how he had stopped Japanese fishing vessels being issued licenses wholesale for fishing on the West Coast by threatening to denounce the Anglo-Japanese treaty.[2]

The most pronounced Canadian viewpoint that Corbett encountered was put forward with no lack of self-confidence by that Toronto stalwart Colonel George Denison.[3] It was, he explained, the United Empire Loyalists, and not the British nation at home, who were responsible for the birth of the Empire and who gave it a special character and flavour. They were worth supporting. On the other side of the coin, he introduced his Pantheon of useless peoples, who included the French, the Americans and the Australians — for the latter he expressed contempt. Corbett found these exclusivist views somewhat rigorous.[4]

Corbett met a few Canadian women at the social functions. Escape from them was one of his more congenial occupations during the Quebec stay. The Mayor of Toronto seems to have assigned himself to Corbett during the reception for the Prince of Wales at the Chateau Frontenac, which dominated the English-Canadian social life of the Quebec scene. The Mayor was 'a fat rather brutal aggressive type of self-made city man' who was openly contemptuous of everything French and indeed everything complex. The Mayor 'prided himself'

---

1 Lt. Gen. Sir Percy H.N. Lake, Inspector General and Militia Council Member in Canada. Admiral Sir Charles Edmond Kingsmill. R.N.; newly appointed Director of the Naval Service of Canada. He was knighted in 1918.

2 Corbett *Diary* 20.VII.08.

3 Canadian Military writer of international stature.

4 Corbett *Diary* 17.VII.08.

on his democratic character. Yet he naively confessed how Lord Grey had won his heart at their first meeting by asking him to give him a light from his cigar, as Lord Grey's had gone out. 'He quite took charge of me, explaining who everybody was and hustled me to the terrace afterwards with one of his great stalwart arms round my waist and the other round his homely little charwoman of a wife'.[1]

In short, it must be said that Corbett found in both the social situation in Canada, and the arrangements made for the grandstanding of the events, insufficient protection from the shirt-sleeved[2] democracy about which he showed little curiosity, and for which he felt a distinct aversion. He was told that better educated English immigrants generally became 'the leading men'.[3]

He did, however, record his impressions of the French Canadians. To put his remarks in perspective, two things must be mentioned. First, that he seems to have formed no impressions as a result of direct contact with people, but rather from English and English-Canadian impressions of them. Second, that it is only incidentally, and largely by conscious reference to the Pageant itself, that Corbett showed any understanding of the fact that this whole pompous affair was meant to celebrate the French origins of Canada. It is true that the Governor-General personally informed Corbett that his idea in promoting the whole thing was to encourage and develop *rapport* between the French and English sections of the population of Canada, together with dedication to the concept of Empire — the latter of which was played down in the original arrangements. He had, he said, found the French cold, and 'sulky' towards his idea in the beginning, and it is clear that they were cajoled and dragged by turns to this brotherhood occasion.[4]

It is also true that Sir Wilfrid Laurier cut a picturesque figure in the gathering, that the Premier of Ontario 'made handsome advances to the French',[5] that post-prandial speeches evoked the required responses, and that the main part of the pageant *did* depict seventeenth-century French Canadian history. What is unmistakable in Corbett's account, as well as in the later account of the pageant, published in

---

1 Corbett to E.R.C. 24.VII.08; CP B/10.

2 He used this description and also 'riff-raff'. Corbett to E.R.C. 24.VII.08; CP B/10.

3 Corbett to E.R.C. 20.VII.08; CP B/10.

4 *Ibid.*

5 Corbett *Diary* 25.VII.08.

French [1] when all was over, is that there were, in reality, two celebrations taking place at Quebec in July 1908. On the one hand, there was a French Canadian celebration of their own past, called forth by English pressure, and tolerated rather than absorbed by the Anglo-Saxons in the interests of national and imperial unity. On the other, was a group of Anglo-Saxons who could tolerate the French nature of the gathering by virtue of the social opportunities it offered, and the sense of power to which such things as the anchored vessels of the Royal Navy gave rise. That military presence, the person of Lord Roberts, the review of the troops on the Plains of Abraham – all betokened a totally different interest; interest in the conquest of 1759. Corbett himself was a personal embodiment of this interest. Between these two groups the contacts were private and superficial as they played out their allotted roles. Just the right touch of irony was occasioned by the fact that British strength, mainly visible in the anchored fleet, represented to the two groups of Canadians present, French and English, protection against each other, although in different ways. It would be hard to find a better example of the real 'Imperial factor' in Canadian history.

To his wife Corbett wrote his views on French Canada. He noted the attempt by the British Government to influence events by sending out the Duke of Norfolk to 'see what influence he can bring to bear on the priests to water down their hostility to Canada and the English'. One of the Duke's chief duties was to make a call on the famous Catholic shrine at St. Anne de Beaupre. Corbett had been there the day before the Duke's visit, where, to his vast amusement, he found a Redemptrist monk, who had been born in Lancashire, 'explaining the almost comic miracles with child-like correctness in his American twang'. When the Duke was shown around, the whole miracle aspect was not mentioned.[2] Corbett, of course, did not find this religious atmosphere congenial, but he noted that their own brand of Catholicism was important to the Quebecois as a *native* religion, for he discovered that the hatred felt by the French for Irish Catholicism was pronounced.

Corbett thought French-Canadians a narcissistic people whose attitudes to other people and political ideas were distinguished by degrees of hatred and suspicion. They were not, of course, intrinsically 'loyal' to a British monarch, but they felt safe under that mantle to

---

1 Camille Roy. *Les Fêtes du Troisieme Centenaire de Quebec, 1608-1908* (Quebec, 1911).

2 Corbett to E.R.C. 20.VII.08; CP B/10.

ignore the details of imperial policy, and yet to huddle there in safety against the pressures of the Americans, Irish-Canadians and English-Canadians whom they disliked in that descending order of priority.[1] His final crushing, but revealing, opinion was that they 'remind me very much of the Irish with their vague longing for nationality and their lack of the qualities and energy by which alone it can be gained'.[2]

Corbett carried out his instructions concerning the attitude of Canada towards naval defence. On 21 July he had a long talk with Admiral Kingsmill, with regard to the formation of a Canadian marine force. Kingsmill was very pessimistic and his pessimism was derived from two opinions. One was that the reservoir of, and facilities for, turning out competent officers were limited, and unhappily they were only available from the Lower Deck. There was a 'total absence of any sense of discipline', and he supposed this impossible to inculcate without a fixed service system. The other discouraging feature was the prevalence of political patronage that was bound to frustrate the sound building of an officer corps. Concretely, he proposed introducing some permanence into the service, employing personnel for at least a three year period, and taking the climate into consideration by employing the hands in the dockyard in the winter. But he was clearly not hopeful and 'seemed to feel all this (was) only a poor substitute for money contributions to the Royal Navy'.[3]

The Governor General was even more discouraging. Corbett asked him 'how Canadian opinion stood with regard to a navy'. Earl Grey said there was none. In his view the country was absorbed in perfecting its communications system in order to bring Far Eastern trade through the land, and, on that basis, to increase the population. Under these circumstances it was no use to try to force them into a more congenial Imperial posture. It was 'no good forcing them — they won't spend money on a naval force'. The Admiralty had no intention of attempting to do that, said Corbett. They only wanted to work with the material at hand; indeed they would have no confidence in any force that did not have the 'heart of the country behind it'. Again the Governor General reported that nothing must be expected, and asked that the matter be allowed to sleep as the Canadians needed time to acquire the strength necessary to a proper defence arrangement. Grey pointed out further that any active measures of defence, especially in

---

1   Corbett to E.R.C. 24.VII.08; CP B/10.

2   *Ibid.*

3   Corbett *Diary* 15.VII.08.

the Great Lakes, would certainly alarm the Americans, who might easily give six months notice and denounce the treaty neutralizing the inland waters. Corbett pressed him to say whether any Canadian naval force would weaken Canada's position with regard to the United States. The answer was yes. Pressed further to state whether a militia might not be prepared on the coast and thus avoid 'arousing U.S.A. suspicions', he 'would not say anything and became thoughtful'. Grey concluded the interview by remarking that the British authorities would do well to be content with the militia system, as it trained more Canadian 'boys to arms'.[1]

General Lake, the British officer commanding in Canada, to whom Corbett talked for two hours on the day before he sailed, was more optimistic. Corbett referred to him as 'a fine fellow with broad and clear views — [the] best authority by far on Canadian defence that I have met'. Lake stated that the local navy or naval militia was not nearly as hopeless as the Governor General thought, but the ministers were corrupt. This, in his opinion, was sufficient reason for delaying a bill that had already existed in draft for three years, till after the next general election. He was also emphatic that any hint to Canadian ministers that the militia proposal would 'be satisfactory to England would do no good'.

Lake wanted a torpedo flotilla, and he already had plans complete for moving it by rail to the Great Lakes when it was needed. Indeed he appreciated Corbett's interest in the defence of the Great Lakes, and provided him with the secret and surprising information that war plans in case of war with the U.S.A. had been worked out. The plans were carefully based on the principle of counter-attack so as to make sure that the Americans crossed the frontier first and could be called the aggressors. Lake revealed that in 1898, he and Captain Reginald Custance, RN, had reconnoitred the Lake coasts of Erie and Ontario. No records of their reports existed in Canada, however, all copies having been destroyed. This was 'done in 1898'. Lake said he was willing to share his information with Slade and that correspondence about it could go in letters marked personal and travel in the Governor General's bag. Another good feature was that the Canadians had the bulk of the shipping on Lake Ontario, also that there were a number of 4.7 guns stored with ammunition at Toronto. Finally, Lake referred Corbett and Slade to General Sir J. Carmichael Smyth's report to Wellington on Canadian defence written during the war of 1812, and

1 *Note on Conversation with Earl Grey,* Naval Intelligence Report. CP B/10.

C.P. Lucas's comments thereon, and indicated that this represented the background to Lake's defence thinking on this subject.[1]

When he arrived home, Corbett passed this amalgam of information on to Slade, leaning most heavily on General Lake's optimism. Slade's reply again revealed the split in Admiralty opinion on Canadian defence. There was also the implicit principle of seeking Canadian defence help and yet concealing both its purpose and its general arrangements from Canadian ministers. It is worth quoting in full.

> Many thanks for your most interesting letter. It is very much as I thought, but I did not think that the corruption was as bad as it is. It makes it very hard to do anything for them, and to a certain extent justifies Sir John's [Fisher's] attitude. For all that, we cannot give up. Canada is a part of the Empire, and however bad they may be it would be the most fatal policy on our part to even hint that in time of danger we would abandon any part of it. It would be the signal for a general disruption and all we should be left with would be the smaller colonies and India. Lord Crewe is very firm about the necessity of keeping our end up in Canada. I had another talk with Sir John about it a short time ago, and he got quite heated on the subject. The fear of making any move because it may arouse the Americans to make further exertion, is I think a very weak argument. If it holds good in North America why should we spend money on our armaments in this country, for we only excite the European nations to try and outbuild us and so bring about still further increased expenses.
>
> I am extremely against the policy of the 'big drum' which so many people like – but a great deal can be done in an unostentatious way which will go far to strengthen our position out there. As I think I have said before, anything which makes American operations in Canada difficult tends to keep them quiet, while the opposite policy is only to dangle a bait in front of them.
>
> I will certainly write to General Lake as soon as I get back, and get what information I can out of him before he leaves. I am sorry he is going, as he is a very good man.[2]

In view of the forthcoming great excitement in Canada regarding the formation of a Canadian naval force this correspondence is revealing of British thought. It reinforces the notion that Sir John Fisher both deprecated the value of Canadian forces and understood the nature of Britain's relationship to America in a forthright way. What Slade meant by his 'unostentatious' policy is not so clear. What is clear is that Canadian defence policy was held to be too important a matter for Canadians to be informed about it. It is also apparent that Canada's value in this connection was not intrinsic but rather for the effect on Imperial greatness if they were not properly defended – although how

---

they could be mollified by what they were deliberately kept in ignorance of is not so clear. When the drum beat in 1914 Canada was not an important military power. Neither, however, did she prove to be a liability to Great Britain.

At all events after his conversations with General Lake, both the work Corbett had been commissioned to do, and the great gathering itself were virtually complete. After a final naval display of illuminations and fireworks it was time to go. The Prince of Wales in the *Indomitable* kept company with the original six ships as they passed up the river and through the Gulf in beautiful summer weather. Outside the Strait of Belleisle, the Prince's ship, to the strains of cheers and Auld Lang Syne, parted company and sped home. Cold and fog dogged the squadron's track across the Atlantic, but the sun came out finally to welcome them back to Brerehaven on August seventh. On the 8th he had crossed Ireland and in the late afternoon took 'tea in my nest again'.[1]

'So ended one of the best months I ever had' wrote the civilian sailor.[2]

1   Corbett *Diary* 8.VIII.08.
2   Corbett *Diary* 7.VIII.08.

7

THE TACTICS OF TRAFALGAR

Julian Corbett was regarded as an expert on the tactics of the Royal Navy in the age of sail. In 1905,[1] and again in 1908,[2] he edited books that set out historical sources which helped to illustrate the development of tactical theory and practice between the times of Drake and Nelson. His book, *The Campaign of Trafalgar,* published in 1910, was mainly a strategic exposition, but it contained two chapters on the tactics of the Battle of Trafalgar. When the Navy Records Society asked him to edit *Fighting Instructions,* a volume of tactical documents to help celebrate the centenary of Trafalgar, this had stimulated a casual interest, and the subject progressively absorbed one facet of his mind. The result was that Corbett was caught up in some of the public controversy over the tactics of Trafalgar that continued, fitfully, until 1913. New historical discoveries occasioned the publication of *Signals and Instructions* in 1908.

Undoubtedly, it was this topical interest in Trafalgar that made him delve back into the historical records to examine the tactical background to Nelson's concepts. As his custom was, he looked for the evidence of continuous development that had assisted his strategic studies and gave his narratives power. Although, in retrospect, it is not possible to say that his acquired tactical knowledge was as sound as his strategic thinking, his over-all tactical knowledge was considerable. When he died in 1922, he still knew more about this subject than anyone else alive, and, by that time, he had at his disposal sufficient new evidence that, had he lived, would have enabled him to write a new book criticizing his earlier ones.

Corbett, of course, did not know everything about naval tactics. This is not surprising.[3] No subject about which naval historians put pen to paper is so capable of inducing them to write nonsense. This is partly because the unwary are inclined to take battle accounts recorded, or given by sailors, at their face value. It is also because the

---

1 *Fighting Instructions,* Navy Records Society, 1905.

2 *Signals and Instructions,* Navy Records Society, 1908.

3 The general discussion that follows, on the problems of writing tactical history is my own. It leans heavily on conversations with, letters from, and access to the MSS of Brian Tunstall entitled 'British and French Naval Tactics, 1650-1815'. The discussion involving Corbett up to p. 8 is confined to his *Fighting Instructions* and *Signals and Instructions* which have not been footnoted in detail.

history of the development of naval tactical activity, theory and practice, is an intensely complicated matter. Faced with conflicting accounts and masses of detail, the tendency has been an attempt to impose a pattern or order on the accounts of battles by participants and/or eye witnesses. This has made it possible for many writers to claim that there is, or was, a difference between formal line tactics and mixed-up unordered fights. This much is clear to everyone. When the detailed investigations, on which these broad conclusions ought to rest are approached, however, the illumination cast on the problems is not great. The tendency has been for diagrammatic simplifiers to reduce half-understood evidence to acceptable conclusions, rather than to probe behind the half-understood evidence itself. Corbett, and W.G. Perrin, who was Admiralty Librarian in Corbett's time, were the only two writers who attempted to master the evidence in a comprehensive way. Corbett came close to gaining a balanced view of tactical development, but not the details of signalling development — about which Perrin had, then, unrivalled knowledge. The fact is, that such a study is a full-time occupation, and only the late Brian Tunstall ever gave it concentrated mental attention. His work explores the subject in a depth that changes the accepted views of naval tactics (and hence readjusts the history of most British naval battles), but his work is apparently still considered too intricate to invite publication in an age where simplification reigns supreme. There have been other 'experts' in the subject, but none of them can make serious claims to have mastered both the overall knowledge and the technique for explaining it: certainly not this present author, who makes no claim to being a tactical expert. Even the great French naval historian, Edouard Desbrière, who probably knew more about the Battle of Trafalgar than anyone else, including Corbett, made no claim to a detailed knowledge of tactical history, and when he and Corbett met they were able to enlighten each other on tactical aspects of that battle.

From the point of view of understanding *accounts* of actions, it must be borne in mind that when great fleets met, their formations covered miles of ocean, and for every viewer the pattern of events was constantly shifting. When battle was joined, vision was often obscured by smoke, or weather; or diverted by the preoccupations involved in the fighting of a ship. Times, often kept by hour-glasses, were differently recorded from ship to ship. The same was true of position reckoning, so that ships' logs represent evidence, but, not infrequently, conflicting evidence. Such limiting factors allow for the drawing of tentative, likely probabilities, but seldom of precise factual conclusions. Corbett understood this, and allowed for it in much of what he wrote.

The other side of the coin is represented by the difficulty in penetrating the minds of admirals commanding, and of individual ships' captains. To even attempt this, the interpreter is obliged to know what tactical movement a particular signal was supposed to mean. Of course admirals and captains often held knowledge in common of particular traditional evolutions. Nevertheless, for moderns to understand both the intention behind an admiral's executive order, and the meaning actually conveyed to a particular captain, involves a knowledge of the system of flag signalling then in use, and the true meaning of each signal as defined in the manuals issued to each.

Corbett's particular interest was in tactics. These, he apprehended, were contained in the 'Fighting Instructions' that dated from Cromwell's navy, and which prescribed certain tactical evolutions. He was interested in prescriptions for line-of-battle formation, which he thought probably existed as an attack method that had been used before 1652 and 1654 when the original Commonwealth 'Fighting Instructions' were issued. But he realized that the original purpose of the 'Fighting Instructions' was not so much to describe tactics likely to defeat an enemy at sea, as to prescribe formations for the sake of British discipline — so that there would be a measuring stick to apply to the courage, intelligence, and place in battle of each particular Captain in each formation. This is an important fact, for from it flowed the nature of the system that lasted for over 100 years. The 'Fighting Instructions' did not prescribe a direct order to each ship, but stated that the fleet was intended to accomplish such and such an effect and that this would be accomplished by executing such and such a manoeuvre. The 'Instruction' thus provided for an effect, and prescribed a method of achieving that effect, all at once, by describing the nature of the signal that would initiate the movement. This jumbling up together of orders, methods, and signal description was cumbersome. Later on, the 'Fighting Instructions' were increased by 'Additional Fighting Instructions', which increased the number of options available, but did not improve the efficiency of the manuals. It is interesting to observe that Corbett was so obsessed with battle tactics that he virtually ignored the 'Sailing Instructions' which accompanied these warfare books. This was logical but unfortunate, since the nature of a battle Fighting Instruction must necessarily conform to, or take into account, the *sailing* order of the fleet before the Fighting Instruction was issued. Corbett's technique, therefore, was to study the Instructions from the point of view of the *effect* that they were intended to produce in battle. That is to say, he was interested in historically determining the nature of tactical changes. He asked himself such questions as 'when did the first line of battle take place?' 'when did British tactics involve breaking the line of the enemy?' 'when did British tacticians plan for breaking the enemy's line; or doubling it?' − and so on.

Consequently, by concentrating on sets of 'Fighting Instructions' issued at different dates, he could tell roughly when such changes took place, and speculate intelligently as to which admiral or naval administration was responsible for the change. There can be no doubt but that by using this system Corbett was able to show change development in tactical dispositions over the years even if he could not always pin-point the precise moment of the innovations or the exact persons who devised them. Since he knew the limitations of his materials, his approach was fairly cautious. For instance, he thought he could detect the genesis of formal and informal tactical thought schools in the Dutch Wars. This conclusion was due to his reposing too much confidence in contemporary accounts of those still shadowy conflicts. Nevertheless, he did no more than suggest his conclusion. It was other historians who did not imitate his caution, who transformed or 'simplified' his suggestions into 'facts'.

Much of the 'Fighting Instructions' material available, covering the early years of the eighteenth century, appeared to Corbett to be fragmentary. His research had made this clear, and he was in no doubt that he was providing materials for a history of British naval tactics, and not writing it. That knowledge did not prevent him from recognizing significant change when it did occur, as it did with the advent of Admiral Lord Howe's thought on the tactical scene. But, since Corbett approached tactical change from the point of view of intended effects, he was not preoccupied with, or even very knowledgeable about, the signals themselves. Howe, however, discarded the old 'Fighting Instructions', and the 'Additional Fighting Instructions' in favour of a new system. He created a Signal Book. In that book were placed the signals in numerical order with each signal requiring the execution of a particular tactical manoeuvre. To complement the Signal Book, he wrote a set of Instructions. These were numbered, and informed the reader how to carry out the executive order that any particular signal demanded. This system was actually invented by Howe in 1776, but did not come into official use until much later. Corbett was somewhat confused as to whether the inventor was Howe or Admiral Kempenfelt, but he understood the significance of the change: it liberated admirals from the tyranny of devising expedients that aimed at adapting new ideas to the cramping effects of the complicated and out-dated

'Fighting Instructions'. The 'Fighting Instructions', as has been seen, were tied to a disciplinary function; the new system facilitated the assertion of the admiral's will in order to secure tactical advantage over the foe, as circumstances might demand.

He also showed how this change came about through tactical experiments in the Channel Fleets, where Howe, in particular, had the great advantage of being able to practise and develop his system. This was important since it had been hitherto held that Admiral Lord Rodney, at the battle of the Saints, in 1782, had been a tactical innovator. The impression was that he smashed the formalist doctrine when he broke de Grasse's line at that fight. Actually the breaking of that line was an accident. Rodney was using the old 'Fighting Instructions' at the time, and they contained no signal or order for actually breaking the line. Kempenfelt had no great tactical talent, and as a practising signaller he was inept. This was partly owing to a lack of real tactical ability but also to the fact that he leaned towards the use of the French tabular system of signalling, that was a *cul-de-sac*. Corbett missed these points about Kempenfelt because of his concentration on tactics as opposed to signalling, but he made it quite clear that the Signal Book system represented the avenue of tactical advance in the future. He thus pointed out the correct path to future historians of tactics.

This background study led Corbett to make points about Trafalgar that were not so complimentary to Nelson's knowledge of traditional tactics. The hero seems to have confused Rodney's action at the Saints with Howe's signal to break the enemy line issued on the battle of the first of June in 1794. Rodney led his column through a break that good fortune opened in the opposing line. Howe's signal, and his attack, were for the breaking of the enemy line by his ships at all possible places, and simultaneously. Leaving aside the question of whether Nelson's intention was sound, there is little doubt but that the concept he used was not in his Signal Book. Furthermore, the 'Memorandum' Nelson wrote some days before the battle was a garbled version of a combination of Rodney's practice and Howe's precise prevision. While it is true that Howe did not embrace the principle of concentration in the way Nelson did, the principle itself was neither 'new' nor 'singular' as Nelson claimed it was. Nor for that matter was the 'principle' of the heavy guarded attack on the enemy's rear 'new' or 'singular'. Indeed, 'Nelson if we may judge from the style of his memoranda, can hardly have been a very lucid expositor'. All this was not, and must not here, be construed as an attack by Corbett on the way Nelson actually fought Trafalgar, but only on his expository coherence, and on the idea that he was a great tactician in the traditional sense of Signal Books, plans, and Lord Howe. Corbett thought Nelson probably explained his intentions verbally, as he had done before the Battle of the Nile in 1798. In any event, it is likely that Nelson was more in a hurry to come to grips with the foe than he was to execute precise manoeuvres: this was what Villeneuve expected, what Nelson had done before, and what happened. Whether Corbett thought that the details were improvised will be discussed in due course.

As has already been noted, Corbett noticed that there was nothing new in tactics that massed a protected attack on an inferior part of the enemy's line – in particular against the rear. Nevertheless, Corbett was cautious in his approach to this problem. He inferred that the manoeuvre bore some relation to the mêlée or pell-mell fighting tactics of some successful English admirals in the seventeenth century. There was also some reason to associate it with the battle habits of such 'General Chase' movements as Admiral Lord Hawke used at Quiberon Bay. On the other hand, because of his mistaken opinion of the place of Kempenfelt in the growth of the Royal Navy's tactical sense he was inclined to trace it through Kempenfelt's knowledge to its French advocate, Sebastian-François Bigot, Vicomte de Morogues. The latter's important book *Tactique Navale: un traité des evolutions et des signaux* was published, first in 1763, with a second edition in Amsterdam, 1779. Kempenfelt probably read it. An English version appeared in 1787. Morogues wrote in praise of the principle of concentration and mutual support of ships *not in a line of battle,* and this, of course, was Nelson's method. Corbett thought Morogues had an influence, but probably not more than that which stemmed from the traditional growth of the Royal Navy. Such a concentration, of course, is not easy to effect on an equal and determined foe. Even Nelson expected to have superiority of numbers over his foes, despite the probability that by 1805 the British were contemptuous enough of their enemies to regard tactics simply as a means of getting at the enemy, not as a substitute for fighting him.

The tactical views and researches undertaken by Corbett, and up to this point outlined, were those put forward in his two edited books for the Navy Records Society. He had much more than this to say about naval tactical history, but their general import here has been shaped by the fact that it was the Trafalgar question that determined his overall inquiry. It is now necessary to look at the kind of questions that the Trafalgar battle raised, as opposed to those he advanced as a general culmination of his researches.

Corbett's influence on the tactical controversy over Trafalgar began in 1905, partly as a result of his comments in *Fighting Instructions*. Looking back, it is remarkable that close argument about these tactics was delayed for such a long time — over a century. Of course, the main general facts about the battle were never in dispute. It was clearly understood that a British fleet comprising twenty-seven sail of the line, commanded by Vice Admiral Lord Nelson, had defeated a Franco-Spanish fleet of thirty-three sail of the line off Cape Trafalgar, with the wind behind the British. After some five hours, two British sections struck a foe strung out in a long line and heading north. The experts knew when the leading British ships cut through the enemy line, the details of Nelson's death, the number of ships taken or sunk, and the main events of the fighting. Indeed, a great deal was known. However, the question not answered was both interesting and difficult. How good a tactician was Horatio Nelson? For a hundred years, death in the moment of victory had protected the great Admiral's thoughts and actions from critical scrutiny.

Three facts called for explanation. First, casualties amongst many British ships were high, especially in the leading ships. Second, eleven days before the battle, Nelson issued a Memorandum, addressed especially to his second in command Admiral Cuthbert Collingwood, outlining his general battle plans. It was, in retrospect, not apparent to everyone whether, in the battle, he had followed those plans partly or fully. Third, since the Admiral died without comment on whether his original intention had been carried out, there was room for speculation[1].

Nelson's Memorandum[2] of 10 October, dealt with two possibilities; attack (there is no mention of defence) on a foe from either the lee, or weather, positions. In 1805, on that immortal day, the British had the wind and so only Nelson's weather plan (in its details) was of much relevance. There were, however, some general principles. First, Nelson anticipated that British ships would advance and attack in two or more distinct bodies and not in one cohesive, but formal, line ahead. One of these bodies would engage and overwhelm a smaller section of enemy force while the other section, or sections, protected that action from interference by the remainder of the enemy force. Nelson assumed that the foe would be in a continuous formal line — which they in fact were on the day of battle; further, he assumed that he would have

---

1   A further possibility, not discussed here is that the very costly action did not enhance the British strategic posture.

2   *The Memorandum* is printed in *Fighting Instructions*, Appendix.

superiority of numbers on that day, which he had not. He planned to attack, personally, the ship of the enemy commander-in-chief, which he ultimately did. Finally, he planned to surrender control of other divisions to their commanders as early as the pattern for the battle seemed set according to his wishes. Whether or when he did that was open to some debate. In detail, his plan assumed that he would be overhauling, from their rear, an enemy in line. Thus the British lee division would fetch along the enemy line just out of gunshot and then go down together on inferior numbers in the enemy rear while the other, weather, divisions would make sure that the enemy rear got no help from their centre and van. In the event the British were in two divisions, not three, since the nucleus of the third division had been detached and was at Gibraltar, on 21 October.

Admiral P.H. Colomb wrote an article shortly before his death in 1898, in which he suggested that Nelson had ordered his fleet to bear up together, early in the morning, and that it went down on the enemy in line abreast formation in two divisions.[1] Since diagrammatic representations had customarily shown the British to have been in a sort of follow-the-leader, or column, formation, this raised real questions. (See Diagrams 1 and 2, p. 121).

In 1905, Henry Newbolt's book *The Year of Trafalgar* appeared. It supported the customary or column theory, although he thought that the two sections had actually struck the foe in somewhat different alignments: the weather line one after another, or, 'in succession', the lee line obliquely, or in a sort of 'line of bearing'. (See Diagram 3, p. 121).

Corbett, in his *Fighting Instructions,* published Lord Nelson's 'Memorandum', and commented on its relationship to the battle as fought. He deliberately wished to begin an argument, for he considered that naval officers generally continued to hold the belief expressed by Lord Dundonald in 1816, 'Never mind manoeuvres: always go at them'. 'The phrase', wrote Corbett, 'is obviously a degradation of the opening enunciation in Nelson's memoranda, a degradation due to time, to superficial study, and the contemptuous confidence born of years of undisputed mastery at sea'. This was dangerous stuff, thought Corbett, but he thought that even the hero captains of Trafalgar were not immune from it since it was only those 'officers who had a real feeling for tactics (who) saw that Nelson was

---

1 Quoted by Admiral Sir Cyprian Bridge in a letter to *The Times* 8.VII.05. See Vice-Admiral P.H. Colomb 'The Battle of Trafalgar', *United Service Magazine,* September 1899.

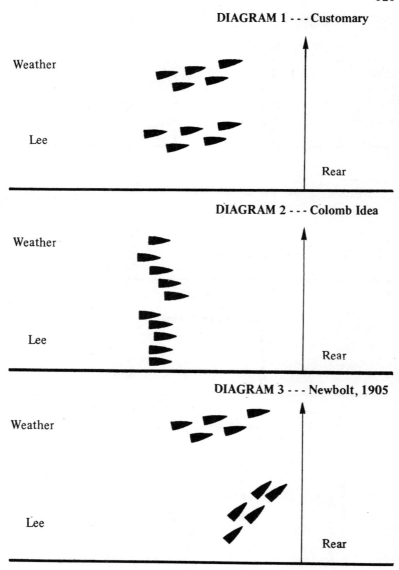

DIAGRAM 1 - - - Customary

Weather

Lee

Rear

DIAGRAM 2 - - - Colomb Idea

Weather

Lee

Rear

DIAGRAM 3 - - - Newbolt, 1905

Weather

Lee

Rear

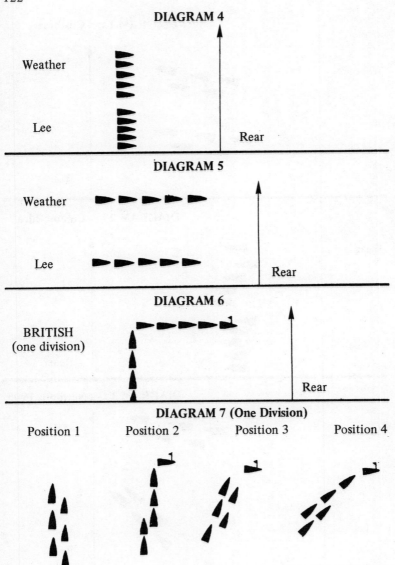

DIAGRAM 4

Weather

Lee

Rear

DIAGRAM 5

Weather

Lee

Rear

DIAGRAM 6

BRITISH
(one division)

Rear

DIAGRAM 7 (One Division)

Position 1   Position 2   Position 3   Position 4

making his attack on what were the essential features of the memorandum'. The distinction many people failed to appreciate was that a difference existed between the 'essential features' of the 'Memorandum' and the way these were carried out on the one hand; and the details of the 'Memorandum' and the degree to which those were carried out on the other. Undoubtedly, the general purpose was to achieve a mêlée of the seventeenth-century type through the application of certain ideas. It was planned to attack by divisions; to concentrate on and isolate one section of the enemy line; to conceal this objective until the last possible moment. All these were plans made for the same purpose, i.e. to produce a general engagement.

In detail, however, Nelson ultimately discarded his plan to approach the enemy parallel, and decided to go down on them so as to achieve a two-column simultaneous impact. Corbett thought that the Admiral had substituted an attack in column, 'a mad perpendicular attack in which every recognizable card was in the enemy's hand'. The risk he took was 'enormous'. This was because the heads of divisions were for a long time exposed to a fire that it was not possible to return, and also because the ships were vulnerable to being doubled on by the irregularly lined foe. Furthermore, Corbett claimed that the column formation was achieved early in the day and in response to signals 76, 76 and 13. In detail, therefore, Corbett held that Nelson had not rigidly adhered to the Memorandum.

Corbett's violent language (viz. 'mad perpendicular attack'), provoked responses from Nelson worshippers. Admiral Sir Cyprian Bridge advised the Navy Record Society that the problem should be re-examined by a sailor expert.[1] *The Times* took the bait. The editor suggested that Bridge supported Colomb's theory and announced that the newspaper welcomed correspondence on the question raised.[2] Newbolt at once claimed that the two British Divisions had struck their enemy differently: the weather line in column, and the lee line in 'line of bearing', but that both had commenced their move 'in column'.[3] It appeared to him that only Collingwood had signalled for 'line of bearing'.

The controversy, mainly between Bridge on the one hand, and Corbett and Newbolt on the other, continued. It turned, for the moment, on what the first signals of the day meant. The key

1 *The Times* 'Report of Navy Records Society Meeting', 6.VII.05.

2 *Ibid.* 8.VII.05, Editorial.

3 *Ibid.* 14.VII.05, Newbolt letter.

instruction was signal 76 which Colomb and Bridge interpreted as ordering 'bear up together'. Corbett and Newbolt thought it meant 'bear up in succession'. The former interpretation would have the effect of making the British approach in line abreast (see Diagram 4, p. 122): the latter would make it in line ahead (see Diagram 5, p. 122). Corbett's and Newbolt's confident interpretation of the 'in succession' theory (despite references to signal books) was shaken by Bridge's assertion that in order to carry out the 'in succession' theory, each ship would need to make and shorten sail to change course properly (see Diagram 6, p. 122) in order not to have a collision at the point of turn. This shifting about would take time, and time was what Nelson lacked.[1]   This forced Corbett to re-examine the meaning of Signal 76, and its historical development, and ultimately to scrap his initial argument.

His final, and more plausible explanation of this point, was that Signal 76 was an old sailing signal that required ships sailing in a loose group led by the admiral to bear up and sail large on a course steered by the admiral, in the lead, or one pointed out by his signal. That is to say, each ship executed the signal individually, saving only that they waited for the admiral's course signal or for her to sail clear and lead,[2] (see Diagram 7, p. 122) 'Your Reviewer' wrote to *The Times* to support the movement Corbett had suggested, but not the historical reason for it.   He thought Nelson had probably explained to his Captains before 21 October how he wanted Signal 76 to be executed.[3] There was no proof for this.

The Times's Naval Correspondent, J.R. Thursfield, wrote a series of six articles to try to sum up what had been discovered so far.[4]   He thought that Signal 76 meant 'bear up together', but dismissed that argument on the grounds that it was pedantic and irrelevant since the Memorandum referred to bearing up together as part of the attack. He noted that the controversy had previously centred on what was clearly the approach. Indeed, he held that it did not matter what the approach formation was, so long as Nelson had accomplished his object of keeping his opponent guessing.   That Thursfield was attacking Corbett is clear when the above sentence, written by him as *The Times* Naval Correspondent, is taken in conjunction with an editorial stating

1   *Ibid.* 19.VIII.05, Bridge letter.
2   *Ibid.* 27.VII.05, Corbett letter.
3   *Ibid.* 22.VIII.06, 'Your Reviewer' letter.
4   The articles appeared between September 16 and 30, 1905.

clearly that Thursfield's purpose had been to challenge the idea of 'a mad perpendicular attack'.[1] Nevertheless, it had not been possible to overthrow the Corbettian assertion that in detail the 'Memorandum' had not been followed on the day of battle.

There was also some argument, in which Corbett did not then take part, as to whether or not H.M.S. *Victory* had turned to port before she made her tactical move to starboard; that is to say, whether there had been 'a feint to the North'.[2] Evidence was not strong enought to elevate these speculations to the height of real argument.

Corbett's consistent interest in Trafalgar, an interest maintained through his lectures on the subject at the War Course, together with his interest in the historical development of fleet tactics, combined to lead him to write the two tactical chapters already mentioned in his book, *The Campaign of Trafalgar.*

It is not entirely clear how much Corbett was indebted to Edouard Desbrière for information on Trafalgar.[3] It is more than likely that he relied mainly on his own British researches. He began the book in early February 1909, and the work was completed by October. In that month, he wrote to *The Times*[4] to claim that a check on the *Temeraire's* log revealed that Collingwood's line of bearing signal was made at 9.00 a.m., not 11.00 a.m. as previously thought. Also, he revealed that the signal book of 1816 had a signal for 'cutting the enemy's line in two columns', and since this signal was new and was not challenged by contemporaries, it stood as good evidence that it represented the actuality of the attack at Trafalgar. In any event, the article was bound to arouse the interest of tactical students in the forthcoming book.

While discussing the relation of the 'Memorandum' to the battle in his book, Corbett rehearsed the *general* arguments of the 'Memorandum' and stated again that they had been followed. However, he explained that the captains who claimed that the 'Memorandum' was carried out *in detail* never, in fact, clearly differentiated between general principles and details. Why, he was not certain. Collingwood, whose dispatch placed him in the same

1   30.IX.05.

2   See Schurman, *Education of a Navy.* pp. 170-4.

3   Col. Edouard Desbrière *Le Campagne Maritime de 1805* (Paris, 1907). An English version, improved by the competent editing of Constance Eastwick in 1933. Brian Tunstall claims that Corbett used the original Desbrière as his 'main authority'.

4   'New Lights on Trafalger', 22.X.09.

categoiy, had a good reason for caution since he maintained 'a lofty determination to ignore any detail which might be turned even remotely to detract from the glory of his dead friend or to suggest in any degree that the victory was not entirely Nelson's'.

Now the 'Memorandum' stated that the lee line was to hit the foe *together*. There is evidence that Nelson wished Collingwood to attempt this. There is, however, no evidence in the 'Memorandum' that clearly indicates how Nelson, or the weather line, was to contain the van. Presumably, it could either be done simultaneously, or one after the other in line ahead. Corbett felt that Nelson deliberately chose the line ahead method, and that he did this because he hoped that speed, and the heavily gunned ships leading, would produce a 'fatal shock'. Since the speed was only three knots, it is not clear that speed would be all that irresistible. Indeed, Corbett seems really to be more convincing when he indicates what Nelson did rather than in attempting to penetrate the Admiral's mind. It may be that Nelson made the best of a situation forced on him by time and the unexpected resolution with which Villeneuve awaited attack after his line had deployed, facing northward. (He had begun the day pointing south). After all, the lee line carried its largest ships up front as well, and the purpose there was somewhat different to that of Collingwood's. In any event, Corbett gave Nelson credit for displaying adaptive genius rather than pedantic adherence to a preconceived formula in the face of altered circumstances. (Having won the battle it was still almost impossible for Nelson to lose the debate!).

The chapter describing the actual battle made reference to Signal 76. The 'bear up together' argument Corbett still rejected. He added important new evidence to support his interpretation that Nelson had used Signal 76 to achieve a similar formation, in practice, on 30 September 1805. Also, he pointed out that from the vantage point of the Franco-Spanish fleet the turn would first look as if the ships were moving together, or abreast, but that this impression would alter, as it did.

In dealing with the state of Lord Nelson's mind in view of the fact that the Franco-Spanish fleet changed direction north as the morning advanced, Corbett did not indicate that the British Admiral had anticipated the move. The attack was to be launched in two distinct bodies, and Corbett felt Nelson's main worry was concerned with whether or not Villeneuve intended flight to Cadiz. It turned out that, while this possibility undoubtedly agitated Nelson's mind for some time, the formation of the British van would serve this purpose equally well in either the contingency of fighting a formal line or chasing a fleeing foe.

In any event, to change formation would take time, and time was at a premium. Looked at from the enemy point of view, it may be seen that two results were obtained. First, the Franco-Spanish van was held immobile by the implied thrust, and secondly, Villeneuve did not know precisely how, or where, Nelson intended to strike. Since we still debate the question now, no doubt Villeneuve was in a similar quandary then. Corbett went so far as to state that Nelson himself was undecided until the last moment. Indeed, he felt that even Collingwood, who had signalled for a bow and quarter line at 9.00 a.m., was unable to finally achieve it — not because he did not wish to, but because Nelson held on with full sail and practically caused a race, making tactical manoeuvre difficult or impossible. Whatever one may think of these moves, they were not those of a cautious tactician.

Corbett did deal with the vexed question of whether there had been a feint to the north. In terms of a deliberate turn to port, he claimed this had not happened; but, in terms of holding on for the enemy van, Nelson had contrived to give the impression, up until the last moment, that he intended to attack it. This was part of the Admiral's 'concealment of purpose' plan.

The conclusion, therefore, was that Nelson 'flung away the security of scientific deployment' and so took a risk that 'almost passed the limits of sober leading'. The proof of the pudding, however, was in the eating. If Nelson gambled, he more or less anticipated that superior British gunnery and ship-handling would ultimately defeat his foes. That, after all, is what happened.

The reviews of the tactical aspects of the book were favourable. One perceptive claim was that Corbett might not have appeared so magisterial had Desbrière's work been available in translation.[1] But even Desbrière did not have Corbett's real strength — viz. 'Mr. Corbett excells as an historian because his strategical understanding is as great as the profundity of his knowledge of the facts, and he never fails to write in such a manner as to command the interest of the general as well as the professional reader'.[2] This is exceedingly high praise for tactical exposition!

The articles that Thursfield had written were later published in book form, and Corbett's book had obviously not agreed with Thursfield's version. Unwilling to let the matter rest, Thursfield wrote a further

---

1   *The Athenaeum*, 2.VI.10.

2   In the *Westminster Gazette*, 28.VII.10.

article on Trafalgar tactics.[1]   In his preliminary remarks, he stated that although Corbett's work was undoubtedly brilliant, the conclusions were unsound, and hence his influence on the Navy, as a War Course instructor, was unhealthy.   No doubt Thursfield was angered by Corbett's statement that 'it is, of course, possible, by selecting fragmentary passages from ill-kept logs and journals, and by calculations based on the various times at which ships alleged they engaged, to infer that possibly a real line of bearing was [not] formed; but the vigour of historical science absolutely forbids such fragile web-spinning to obscure a question which is illuminated by *direct and unimpeachable evidence* to the contrary'.[2]   This was strong controversy, and here Corbett seems to have stood on his establishment reputation as an historical expert.   In any event, the historian offended the journalist sufficiently that the latter called on the press for an Admiralty Committee to investigate and pronounce on the subject, undoubtedly with the purpose of discrediting Corbett in the eyes of British sailors.   Thursfield, however, while he was successful in securing the Committee, was the ultimate loser, for the Committee declared for Corbett.

Nevertheless, at the time of the Committee's appointment, Corbett felt that the news of its formation was ominous.   They are going to 'sit on my book'.[3]   Moreover, he felt that Admiral Sir Cyprian Bridge and the Chairman, Admiral Sir Reginald Custance, were unlikely to do him justice.   The historian, Sir Charles Firth, was also a Committee members, and its secretary was W.G. Perrin, the Admiralty Librarian.   Corbett complained officially,[4]   and took the precaution of inviting Firth to lunch where he impressed on the latter 'the necessity of historians asserting their rights with "No"s'.[5]   Firth asked for his opinions.   Actually, Corbett need not have worried so much.   When Fisher (about whom Custance was almost paranoic) was not involved, Custance generally displayed fairly balanced judgements.   Bridge was no dogmatist.   Firth was intelligent, and W.G. Perrin had strong carefully formed views — along Corbett's line of reasoning.   Perrin had provided much of the signalling information for Corbett's book.[6]   There-

---

1   In *Brassey's Naval Annual*, 1911.   A less impressive attack on Corbett was written by Captain Mark Kerr, RN, in *The Nineteenth Century*, October 1911.

2   *The Campaign of Trafalgar*, p. 372.

3   JSC *Diary* 2.IV.12.

4   JSC *Diary* 4.IV.12.

5   JSC *Diary* 17.IV.12.

6   Tunstall information.

fore, since Perrin wrote the Report,[1] the result was never in any real doubt, and Perrin carefully handled the evidence so as not to use the work of people who had written since 1905 — with the exception of Desbrière whose authority gave strength to the whole. On every important point the Committee supported Desbrière and Corbett against Thursfield and the British literalists without ever mentioning either Corbett or the literalists by name. No doubt this result helped Corbett to forget the presumption and arrogance shown by the appointment of the Committee in the first place. No doubt the Board of Admiralty held a high view of its competence to pronounce authoritatively on almost anything referred to it. History certainly did not daunt them, as the self-confidence of this committee showed. Yet the historian is humbled by the competence that, in fact, *was* displayed.

Corbett's judgements on the tactics of Trafalgar were balanced, judicious, and based on an historical method of interpretation. This is not to say that he did not change his position, or that he was invariably correct. What he did do was to challenge the idea that all speculation and consequent deduction about the battle were equal in value. This is where he and Thursfield really differed. Thursfield wanted to find the truth, to be sure, but he was willing to find it at the ends of many avenues of approach. Corbett strove to confine himself to approaches that were confined by the rules of historical evidence. For instance, historical facts could be discovered by the simple use of original sources. But for those facts to be of use to Corbett they had to be strung out intelligibly against an historically determined background. Anything else was 'cobweb spinning'. We cannot ever know the exact relation between the 'Memorandum' and the 'Action', but we can know that there is a reasonable way to approach that relationship. For Corbett, the reasonable way was the historical way, and he illumined a good deal by using this approach.

The author has endeavoured not to let his own views on the tactics of Trafalgar trespass on those of Corbett, for this appreciation concerns Corbett and *not* the battle, which is still open to different interpretations. To assist the reader in understanding the level of Corbett's tactical writing it is necessary to repeat that the two chapters he wrote on the battle were the work of one who knew more about the material he handled, *in its general tactical setting,* than even Desbrière. It is not necessary to prove him right on all, or even most, points to appreci-

1   The assertion is made in writing by Perrin on the copy of the Report in the Public Record Office, London.

ate that he dignified and lifted the controversy by his participation in it. Only by appreciating the depth of his labour and the wonderful subtlety of his mind is it possible to understand the sense of horror with which he viewed an Admiralty Committee, as he put it, about 'to sit on my book'. The Admiralty were mistaken in one thing. They regarded their pronouncement as final, or semi-divine. In fact, the god of tactics had already given utterance.

8

THE RUSSO–JAPANESE WAR

A general description of the first British Official Histories, dealing with the Russo-Japanese War, has been penned by Professor Jay Luvaas.[1] The origins of these books, at least so far as naval interest is concerned, has not been thoroughly probed. Indeed, it is not generally known that an entirely separate naval history of that war was written for the Naval Intelligence Division at the Admiralty: a work that still exists in two printed volumes in the Naval Library. It was written, between 1911 and 1914, by Julian Corbett.[2]

The connection between this 'confidential' history, and the public productions of the Committee of Imperial Defence was intimate, and is revealing. A study of this relationship provides insight into the reasons that led Julian Corbett towards official history. It also adds to knowledge about the way in which official maritime history in Great Britain began. Departmental friction, the high confident casualness that the man of war exhibited when dealing with men of letters, and the quixotic effect of personality in determining the shape of future events, are discernable as this almost comic-opera train of events is examined. Comedy aside, however, a review of these events provides a background to understanding the mentality of those who were involved in collecting material for, writing, and producing, the subsequent history of the First Great War.

It was natural that the Royal Navy, a service that served both as tutor and model for the development of the Imperial Japanese Navy, should be interested in the actions and activities of its *protégé* in war conditions. The C.I.D. began collecting materials for such history as soon as the Russo-Japanese War ended in the autumn of 1905. One man who was keenly interested in the way that such materials should be used was Captain Charles Ottley, R.N. In 1906, Ottley was

---

1 See Luvaas, 'The First British Military Historian', *Military Affairs*, XXVI, no. 2, (1962), pp. 49-58. The CID history was written under the direction of Sir Ernest Swinton and entitled *Official History (Naval and Military) of the Russo-Japanese War*, 3 vols. (London, 1910-20). As Luvaas points out, vol. III was completed by 1914 but not published until after the First World War. Most of the preliminary work and organization was done by Colonel Neil Malcolm, who was succeeded by Swinton in 1910.

2 Julian S. Corbett Ll.M., in consultation with Rear Admiral Sir Edmond J. Slade K.C.I.E. K.C.V.O. *Confidential – Maritime Operations in the Russo-Japanese War 1904-05.* 2 vols. Issued under the Direction of the Admiralty War Staff.

Director of Naval Intelligence. One of the men paid by his Division, within the Admiralty, Major E.Y. Daniel, was engaged to translate the Russian materials relating to the war. He, Daniel, was a linguist, not a literary master. No more was he a professional Naval Officer, having been loaned to the N.I.D. by the Royal marines.[1]

The services of an author were required to write a coherent and instructive narrative. As a beginning, Ottley thought that Daniel should be assisted in arranging the evidence by some intelligent sea officer of experience. Once this was done then the actual writing, he thought, might be entrusted to a man who had made literature his life's work. Among these, were 'Professor J.K. Laughton, Mr. Julian Corbett, or Mr. Henry Newbolt . . . and many more'.[2] To ensure professional guidance, Ottley recommended that the selected writer ought to be placed under the supervision of the Secretary to the Committee of Imperial Defence, Sir George Clarke because 'no abler non-professional naval writer exists'.[3]

Ottley had no personal objections to the naval history being written at the C.I.D. He had a dual purpose in mind in bringing the subject to their Lordships' attention: to make sure that the result would be well written, and to ensure that the work would meet the needs and requirements of the naval service. The question of where the final departmental responsibility would lie, and how it would be financed, did not worry him at this stage. Consequently, Daniel continued his work at Portsmouth, and he was given assistance in sorting and arranging by Captain Thomas S. Jackson, R.N. who it was thought might get some assistance from Corbett when the latter visited Portsmouth on his War Course lecturing duties.

Clarke, on the other hand, whose days at the C.I.D. were drawing to a close, wanted the final responsibility for official histories (one concerning the navy and the other the army) to rest at the C.I.D. Applications to the Treasury by both the Admiralty and the C.I.D. for funds caused the Treasury to decide that that naval work would be the responsibility of the navy alone. Jackson and Daniel carried on, therefore, and Clarke wrote to acquiesce as 'the drawbacks of dual responsibility will be avoided'.[4]

1 PRO ADM. 1/7878 Minute Charles Ottley, the Director of Naval Intelligence; for Admiralty Board. 4.VIII.06.

2 PRO ADM. 1/7878 Minute, Ottley to Adm. Board 14.XII.06.

3 *Ibid.*

4 PRO ADM. 1/7878 Sir George Clarke (C.I.D. to Adm. Board), 4.VI.07.

Ottley had not forseen his transfer to the C.I.D. to succeed Clarke (24 August 1907) when he wrote his original memorandum. But he had dimly appreciated that some naval control was necessary to ensure that the ultimate production would serve to meet educational naval needs as the navy saw them. Consequently, it was not long before the evils inherent in the looseness of the working agreement were revealed. As his day of removal to the C.I.D. approached, and presumably he had some suspicion that it was imminent, Ottley warned the Board of Admiralty that Jackson would be posted in the natural course of events and although funds for the work of preparing naval materials existed, continuity for that project was not assured. Consequently, Ottley sought authority to engage Mr. Corbett 'or some other literary expert' to do the composition, 'naval Officers having little time to spend on such lengthy works . . . in any event Corbett's terms ought to be ascertained'. In the meantime, Daniel and Jackson could work on until 'the end of the present financial year'. The Board agreed with the last portion.[1] Sleeping dogs were let lie. Corbett was not approached.

When he moved to his new position at the C.I.D., Ottley knew that he was supposed to produce both a military and a naval history of the War. But he also knew that the other naval history he had commissioned, at the N.I.D. was going ahead. He was aware as well that confidential and other material, now available subject to the control of his successor at the N.I.D., Captain Edmond Slade, might be very useful in the production of the C.I.D. naval history. He therefore proposed co-operation. Fisher, the First Sea Lord, shrewdly minuted 'Treasury might well object to pay for history in two separate compartments'.[2]

Slade, for his part, at once recognized the importance of what Ottley was attempting to achieve. He may or may not have realized the force of Fisher's comment on a divided operation. But as Chief of Naval Intelligence, he knew that there could be no publication of much of the secret material gathered through his Department. Therefore he felt that there should be a 'confidential' history, and, since it alone could point up the real naval lessons of the war, the task of writing it should be entrusted to a man who could make sense of the materials. His friend and associate, Corbett, was obviously that man. Slade wrote 'I am of the opinion that he is by far the best man to undertake this work, from his position as a lecturer on Naval History at the War College he is in intimate touch with the Service, and his published

1   PRO ADM. 1/7878 Ottley to Adm. Board 11.VI.07.

2   PRO ADM. 1/7878 2. VII.07.

works on Naval History show a grasp of strategical and tactical questions which is greatly superior to that of any other writer with whom I am acquainted'.[1]

Thus while the production of the histories at the C.I.D. proceeded, the relationship that bound that committee to the Admiralty in the production of two naval histories was not clear to everyone. Theoretically, the C.I.D. was the place where the thinkers of the two services could be brought together in a spirit of fruitful co-operation, but, of course, service rivalry between the army and the navy had caused the First Sea Lord to look at most of what went on at the C.I.D. with suspicion. The matter was complicated by the ambivalence resulting from this mistrust. Furthermore, there was, at this stage, no evidence that either the writing of the 'confidential' or the C.I.D. history excited the intellects of members of the Admiralty Board, much less impelled them to action. In 1907-08, when matters of important military orientation hung on the decisions reached concerning ship-building plans and fleet disposition, it is not surprising that history was somewhat neglected.

Ottley pushed on as best he could with his work at the C.I.D.[2] For the Navy, Commander Luce, who had succeeded Jackson as Daniel's partner, prepared a preliminary manuscript of a naval history that turned up on Slade's desk in the autumn of 1908. This production did not impress the D.N.I. and he passed it on to Corbett. The manuscript at once struck the historian as a disaster. He wrote in his Diary[3] 'at tea came letter from Slade enclosing from Ottley "comments" on Naval Strategy for C.I.D. history of Russo-Jap. war – which Ottley thought not good'. Slade wanted Corbett to improve it. 'I wrote him a strong letter stating that it was useless – playing at it – and that I could have nothing to do with such amateurish stuff and thought the Admiralty ought not either. It is going back to where he began – trivial stuff without a spark of understanding of what strategy means – done by a Commander who could not possibly know enough . . . I told Slade it was trifling with the whole thing and he should protest at all the N.I.D. work being wasted for lack of proper treatment'.

Such a vehement reaction made Slade realize the need for a more

1   PRO ADM. 1/7878 Slade (DNI) to Adm. Board 14.XI.07.

2   PRO ADM. 1/7878 Ottley (C.I.D.) to Adm. Board 6.XI.07.

3   Corbett *Diary* 17.X.08.

sensible arrangement.[1] He placated Corbett by stating that he had protested against the C.I.D. history. He explained that secrecy was vital because the Japanese, as allies, had been good enough to supply confidential information. The word 'secrecy' had been introduced, and secrecy was a two-edged sword, as Corbett would find out. Meanwhile, Slade dilated on the need for an author. He, himself, was too busy. He had considered Captain Lowry at the War Course, but the latter was 'not clear enough on the principles involved'. Admiral Wm. Henderson was also considered. Then Slade was posted to India.

Slade's successor as D.N.I. was Admiral Bethell.[2] He agreed with Slade's view that Corbett was the man to write the N.I.D. history. At once he offered the historian a permanent post in his Division at the Admiralty. Corbett was overjoyed at the prospect. He wrote in his Diary that such an appointment represented the 'summit of his ambition'.[3] At last his true worth was recognized and he was to serve in the service he so admired in the way that would best use his talents. The next day he wrote to Bethell to accept, providing that the appointment would not entail regular attendance at the Admiralty.[4] At that point, however, Fisher sent for Corbett and advised against acceptance, since no promotion could be expected in such a static post.[5] Corbett took the advice. Slade was also against it and wrote from Ceylon to say that the appointment would not be looked upon with favour by senior officers at sea.[6] This was something of a commentary on the slightness of the rapport Corbett had established with serving sea officers. It is all the more revealing in that Slade, through his cumulative experience, was probably better placed than anyone else to really assess Corbett's overall impact. The man who was most sympathetic to the historian's ideas was clear that the desired service-wide acceptance of them had not been attained.

Of course both Fisher and Slade were right, but it is another question whether the reasons they gave to Corbett for rejecting the post were, although sensible, the most important. The way to muzzle or control an historian is to put him into a post where his work may be censored. The Admiralty was an ideal place for this: a place where the need for secrecy could be used to justify all sorts of behaviour (as

1   Slade to Corbett 19.X.08 CP.B/13b.

2   The Hon. Sir Alexander Edward Bethell.

3   Corbett *Diary* 20.IV.09.

4   By which he meant keeping regular office hours.

5   Corbett *Diary* 24.IV.09.

6   Slade to Corbett 30.IV.09 CP.B/13b.

Fisher well knew). The very citadel of the 'secrecy' mania at the Admiralty was the Naval Intelligence Division. It seems that Corbett was terribly naive about such things at that time. Certainly he did not then appreciate the lengths to which powerful men would go either to protect their own views, or to obliterate those with which they disagreed. The incident also shows that Corbett had a powerful urge for personal recognition, or an equally strong, but misguided, idea that naval history could educate a navy, not only from within the service, but from within the citadel of its bureaucracy — among the powerful at the Admiralty. In any event, for the moment he was saved from this particular urge to cloister his talents.

It must, however, be made clear that if Bethell's desire had been simply to remove a troublesome file concerning the Russo-Japanese War from his desk, Corbett did not know it. The historian had not been approached officially in any way concerning its writing. Meanwhile, he was asked to lecture on the Russo-Japanese War to the Naval War College. The fact that Corbett agreed to lecture on this subject, however, posed a problem for Ottley at the C.I.D. Corbett's opinion of the C.I.D. history was low.[1] But now that Corbett was to reveal his views to the War Course, it would mean that the C.I.D. history, if it were produced, would face at least that competition. For it was always clear that Corbett and Slade thought that military men in both the Army and the Navy looked on the Germans as the great exemplars in writing military history. Since their association in 1906, they had been opposed to this viewpoint. It was Slade's opinion that the lectures should take the form of timeless commentary and not mere detective work: that they should show the senior naval officers how the methods of the old sail navy were still relevant. 'I do not fancy that is what you are to do', wrote Slade, in reference to the proposed lectures.[2]

Meanwhile, the C.I.D. history was being completed. The whole question of historical writing for service instructional purposes came up again, as the Treasury were pressing for the abolition of historical work at the C.I.D. Bethell wanted the naval side brought back to the Admiralty and connected with the War Course and he knew that this subject was soon to be aired at a sub-committee meeting of the C.I.D., so he asked for Corbett's help in securing the acceptance of his viewpoint. Corbett at once grasped the reason for Bethell's request: presumably the reason for the D.N.I.'s interest in him. Generally

---

1   Corbett *Diary*. 24.IV.09
2   Slade to Corbett 30.IV.09; CP B/13b.

speaking, soldiers knew more military history than did naval officers, therefore military history produced at the C.I.D., in the name of co-operation, would be dominated by the army men. With this unpalatable conclusion Corbett agreed.[1] He prepared a paper outlining the value of acuracy and competence over flair and co-operation.

Armed with Corbett's argument, Bethell attended the C.I.D. sub-committee on Pay and Functions of the Secretariat, which sat on 26 November 1909.[2] The Committee included the First Lord (Reginald McKenna), the Secretary of State for War (Haldane) and Lord Esher.

Bethell contended that there was a real need to continue with the production of historical work, once the specific Russo-Japanese studies were complete. But he considered that the naval instructional value of material already produced was limited. The Navy needed something more. That a special naval history was wanted was owing directly to the fact that naval officers competent to write what was needed did not exist. A competent, learned civilian, if properly supported by technical advisors, could fill the need. General Ewart, speaking equally frankly, stated that the army appreciated the need for intelligent military history production but opposed the use of civilians. What was needed to help educate officers was a supply of reliable military texts for formal examination purposes and he claimed civilian writers often failed 'to bring out the lessons to be derived from the wars with which they deal'. The sub-committee concluded, loosely, that the C.I.D. ought to continue with the work, but that civilians might be preferable. Really nothing was settled.

Bethell used the sub-committee's loose approval of civilians to request formally that Corbett state his terms for the writing of a history of the Russo-Japanese War. What they wanted, responded Corbett, was 'strategy illustrated by historical analogues'.[3] His terms were £500 for six months work. Bethell then wrote to Ottley asking for the £500. As a result, Ottley, rather incautiously, wrote to the Treasury objecting to a purely naval history being written by a civilian and falling against the C.I.D. budget.[4] The Treasury Board seized the opportunity to declare first that history was not a C.I.D. affair and,

1   Corbett *Diary* 16, 17, 18.XI.09

2   PRO ADM. 1/7878 *Report* of a Sub-Committee appointed to consider various suggestions regarding the Pay and Functions of the Secretariat of the Committee of Imperial Defence.

3   Corbett *Diary* 9.XII.09.

4   PRO ADM. 1/7878 Bethell (DNI) to C.I.D. and Adm. Board 9.III.10.

second, that 'it should be compiled by a naval officer rather than by a writer such as Mr. Corbett and the whole charge of it should fall upon Naval Funds'.[1] The Secretary of the Admiralty Board, Graham Greene, however, minuted on this the opinion that the service had no naval officers who could do the work.[2]

The Board's view of this, finally given in June, was that Daniel should stay at the C.I.D. while he was needed for the C.I.D. history, and that Corbett should write the naval history. Both costs should fall on the Navy. This was 'the most efficient and economical method of preparing the history desired'.[3] At this stage, Corbett was consulted. He had held consultations with various people about the C.I.D. work and concluded that its chief demerit appeared to be caused by slavishly following the 'German history' method. But he suspected muddle over the whole concept and prudently refused to correct the C.I.D. naval MSS without a contract being signed.[4] The Treasury agreed to this if Corbett's work and that of the C.I.D. were kept separate and the cost rigidly kept down and 'not to be exceeded under any circumstances'.[5] Terms were worked out by September.

Corbett's objection to being involved with fixing up the C.I.D. history was directly professional. For him there was a right way and a wrong way to write naval history: wrong history was bound to result from imperfect methods, and imperfect methods of writing military history were non-British methods. Nothing could illustrate more clearly Corbett's ultimate concern that naval officers should not be corrupted into regarding their profession from a continentalist as opposed to a maritime, viewpoint.

The Treasury was interested in this question of whether history should be written at the C.I.D. or the Admiralty, from the point of view of preventing the proliferation of what appeared to be similar tasks. Proliferation would doubtless mean more expense. The attention of the financial experts had been specifically drawn to the question by Ottley's objection to the C.I.D. paying for a purely naval work. This query had raised the whole matter of payment of salaries at the C.I.D. One example, among others, was the case of E.Y. Daniel.[6]

1 PRO ADM. 1/7878 Treasury to C.I.D. and Adm. Board. 9.III.10.

2 PRO ADM. 1/7878 20.V.10.

3 PRO ADM. 1/7878, Adm. Board to Treasury 27.VI.10.

4 Corbett *Diary* 25.V.10.

5 PRO ADM. 1/7878 Treasury to Adm. Board 12.VIII.10.

6 PRO ADM. 1/7878 Adm. Board to Treasury 27.VI.10.

Major Daniel, who sometimes worked at the C.I.D., had actually been seconded from the Royal Marines by the Admiralty. He might have been forgotten about had it not been for the fact that when he retired from the Marines his salary (to keep him on as a translator of history) had to be re-negotiated through the Admiralty and a special arrangement made. Thus when the Treasury came to consider paying for a more historical production, Daniel was their case precedent, and so the Admiralty was favoured by them over the C.I.D.[1]

On such seemingly small matters do bureaucratic decisions turn. Indeed the whole genesis of the Russo-Japanese War history cannot always be followed as a matter of high seriousness. It is clear that at the Admiralty no one, certainly not Fisher, considered the production of naval history as a matter of great consequence. Admiral Bethell, who supported Corbett's appointment, was not a man who had great influence, either personally, or owing to his position. No doubt the First Sea Lord disliked Directors of Naval Intelligence with pretensions to power. Even if Bethell was serious the desultory nature of the circulation of the file does not indicate that he was moved by any sense of urgency. While it is not possible to state what Admiralty Board members said to one another, it is possible to suggest that they treated the subject lightly, except when it became a question of whether right naval thinking was safe in the hands of the C.I.D. Fisher was not pro-C.I.D. and the Board generally disliked the idea of turning any naval business over to that body where army influence was thought to flourish. Ottley at the C.I.D. wished his own power increased and his office to acquire more status. He was not taken seriously. One thing is certain: concern for scholarship was not a factor in this atmosphere of service rivalry and Treasury desire for economy.

Finally, it must be stated that no one, outside Bethell, his predecessor Slade, and perhaps Ottley, really understood what the arguments were about, and probably not one of them ever went to a meeting with the subject well in hand. Corbett was quite right to refuse to work for these carefree administrators without a contract. He was wrong to think he might impress them with his finished work — contract or no contract — as we shall see.

However, Corbett's letter of acceptance to Graham Greene must have been refreshing to the Admiralty Secretary. He had no intention,

---

[1] PRO ADM. 1/7878 Corbett to Graham Greene (Adm. Board Secretary) 23.IX.10.

Corbett wrote, of writing a microscopic account 'nor of dealing with such matters as the effect of shot, armour etc. Elimination and compression is what you have a right to expect when you employ a professed man of letters, and an historian who cannot get all that is worth telling of two short campaigns into two ordinary volumes I should consider did not know his job — that is if he is given a fairly free hand . . . and personally I am anxious to show that these naval staff histories can be produced efficiently at no great cost. It certainly ought to be a question of hundreds rather than thousands'. This economy-mindedness impressed the Board and they were inclined to go for the Corbett plan providing his general purpose was made clearer and that he would agree to submit his chapters to the Directory of Naval Intelligence for approval as they were written.[1] Corbett agreed. He informed their Lordships that he intended to take a broad strategic approach, and to emphasize the 'interaction' of military and naval operations. As far as a submission of chapters was concerned he was 'very sensible not only of the advantage but of the necessity of this course being taken at every step'.[2] This supervision was to prove easier to write about than to suffer. But the agreement was finally struck. Not because there were no more objections to a civilian doing the work; there were, but the Navy had no professional who was capable of it.

Corbett next looked to the kind of source material he could expect to find. One reason for the Admiralty wishing to write its own history was that its Japanese allies had provided the Board with a good deal of secret information, especially concerning the origins and opening moves of the war. The Japanese for their part, were sensitive about the lack of frankness they experienced from the British allies. Under these circumstances they might be diffident about providing the secret information their allies required. This was especially the case when one considers that they did not even know that the material they provided was being made into a book. How much should they be told and how much should they be asked to provide? These were sensitive questions and hence referred to the Foreign Office. 'So here is another hitch when I thought [that] all [was] settled', wrote Corbett wearily.[3] Despite apprehensions for the future, however, existing materials were made unreservedly available to Corbett even to the extent of his using British Admiralty-Foreign Office correspondence

1 PRO ADM. 1/7878 Adm. Board to Corbett 7.X.10.

2 PRO ADM. 1/7878 Corbett to Adm. Board 10.X.10.

3 Corbett *Diary* 27.X.10, 1.XI.10; 10.III.11; 14.III.11.

concerning the antecedents of the Russo-Japanese War, and he was given Room 43 at the Admiralty to work in. By the time it was also decided that the Japanese would 'probably' get no copy, so that 'criticism could be outspoken'; it was July 1911, and Corbett had written nine chapters.[1] On 8 January 1912, Corbett delivered chapters 10-12 to the D.N.I. who was then Captain T.S. Jackson,[2] and a new arrangement for criticism of the chapters was worked out. Before going on to discuss those arrangements it is necessary to explain some of the reasons for them.

When Corbett took the first nine chapters in to Bethell in July 1911, he learned that when the C.I.D. history had first come up, years before, the army men on the Committee had been opposed to his writing it. Corbett wrote; '[I] told him I knew it because they are hypnotized by Germany and forgot we had ideas of our own of wh[ich] Germans knew nothing'. It is important to emphasize that Corbett had made enemies in the Army, and the persistent opposition to his ideas by the soldiers did nothing to help his cause. His *Diary* contains many references to his ideas being opposed by the dominant continentalists − both at the War Office and at Camberley. The army men made two points about Corbett; that he was a civilian and hence prone to error on military affairs, and secondly, that his strategic views were unsound. They knew, of course, of his part in the invasion enquiry. We have already seen that some of Corbett's purely naval views were too rarified to be acceptable to most naval officers, and what is not understood in this world is usually condemned. Therefore, it must not be thought that this persistent army opposition fell on deaf ears. Furthermore, it is doubtful if Corbett ever understood, before 1914, the extent to which the army concepts of strategy were dominant. Whether the army thinkers were right or wrong is a question of judgement, but that most naval officers did not really grasp the nature of the anti-army case, let alone press it home politically, is clear. That Corbett was able to maintain himself at the Admiralty with Fisher gone and on such a slim contract is a minor miracle in these circumstances. Certainly his direct influence with the Admiralty Board at that time was not profound.

There were, however, reasons relating to personality and to changes in Admiralty organization that were also responsible for the altered organization that was to face Corbett's contracted history. Winston

1 Corbett *Diary* 3, 6.VII.11.

2 Corbett *Diary* 8.I.12.

142

Churchill's new Naval Staff reforms altered the position and functions of the Director of Naval Intelligence somewhat, and he now functioned more directly under the Chief of Staff. The Chief of Staff was Admiral Sir E.C. Thomas Troubridge, and, as has been seen, the successor to Bethell as Director of Naval Intelligence was Captain T.S. Jackson. When Corbett went to call on Jackson on 22 January 1912, he found him 'anxious [that] my work should remain in his division and not to be taken by Ballard' who was Director Operations Division. Two days later Jackson took Corbett to see Troubridge, where after a 'long and satisfactory talk'[1] it was decided that Troubridge would be Corbett's chief and Jackson and Ballard would both criticize the work, with Corbett to be called in when the judgement of these two differed.

Like most arrangements made with men of power concerning (in their eyes) non-vital work and involving a number of people, this one was not fruitful. When Corbett took chapters 18-26 to the Admiralty in March, he found that Troubridge was anxious to read the typescript as soon[2] as the manuscript was transformed into print. A few days later, on 22 March, Jackson agreed with Corbett's fears that Troubridge would likely try to make big 'violent' changes in the manuscript, and therefore the sooner it was removed from him the better. But by July neither typing nor criticism was done, and Corbett, whose work was held up thereby, protested.[3] This had some effect, but the situation was not simple.

What had happened was that Troubridge was under the impression when he was appointed C.O.S. that he had been placed in charge of a new and influential department. This was not so. The power structure in the Navy did not go through him. Bethell had told Corbett when Troubridge's appointment to the new Staff position was made that 'all [the] service was laughing at Troubridge . . . nothing was changed'.[4] One must suppose that this did not dispose this naturally difficult man to be any more keen to co-operate with anybody, and certainly not with a semi-intellectual like Slade. For it was to Slade that Corbett wished to send his manuscript when it could be pried loose from Troubridge — officially that is, for Corbett was already consulting Slade chapter by chapter as he went along. Finally, the Admiralty Secretary, Graham Greene, threw his powerful support to

---

1 Corbett *Diary* 22.I.12; 24.I.12.

2 Corbett *Diary* 5.III.12.

3 Corbett *Diary* 1, 12.VII.12.

4 Corbett *Diary* 8.I.12; 9.II.12.

the Slade idea and the thing was done.[1] Corbett wrote, feelingly, 'a great relief'.

By the end of the year, the Slade collaboration was getting on famously. On 6 November, Corbett recorded an interesting decision in his *Diary*. For security reasons, there were to be only six copies of the Japanese Confidential History issued.[2] This ruling was to make the history next to useless when it finally was printed. Also at this time he had difficulty with Slade. When he received the proofs for Volume I, Corbett discovered that Slade's name preceded his on the title page. He protested, and the final copies advertised that the book was written by Corbett 'in consultation with' Slade.

From this time until Volume II was completed, and the proofs were being corrected while the ominous events of July 1914 relentlessly progressed, Corbett had no further trouble with the history except in the writing of it. But his position was difficult. His work threw him into close contact with the C.I.D. because of the convenience in using their sources. Yet he was not of that body. If there were future histories, where would they be written? He did not know. There were, however, some rewards. Hankey, the Secretary of the C.I.D., had read Corbett's new book, understood it and liked it. Furthermore, he had observed first hand and understood the difficulty of writing useful history under the combined handicaps of power maniacs, divided responsibilities, and secrecy. He and Corbett had a long talk on the subject in November 1913. Corbett recorded it in his cryptic diary style 'to C.I.D. where had long talk with Capt. Hankey over future of historical section and getting work produced with civilian help. Lord Esher came in and went on regarding same subject — but more vaguely. Hankey seems to have got all my ideas on his own so we entirely agreed on lines that should be adopted. . . .'

In this conversation with Hankey, Corbett also informed him that he was planning to secure publication of a naval and military series through the Cambridge University Press. This proposal stemmed directly from his first bout with official history and its attendant secrecy. Such work, Corbett thought, ought to secure scholarly as well as military recognition. Hankey understood and agreed. This was an important conversation since Hankey's understanding of the real problem of official history was to save Corbett's wartime work from severe interference, and perhaps ruination.

1 Corbett *Diary* 23.VII.12.
2 Corbett *Diary* 6.XI.13.

The completed history, in two volumes, was titled *Maritime Operations in the Russo-Japanese War 1904-05.* Only six copies of Volume I were produced by the Admiralty. Of Volume II over 400 copies were produced. Although marked *Confidential,* Corbett stated that the production was for use by naval officers generally, although not freely by officers of lower rank. It was not to circulate to officers who were retired. This was because it contained material that had been provided by the Japanese Government. It is clear from reading Corbett's Introduction that the important Japanese source material was translated by Naval Instructor Oswald T. Tuck, R.N. under the direction of the Naval Intelligence Division. Daniel had translated the Russian material. French translations of Russian histories had been undertaken by various persons engaged on the C.I.D. histories.

The material, wrote Corbett, was not complete enough to explore the causes of the war as thoroughly as he would have liked. Also, the combined operations discussions were not capable of being rendered complete because of gaps in the evidence. This was caused partly by separation of function between the Japanese naval and army commands. However, from his experience with this material, he was able to state that the 'inter-service relations as they worked out in the war are of the highest importance to ourselves'.

Thus the history of the Russo-Japanese War, by Corbett, was completed just before the First World War began. The secrecy and muddle over its beginnings emerged to contain it when it was concluded. The First Sea Lord, Prince Louis of Battenburg, an intelligent man, read it before the war began, but he was soon hounded from office by the Germanophobia that occurred during Britain's entry into the war. So it lay on the shelves of the Admiralty Library unheeded and forgotten by any but Slade, Corbett, Prince Louis and perhaps a few others through two world wars. Corbett, who did not need the money, was some £1,000 richer, if that meant anything.

The Russo-Japanese War history was written to demonstrate how the priceless lessons of naval warfare were revealed by that conflict. It was aimed at British naval planners. Corbett's other histories, although privately published, had similar objectives. Nevertheless, this was his chance to show his readers that lessons deduced from the historical consideration of sail warfare could also be extracted from the historical study of modern ironclad warfare. His purpose was to use a modern event to show that warfare involving an essentially marine nation was different in many essentials from conflict where sea power has no great, or at any rate predominant, role to play. In this sense he wished to demonstrate that 'continental' type warfare was different from warfare involving significant maritime content.

The book did consider tactics. In its detailed consideration of mining, torpedo work, and battleship contact he was able to discuss the main preoccupations of his contemporaries and the spectacular Tsushima fleet action made a fascinating study. But it was in the field of strategy, in the interplay of the separate services and their direction in an essentially maritime war that he was able to achieve his most striking effects. In order to accomplish his aims he merely repeated his usual method of writing historical narrative. But in writing for a predominantly professional audience about a recent event he felt constrained to point out that this method was not the same as that usually employed in the then fashionable German Staff histories that exercised such a 'pernicious' influence on most British soldiers and sailors. This 'continental' method was to narrate the passage of events and then to draw up conclusions, or lessons, at the end. Such a technique had been employed in the separate British C.I.D. histories of the Japanese War, and in the histories written by Japanese and Russian authors, with the result that army and navy activities were treated separately from each other and consequently reached two separate conclusions. Corbett's method, as he explained it in his preface, was to write a continuous, self-revealing narrative showing how sea and land events impinged on each other and affected each other in conception, execution and result. In this way political objects, geographical pecularities and command machinery could all come in for their requisite share of on-going analysis. Since his work was not to be circulated to the Japanese he had the additional advantage that he could make comments on professional decisions unfettered by any sense of exaggerated deference to the powerful men who, in the natural course of the war, made mistakes. After all, Britons would think it natural that foreigners should have made mistakes; indeed they would expect such a record to appear.

Corbett adopted the technique of looking at the developing events from a Japanese perspective. This was because the Japanese were an island power off a vast continent, and thus provided a welcome opportunity to compare and contrast the Japanese and British situations, just as he constantly compared the Japanese methods for dealing with particular naval situations to the processes employed by British sea-practitioners during the age of sail. Also, like most navally-minded Englishmen, Corbett took a pride in the knowledge that English naval architecture and naval example had been closely followed in Japan.

A geographical similarity existed between the two countries, in their strategic situations, but was not exact. Whereas England had no programme involving the occupation of Holland, Japan regarded Korea differently, partly for traditional reasons, but mainly because Korea was a peninsula with good concealed harbours; an appendage to Asia that Japan actively wished to possess or control. Influence in Korea was vital to the control of the water separating the islands from the continent generally, and control of those waters was the cornerstone of Japan's military-cum-national policy, just as control of the English Channel was Britain's policy.

Undoubtedly the war was caused mainly by the fact that Japanese home security and Russian Eastern maritime commercial ambitions both required control, not shared occupancy, of the Sea of Japan. Predominant interest in Korea was Japan's guarantee for securing Japanese control. After the British took Weihaiwei in 1898, the Russians obtained a lease on Port Arthur and the Liaotung peninsula. The Japanese then prepared for war. Corbett made it clear that the Russians, or some of them, understood very well the essentially maritime and limited nature of the war that their pressures in the Far East made almost inevitable. They were aware that it would not be a war of total territorial conquest or overthrow. They thought, Corbett asserted, in terms of the Sevastopol campaign in the Crimean War and not of Sedan and the Siege of Paris.

If Corbett's perspective was Japanese oriented, he was not without sympathy and understanding for Russian problems. Certainly Russian opinion that the war would be limited and maritime was intelligent enough, and Corbett appreciated that in St. Petersburg they understood the advantages and disadvantages that water conveyed. Their chief difficulty was that while steady pressure, including army interest in support of Russia's commercial expansionist plans in the Far East built up, naval opinion which saw the difficulties inherent in the position on the spot, was not able to either dominate or even restrain policy. Certainly the naval people in St. Petersburg saw that if Russian squadrons existed in both Port Arthur and Vladivostock, not only would a Japanese landing on the west side of Korea be a risky operation, but this strategic stance would appear to threaten Japanese control of the Sea of Japan. Therefore, despite local Japanese numerical naval superiority, and the fact that Port Arthur was vulnerable to being cut off at the end of its peninsula, the strategic advantages were not entirely Nipponese. The unfolding of events bore out this assessment of Corbett's and hence the real strategic interest of the history turned on how each side reacted to this strategic situation. It is well to bear in mind the fact that Russian responses were conditioned by the Anglo-Japanese Alliance of 1902. Corbett pertinently quoted Admiral Alexiev's comment that the very thought of British intervention 'paralysed' Russian iniatives by sea.

So the Russians held good naval cards. Why, aside from the inhibiting effect of the British threat, did they not properly prepare to take advantage of their sea chances? Partly, said Corbett, it was the lighthearted way in which the extreme imperialism of interested men inhibited the development of sane diplomatic and military preparations. More important, there was no Naval War Staff. Corbett had written this part of the book before Churchill appointed his rudimentary staff in London and the material was put forward as a cautionary tale. The Russian Naval Service needed a body capable of exhaustive study in order to face the Imperial Council 'with the weight of argument and authority which such expert study alone can give'. St. Petersburg had never been made forcibly aware of the need for Far East sea reinforcements, and they thought they could plan such matters on an *ad hoc* basis! Even if reinforcements had gone out the Russians did have a real problem. On which base should they concentrate? Corbett, arguing on the basis of Kempenfelt's base selection problems in 1782, thought that the Yellow Sea should have been disputed by the smallest possible force and the rest should be used for diversionary purposes to keep the Japanese off balance in the Sea of Japan. More ships would have helped this chance, and the principles were understood by some, but what was needed was the consistent application of some policy. This, in turn, could only come from strong executive orders based on accurate *staff* information.

The Japanese advantage was that they had a good naval staff whose opinions were respected and influential, but not dominant. This was as well, since the sea was the key to their whole plan. Japan itself was not vulnerable to invasion unless a war of annihilation were launched against it, and this was understood to be impossible given the overall Russian situation; and the cautious responses of the Russian Foreign Minister, Count Lamsdorf, had made this clear. Therefore, the only kind of war that made sense, since no one expected the Japanese to march on St. Petersburg, was a limited one with a geographical objective, viz., to isolate a piece of strategic territory (in the Kwantung Peninsula) and hold on to it in such a way that the price of recapture would be too high a price for the Russians to pay. To achieve this result was a matter totally dependent upon the exercise of sea-power in a decisive manner.

However, Japan, like Russia, was a country dominated by army traditions. The Navy was the service to be proved. This produced disadvantages as the war went on for in a pro-army society the real function of a navy was not generally understood except for the expectation that the fleet would win spectacular victories. When all this is said, however, the input of the Japanese Naval Staff into the joint service and state Imperial Headquarters Staff was strong, and with a few significant exceptions, kept nervous response to naval operational moves to a minimum.

Certainly Corbett thought that sanity with regard to sea strategy reigned in the mind of Admiral Togo, the Japanese Naval Commander in Chief. He wrote:

> The Admiral's view of his functions was characteristic of his unfailing grasp of combined problems and was in full accordance with our own traditional practice. Where the main offensive movement rests with the army the logical function of the fleet is defensive and was always so regarded in our Service. It may be that it cannot perform that function without destroying the enemy's fleet and this will always be so if the enemy's fleet is active and badly handled. But where it is not so handled and when topographical conditions make it possible to prevent its interfering with the army's movement, it was never our practice to postpone that movement in order to enable the fleet to carry out elaborate offensive operations with a view to securing a complete decision. Desirable and eventually essential as decision is, in these cases it is not always the paramount necessity of the opening. For Japan that necessity was the immediate success of the military and not of the naval offensive.

When the war began the Japanese attacked Russian ships in Port Arthur by torpedo. Nineteen torpedoes were fired. Three Russian ships were hit; none were sunk. It was a disaster. Despite other torpedo attacks, a pitched battle, and considerable mine-laying, the last Russian ships did not surrender until the next year along with the harbour itself. For Togo, and the Imperial Staff in Tokyo, this failure raised the question of whether the army could be ferried to its disembarkation points on the *west* coast of Korea in the face of undestroyed shipping in Port Arthur. The Russians had felt that the Japanese would not attempt a western Korean landing owing to nervousness concerning the Port Arthur squadron and had expected them to land in eastern Korea, march north-east over lengthy and difficult routes to the Yalu River, and thence to attack the Mukden-Port Arthur railroad. To prepare against this the Russians had time. The Japanese, however, with splendid strategic courage elected to escort and protect their army to landing places, even eventually on the very edge of the Nanshan neck that attaches Kwantung to Liaotung. Meanwhile Togo had detached one squadron to operate in the Yellow Sea side of the Straits of Tsushima — responsible for army lines of communications with Japan, and to watch for attempts of the Russian Vladivostock squadron to join that in Port Arthur, or otherwise interfere with the naval-military operations in the Yellow Sea. This Force was commanded by Admiral Kaminura.

It took a great deal of courage to proceed with the army movement in the face of undefeated fleets. But with good nerves and by obeying the laws of probability it was possible to go ahead, securing local command of the sea for covering purposes with what naval force the Japanese could muster. As Corbett pointed out, in line with his teaching, they did not have overall command of the sea. That their plan was good enough to have obtained such command does not alter the fact that they did not obtain it by either an attempted decisive strike or attempted decisive battle. The Japanese proceeded, but their balance was precarious and vulnerable.

Its vulnerability was demonstrated by the cruises south of the Vladivostok Squadron. In June, July and August 1904, this Russian squadron made three cruiser sorties south and each time disoriented Japanese movements in the Yellow Sea. During the August cruise Admiral Iessen attacked shipping off Tokyo Bay, and the Imperial Military Staff panicked and recalled Togo from the Yellow Sea. This, wrote Corbett, showed the strategic vulnerability of a naval situation ultimately dominated by army personnel. Calm was restored when Admiral Iessen went back to port. The course of war was only slightly affected. But Corbett's points were forceful.

Why did Kaminura fail to destroy Iessen? He had, wrote Corbett, a 'loose hold on fundamental principles . . . a recurring tendency to confuse the two functions of the two sections of his force (four armoured cruisers, four protected cruisers and a numerous flotilla) a restless anxiety "to seek out" the enemy's fleet with his battle division, or with his massed force, on any alarm and on quite inadequate information. The result was that not only did he miss decisive contact, but he permitted the enemy to penetrate the vital area from which it was his primary object to exclude them'. Corbett added that he may have done it to satisfy public opinion, or to enhearten his crews. It was Corbett's best exposition of his teaching that big battle was desirable but that the wish for it was no reason to dart here and there in careless disregard for the general rules of naval strategy.

Thus did the Russo-Japanese book fit into the main stream of Corbett's naval patterning. You could fight a successful war without 'command of the sea', in general terms. The Japanese had done it. It must be mentioned that he shared the general opinion that the death of Admiral Makarov was the premier Russian disaster. Had that restless soul remained alive the tension on the Japanese supply lines would have been more severe and perhaps unbearable, and the effects of the Vladivostok sorties might have been crucial.

Most commentators make the unfavourable comparison between the Russian and Japanese expertise and morale — unfavourably toward the former. Corbett's view was different. He thought their lack of morale was traceable to general lack of leadership and he quoted approvingly Makarov's comment about 'the inability of the captains to handle their commands in a seamanlike manner'. This was important since anyone studying the effect of leadership, before Makarov was killed in a mine explosion, will not need to be instructed on the importance of the personal factor in naval war.

In conclusion Corbett's book taught that with relative equality at sea combined operations can be prosecuted successfully by a determined power cognizant of the real deployment requirements of sea power. He implied, but did not state, that luck was a factor in the war. Makarov was killed by a mine. But then the Japanese laid the mine.

It may well be asked why this account of Corbett's treatment of the Russo-Japanese war is confined to what may appear to be very arbitrary selections of significant explanation and information? Precisely it is because his fundamental purpose, method and habit of treating sea strategy are understood by isolating these features. He expected, as a matter of course, that students of war would be interested in the use and effectiveness of various kinds of modern naval hardware. Corbett dealt with these matters in an authoritative and detailed fashion − and the particular specialist may read him now, as he could then, with profit. But Corbett was determined to resist allowing the war to be considered merely from the point of view of one or more technical specialities. In the same way he understood the nature of the argument of those who put the blame on inferior personnel, lack of morale or incompetence − yet he refused to succumb to the temptation to write the Russians off with sweeping generalities. He knew, and his treatment of Makarov showed it clearly, that men made a difference. Nevertheless he declined to discuss the war as if the result were a foregone conclusion. Corbett would not be dominated by any simplistic explanations although he illumined many casual factors as he proceeded. His purpose was to make his readers see that sea warfare had rules which conferred special advantages in the present as they had in the past. 'Engage the enemy more closely' was not enough of a guide for every situation.

For those reasons he put the conflict in historical-strategic perspective and he served no special interest except so far as he obviously wished to instruct British strategic planners: to make them think. He carefully discussed strategic options that had historical sanction and then tested them in the light of the conditions of the dreadnought age and in the light of the new technology. Thus, while most histories of the war had specialist axes to grind, his did not. He only wished modern naval planners to see that sea options enforced restrictions and advantages that could be predicted.

It seems likely that had this book been read by thousands (or even hundreds) of aspiring naval leaders in Britain, he would have found his main concerns neglected in favour of his tactical hardware information — which he would have been the first to admit, was very important. But if the reception of his lectures at the War College is any guide, he would have been accused of showing how the Japanese won the war almost by accident, whereas his purpose was to show that their methods involved risk. All war involves risks and they were surmounted in this case study, showing, as Corbett wanted also to show, that the Japanese understood those risks, calculated the chances, and then acted (despite one failure of nerve) and ultimately triumphed. An audience that really wanted to hear 'never mind manoeuvres — always go at them' would have regarded anything. militating against this simplistic nonsense as close to treason. It was not treason and it was worth study. Until submarine hunters in World War I adopted attachment to convoy as the place to meet the foe, the submarines exerted the same effect on their opponents as the Vladivostok squadron had exercised on Admiral Kaminura.

9

JULIAN CORBETT AND THE WAR

When the First World War broke out, the Royal Navy was ready for the conflict. At least it was ready in *matériel* in so far as it outnumbered Germany by a significant margin in fighting ships. In five months the German surface raiders, who initially menaced Empire trade, were either sunk or bottled up in harbours. When the test of fleet action came in 1916, the Royal Navy, while it did not achieve a tactical victory of great or Nelsonic proportions, sufficed to drive the German High Seas Fleet into its home ports — whence it never again emerged in strength, except to surrender and scuttle itself. There was, of course, the submarine threat — which British sea officers did not predict or prepare for, and while much ink has been spilled to show how nearly that form of sea warfare came to throttling the island Kingdom, the fact remains that the employment of convoy did prevent the enemy submarines from actually accomplishing their objective. On all fronts the fight for the sea was successful. The might and majesty of Britain's sea service was tested by an energetic foe and not found wanting. Tribulations, disasters, mistakes there were, which spawned recriminations later, but the ultimate disaster, loss of sea command of the approaches to the United Kingdom and of those to her dependences abroad, did not occur.

And yet . . . there lingers over the wartime performance of the Royal Navy an aura of dissatisfaction. No new Nelson emerged. The prosaic and actual work of maintaining sea communications was the daily, almost routine, lot of the fleets and ships. It is true that the anti-submarine campaign provided some extraordinary activity, but Jutland, like the Dogger Bank the year before, did not prove to be the glorious new Trafalgar that the public and the sailors, in their hearts, had come to expect as their due. The fact was, that the changed circumstances of modern warfare made it virtually impossible to equal the record of the last days of the sailing ship age. Nevertheless, changed circumstances were not taken into consideration by most people in Britain whose expectations remained pitched extraordinarily and unrealistically high. The resulting discrepancy between expectations and results formed the matter of naval disgruntlement both during and after the War. The public, of course, was generally ignorant about the way in which sea-power worked and this ignorance was fed by the popular press and abetted by a feeling amongst some officers in the service who were unimpressed by their leaders. The Fisher-anti-Fisher cleavage in the navy did not help matters.

A more realistic field for criticism lay on the strategic level. The real problem during the war had been the price that the Royal Navy had paid for strategic thought that over-concentrated on battle, as opposed to the end or purposes that battle was supposed to achieve. For the British fleet was not trained, as fleets had been in the days of Hawke and Nelson, to give the British army mobility and point by transporting soldiers in security to new places of action. It was not trained in the concepts of combined operations. Much of the fiasco at Gallipoli was caused because this training had not taken place, and because the grand slam or big battle advocates believed that the Grand Fleet always commanded priority − a notion that tended to make *any* transfer of fighting power from that body next to impossible. This kind of reasoning also caused the dearth of escort vessels that predisposed most admirals against convoy until the eleventh hour. This strategic fixation and not the relative merits of various Grand Fleet admirals was the cause of much wartime paralysis. But on top of this, all critics persistently missed the fact that a seemingly inactive navy, by holding the correct positions in force, was able to strangle her enemy from the sea. Spectacular moves were not necessary in this kind of war.[1]

Julian Corbett, at the outbreak of war, understood all of this. The defects in strategic approach were the very things that he had lectured on and written about for fourteen years. His books had been intended to dissipate the ignorance about the fleet's real function − a function that should be obvious to readers today. In the *matériel*-centred world of Fisher and Jellicoe, however, strategic thought had been somewhat neglected in a welter of steel and equipment. The wonder is that such a non-*matériel* thinker and historical interpreter as Corbett was still in demand as a lecturer to the War Course by 1914. Nevertheless, he *was* in such demand, and there were *afficionados* in positions of importance who kept him in touch with the naval service. As a result, Corbett was placed in a position where he could chronicle the activity of Britain's sea-power for present and future readers. To bring this thinking to the foreground was his purpose, both in advising the men in power during the progress of the war, as well as by describing events against that kind of background when he came to write his history. That his pedagogical purpose was a great success it would be rash to claim, but certainly some of it must have penetrated the minds of readers of his narratives.

However, this achievement lay in the future. At the outbreak of the

---

1 See Marder, *From the Dreadnought*, vol. II, pp. 48-50 for similar argument.

War, Corbett had no official standing beyond the fact that he had been a lecturer at the War course for nearly fourteen years, and had written the history of the Russo-Japanese War under Admiralty contract. On the other hand, his influence was greater than that. He was known, respected, and had been used by Fisher, who was soon to return to the premier professional post in the Navy as First Sea Lord. Of more immediate importance was his intimate relationship of many years standing with Edmond Slade, who was attached to the War Staff and who had good reason to appreciate Corbett's ability to produce intelligent ideas and to draft them swiftly to fit the needs of all levels of service and government. His other great strength turned out to be his ever-closer relationship with the Secretary of the Committee of Imperial Defence, Maurice Hankey, who never forgot a useful man, and who was to become more and more important as the secretarial functionary who stood at the centre of political events and facilitated the interweaving of the various pieces of governmental machinery by which the complicated British power structure functioned in the First War.

It was as a result of these contacts that Corbett eventually became the official historian of the War. Also because of these contacts, a man with a far from representative view of the strategic function of the naval service came to write its history. Ironically, many of the effects that he looked forward to were produced by men who did not share his theoretical approach — men who confused ends and means. For whatever reasons, however, the Navy had managed to secure the services of the best man in the world to write up its wartime exploits. No one else, anywhere, was capable of such a vast subject, and yet of treating individual sea actions with authority, just as no one else had an equal capacity to translate planning, action and result into flowing narrative characterized by an accomplished prose style. Actually, as they had discovered over the Russo-Japanese War history negotiations, the sailors really had no alternative to Corbett.

Suddenly, in early August 1914, the military men whose presence adorned London society became dramatically important. The Admiralty buildings became a hive of activity and sluggish brains made valiant attempts to grapple with the complexities of war in the machine age. Telegraph and post worked overtime to move vessels on the deep in response to the decisions made at the centre of the hive. To guide them, there existed the necessary set responses to emergency set out in great detail in the War Book, but, as time advanced, new situations and possibilities revealed themselves to naval officers not geared to deal with more subtle unplanned factors. Corbett went down to the Admiralty, watched the self-consciously serious movements of the warriors and returned home sadly, feeling, as he wrote 'out of it with no work to do'.[1] Relief for him however, was being prepared. Slade, on the War Staff, realized at once how much Corbett could contribute owing to his ability to produce original memoranda without being coached. Some subterfuge was necessary to allow him access to secret material, so it was submitted that Corbett's historical-legal training would be useful to assist in the preparation of the periodic situation reports that would obviously be needed. In the meantime, Corbett had been unofficially approached by the C.I.D. historian, E.Y. Daniel, who wanted help with an envisaged history of the War.[2] He declined the latter (although he declared his interest) until such time as he was officially asked, but he agreed quickly to Slade's proposal. He was thus catapulted into the heart of naval life, and anxiety gave way to service.[3]

Of his potential usefulness there could be no doubt. The question was, how could the service best regularize the sudden appearance of this civilian. Slade's submission urged that Corbett be taken on officially as author of the 'Historical Journal of the War' but the real purpose was to have him 'at hand to discuss strategy and draft memoranda, embodying ideas of staff as Sturdee could not do it'.[4] Almost at once, and before the appointment became official, Corbett went to work.

Simultaneously, Corbett began to interest himself in the tentative planning that was taking place with a view to recording the history of the war. The planning of war history was as important as it was vague and neglected, and, because it was neglected, difficult. In April 1914, a decision had been taken to wind up the historical operations at the C.I.D., and had there been no war, the Russo-Japanese War history team would have been broken up when the final volume of the C.I.D. history was completed.[5] As a consequence, it was by no means axiomatic that the historical work concerning this new war would devolve on that body. However, Corbett (now working at the Admiralty) discussed the matter with Major E.Y. Daniel, Commander

1   Corbett *Diary* 2.VIII.14.

2   Corbett *Diary* 7.VIII.14.

3   Corbett *Diary* 10.VIII.14.

4   Corbett *Diary* 10.VIII.14.   Admiral Doveton Sturdee. Sturdee was Chief of Staff.

5   Corbett *Diary* 2.IV.14.

Tuck, and Leopold Amery on 11 August.[1]   At first, it was proposed to lodge the historians in the Admiralty Library, but the final decision was to keep it all at the C.I.D. – at 2 Whitehall Gardens.[2]   Corbett spent the next few days arranging the details of office procedure.   Graham Greene, the Secretary to the Admiralty Board, was irritated to discover all this going on before Corbett's appointment was official,[3]   but it became so on 24 August.[4]

His duty, aside from writing memoranda for the Naval War Staff, was to prepare a daily record of the war's progress referred to variously as the 'Journal of Historical Events' and the 'King's War Diary'.   To do this, he had to have access to naval documents normally very secret, and he arranged at once to peruse them on the C.I.D. premises.[5]   But Hankey proposed, as early as 18 August, that since the Prime Minister wanted materials collected with a view to a history, the facilities at the C.I.D. be used.[6]   Daniel was at the C.I.D., and the Admiralty Board agreed that the collection and collation take place on those premises, and that Naval Instructors O. T. Tuck, and R. C. Cummings should be transferred to assist him.   It was further proposed that the work at the C.I.D. be supervised by an advisory Sub-Committee and the Navy nominated Slade and Corbett to represent them on that body. Corbett was 'willing to give his assistance, and the question of his remuneration need not be entered into at the present stage'.[7]   The complete Sub-Committee contained, as well, Colonel the Honourable M.G. Talbot, representing the War Office, and Hankey for the C.I.D. with Daniel acting as Secretary.   This was the small beginning from which the official history eventually sprang.   The first meeting was held in mid-September.[8]

Corbett's first task in this line of work was to draft a memorandum for the Historical Sub-Committee on the progress of the war during its first month.   Shortly afterwards, he revised this work for presentation as a Cabinet paper, and consequently he was given access to a very wide range of material indeed, including the Grand Fleet papers for the

---

1   Tuck and Daniel were at the Historical Section of the C.I.D. Amery just happened to be there.

2   Corbett *Diary* 11.VIII.14.

3   Corbett *Diary* 15.VIII.14.

4   Corbett *Diary* 25.VIII.14.

5   Corbett *Diary* 28.VIII.14.

6   The identical letter was sent to the War Office and to the Admiralty.

7   PRO ADM. 1/8391. 18.VIII.14.

8   Corbett *Diary* 15.IX.14 and PRO CAB 42/1, 27.VIII.14.

month of August, together with a verbatim account of the proceedings of the War Council during the opening days of the war.[1]   This important paper which was finally printed for the Cabinet on 10 October, purported to place the commingling events of the first month of feverish warlike activity in navally-oriented perspective and juxtaposition for the use of statesmen.   Although military activities were also described, the main emphasis was upon naval affairs.   It was an odd situation.   Not until the last minute was the ultimate position of the British Expeditionary Force, in line with and to the left of the French armies, decided upon.   At sea, however, naval movements proceeded according to prearranged plan, and yet the carrying out of this clearly defined sea role was 'greatly more complex' than that of the land force.   Furthermore, the uncertainty regarding the army's destination meant that the Navy had to set the Army's secure passage towards the place of their ultimate combat as a priority commitment. Corbett saw this fact without giving it undue emphasis, but later he stated bluntly to Sir Henry Jackson that 'in this war (the) navy was subordinate to (the) army'.[2]   He was not pleased.

This French deployment, that gave the Army priority over the naval service, did not sit well with Corbett. Hankey, whom the war was to raise from Secretary of the C.I.D. to the post of Secretary to both the War Cabinet, and the Cabinet, agreed. He told Corbett that he had put in a 'special memo' urging that the army not be committed to France, but found that 'the W.O. would not have it'. The two men agreed that if the Army had been originally at sea ready for deployment, it would have been worth double its value if 'thrown on German communications for Ostend, or Antwerp'.[3] It is important to realize, for an understanding of Corbett's approach to the war, that Hankey was, at heart, on the naval side when it came to rivalry between the services and when questions of strategic priority came up. Indeed, in April of 1914, he had announced that the doctrine of amphibious attack had vanquished the continentalist fixation.[4]   Seldom has a statement been proven to be so wrong-headed, but it gives a good indication of Hankey's general strategic thinking.

1   Corbett *Diary* 15.IX.14 to 7.X.14.   See also Proof Copy RCP *Historical Report on the Opening of the War.* Hankey wrote an appendix on the economic problems at the war's beginning.   The final Cabinet copy went forward under Hankey's name.   In the Richard Corbett Papers Julian Corbett has unmistakably signed his name to the final document.

2   Corbett *Diary* 9.IX.14.

3   Corbett *Diary* 25.VIII.14.

4   Corbett *Diary* 2.IV.14.

However, once the deployment of troops was made, Corbett was convinced that small slightly trained amphibian attacks were not viable as substitutes for more intensive combined operations. As early as 11 August, he was disturbed to realize that some important people apparently wished to promote swift offensive measures in the naval war, despite the fact that 'our position at sea gives us all we want', a view, incidentally, shared by his friend Captain Richmond.[1] He prepared a memorandum on the inadvisability of 'attempting (an) offensive against (a) skulking enemy'.[2] It soon transpired that the apostle of the offensive was Churchill, the First Lord, who, as early as 18 August was advocating the formation of a naval brigade to serve with the Army 'which nobody (i.e. at Admiralty) seems to want'. Corbett supplied the Staff with a memorandum showing how Churchill's plan would infringe Dutch neutrality.[3] The Board, at the time, declared for the expedient of a naval demonstration off Ostend, but a modified Churchill plan eventually was carried out. It proved to be too small an effort to produce any dramatic effect on the German movements. What it did show was that Churchill could overrule his naval experts, that he hungered for action, and that he ignored naval advice 'which had been working out for years at the War College'.[4] Before the naval brigade operation was put in, Churchill had insisted, against staff advice, on laying mines to protect the mouth of the Channel. He was under Cabinet criticism for the loss to a submarine of cruisers *Aboukir, Hogue,* and *Cressy.*[5] The mines had no sooner been laid than it was necessary to sweep a path through them to keep up communications with Antwerp, an operation to which his advisors had also objected. Jellicoe's comment on the loss of the cruisers had been a sensible, 'We must expect this'.[6] But for an Admiralty that was becoming increasingly nervous, and had submarines 'on the brain',[7] Churchill's pushes and pulls were doubtless very unsettling.[8]

---

1 Corbett *Diary* 11, 13.VIII.14.

2 Corbett *Diary* 13.VIII.14.

3 Corbett *Diary* 18, 20. 21.VIII.14.

4 Corbett *Diary* Sir Henry Jackson conversation with Corbett 5.IX.14.

5 Corbett *Diary* 30.IX.14. and 1, 5.X.14, and PRO. ADM. 137/65 Jellicoe to Churchill. 1.X.14.

6 PRO. ADM. 137/65 Jellicoe to Churchill. 30.IX.14.

7 Corbett *Diary* 29.IX.14.

8 Churchill really was perplexed. He believed in naval primacy but had not thought out the implications of the continentalism that the French commitment entailed. For a brilliant discussion of this problem see, Nicholas J. D'Ombrain,

In the meantime, the work of collecting historical material went on. Corbett found his War Office opposite number, Colonel Talbot, highly unsatisfactory and disinclined to do anything. Subsequent meetings strengthened this impression. When Corbett wanted materials from the War Office to include in his Cabinet Paper summarizing the first month of the war, he was given nothing by the soldiers, whereupon Hankey was moved to give Corbett access to the War Council minutes, previously mentioned.[1] When his Paper was nearly completed, the War Office did provide a 'useless . . . accusing and narrow-minded criticism of ministers for not doing all that (the) W.O. wanted. (The) W.O. really makes me sick', he wrote, 'with their hidebound ideas and ignorance of political pictures'.[2] Strong words were these, but the military men were not co-operative.

Hankey's trust in Corbett increased. As early as 10 October, 1914, he mused aloud to Corbett on the form that the eventual history ought to take. The exact words recorded by Corbett are worth quoting for they bore directly on the future arrangements for the publishing of the history. Hankey suggested 'something that could be published officially but in my name and by (an) outside publisher so that I could have (the) profits. (He) also said (that) Balfour told him that he was delighted to hear that I was doing the job'. Hankey promised to put it to the Prime Minister on the 'first chance'.[3]

In mid-October, Corbett had a minor operation that kept him from work until the end of November. Thus he missed the gloom over Coronel, and returned just in time to be able to pen congratulations to Admiral Sturdee who commanded the successful action off the Falkland Islands. In the meantime, Fisher had been brought back as First Sea Lord, and in December he discussed his views on the progress of the war with Corbett. They agreed that the German Fleet would not come out to fight in ordinary circumstances. Expedients were needed. Corbett, consequently, prepared a memorandum for the First Sea Lord on the value of a fleet attack to gain command of the Baltic. This projected operation may or may not have been feasible. What is important to understand is that it was intended, both by Corbett and Fisher, as a dramatic stroke against Germany if the policy of 'passive' sea-control did not prove sufficient to strangle the German economy. It was not immediate, but meant to be thought through very carefully.

'Churchill at the Admiralty and CID 1911-1914', RUSI *Journal,* March 1970.

1   Corbett *Diary* 19.IX.14.

2   Corbett *Diary* 6.X.14.

3   Corbett *Diary* 10.X.14.

Its main ingredient was to be a sowing of mines in the North Sea on such a large scale as to immobilize the High Seas Fleet first, and then other consequences would follow.[1]   Corbett's only objection was that if the British could sow the North Sea with mines, then presumably the Germans could do the same in the Baltic.   The question of the morality of such wholesale minelaying was foreseen by Corbett and Fisher.   Despite this difficulty the scheme ought not to be lightly dismissed.   The War Council was not impressed by Fisher's Baltic scheme, but it should be borne in mind that his intention was 'hastening the end of the war by getting command of the Baltic — combined with his method of making sure of the North Sea'.[2] Strategic- ally, this much-canvassed idea had something to recommend it, but as Corbett was subsequently to find out, even an advocate of stratagems such as Richmond did not think the operation was tactically feasible in the face of mines and submarines.[3]

This memorandum on the Baltic was in Fisher's hands almost at the same moment that Churchill began to look for fields of activity further from home.   Corbett wrote a memorandum on the East African operation for Churchill, about which he knew a great deal since he had seen the minutes of the Overseas Attack Committee of the C.I.D. for his Cabinet Paper in September-October of the previous year.[4] What- ever one may think of the Baltic proposal, it is tolerably clear that Churchill resisted it in large measure because it would affect his own schemes that were centring on the Dardanelles.   For Hankey told Corbett late in January that the Baltic memorandum (about which Hankey admitted having been consulted) had made Churchill angry. Also, Hankey claimed that Fisher had read Corbett's books and imbibed their principles.   Consequently, in Hankey's view, Fisher appeared to be a moderating influence on Churchill, and he thought that the First Sea Lord was only retained in his position because Churchill was afraid that in a trial of strength the First Lord himself, and not Fisher, might be the victim.[5]

In view of this interesting opinion, it is useful to connect it with the conflict in the autumn of 1914 between the civilian head of the navy

---

1   See Lord Fisher *Records,* Chapter XV 'The Baltic Project' (London, 1919), pp. 217-24.   Fisher acknowledged Corbett as the author, p. 217.   Also Fisher Papers, Lennoxlove, Corbett to Fisher 19.XII.14.

2   Corbett *Diary* 17.XII.14.   The paper was delivered to Fisher 21.XII.14.

3   Richmond to Corbett. 6.XII.15. CP/B6.

4   Corbett *Diary* 18.I.15.

5   Corbett *Diary* 26.I.15.

and his professional advisors. Furthermore, in January, Fisher was forced to be very firm to prevent being 'bounced by Churchill into reckless coastal attacks'.[1] Even in May, Hankey reported that the Admiralty could deal with any submarine menace if 'Winston would let them concentrate and not occupy them with wildcat aviation schemes that never came off'.[2] Consequently, it may be conjectured that perhaps the controversy over the Dardanelles Operation, that culminated in political disaster for each, had its roots not so much in the merits of the case, but rather in a power struggle between the two pugnacious men. This is an important matter, since if the Baltic scheme did not enthuse the professionals at the Admiralty, they were on Fisher's side in opposing the Dardanelles proposals. Once the operation was determined upon, Hankey, like Corbett, and along with the pre-ponderance of service opinion, wished to make certain that the Navy did not try to force the Straits alone. A week and a half before the Fleet went ahead with Churchill's plan that combined failure and the world-wide advertisement of British intentions, Hankey had asked Corbett to write an historical appreciation of Admiral Duckworth's attempt on Constantinople with the fleet alone in 1807. This Memorandum showed how Sir John Moore advised against taking the ships into the Sea of Marmora without troops to hold the Dardanelles. Duckworth went without land forces, was becalmed in Marmora, so the Turks reinforced the Straits' defences through which the Admiral was lucky to retreat with only damage and gunfire casualties. Corbett argued the danger of a second humiliation in prestige, and a second angering of an expectant Russia if another fiasco resulted, which appeared likely.[3] Whatever the strength of these views, they were put forward to prevent the Fleet from attempting the Straits unsupported by troops. When the naval attack failed, Fisher used Corbett's arguments to influence Kitchener in an attempt to get War Office support against Churchill's continuing this policy. It was necessary to go direct to Kitchener, said Fisher, for although 'Kitchener was not too brilliant and rather slow on the up-take' he was still the best of the bunch. In any event, Corbett was assured that his original Dardanelles Memorandum eventually helped to convince the War Council to consent to troops being sent out to help the Fleet. Furthermore, he wrote to Fisher to show him how it was possible that a determined feint at the Bulari Isthmus at the neck of the Gallipoli Peninsula, as

1   Corbett *Diary* 25.I.15.

2   Corbett *Diary* 10.V.15.

3   PRO CAB 24/1 5.II.15.

that at Nanshan had in the Russo-Japanese War, could force the Turks to withdraw all their troops in the Peninsula.[1]

By March, Corbett was convinced that Baltic operations were impractical. Under pressure, Fisher was becoming more difficult to deal with. But there was one more scheme in him. That was to make an attempt to secure the port of Alexandretta in northern Syria and to link that by railway with the valley of the Euphrates, which Britain was to govern by setting up a puppet ruler on the same basis as the Khedive ruled Egypt. Corbett drafted an elaborate memorandum on the subject which provided 'moral' and strategic reasons for such an enterprise, as well as sage advice on how to calm the French who had an interest in Syria.[2] Corbett found that Kitchener, as well as some officials at the Foreign Office, agreed with his proposal.[3] In a private letter to Fisher, Corbett urged the importance of this step in the provision of oil supplies for the Fleet.[4] The most interesting paragraph of this memorandum is item ten which reads: 'Clearly it is our right and our duty, if we sacrifice so much for the peace of the world, that we should see to it we have compensation, or we may defeat our end.' It was argued that progress would follow the flag along the oil and railway lines. The idea of an Empire of power was still green in the days before the second Battle of Ypres. The same kind of thinking which involved the outmanoeuvring of the French in the near east motivated Colonel T.E. Lawrence in his negotiations with the Arab leaders over this whole period.[5]

The majority of Corbett's time was spent collecting information for the Historical Section and attempting to organize properly the growing mass of material. The first Report of the Historical Section's Sub-Committee was made in early January of 1915.[6] It was determined, at that meeting, to approach the well-known military historian, Sir John Fortescue, with a view to his collecting and arranging the military (army) material. The Report stated that Colonel Talbot, while not engaged in an extensive operation, did serve as a receiver of departmental and sectional papers concerned with the Army role, and

---

1   Corbett *Diary* 1.III.15; CP/B6. Also Corbett to Fisher 1.III.15.

2   Printed Admiralty Memo for C.I.D.   'Alexandretta and Mesopotamia'. 17.III.15. CP/B7.

3   Corbett *Diary* 17.IV.15.

4   Corbett to Fisher 17.III.15. CP/B7.

5   See Phillip Knightly and Colin Simpson, *The Secret Lives of Lawrence of Arabia* (London, 1969) especially p. 39.

6   PRO CAB 42/1. 20.I.15.

of the unit war diaries. The multifarious material relating to the naval side, was, when no longer required at the Admiralty, passed to the Historical Section for processing. The collection included more than naval records. It embraced documents involving the Colonial Office and Foreign Office that were considered valuable as a base for broad strategic history. The permanent staff, aside from the members of the Sub-Committee, included the two naval instructors, Mr. Tuck and Mr. Ainslie; a confidential clerk at the C.I.D., and 'three gentlemen who donate their time free of charge'.[1] It was recommended that all relevant available materials be collated at once and that Fortescue soon could be encouraged to go ahead with the army side. Corbett, for his part, had had access to most of the important naval materials for the whole of 1914.

The forward movement of the whole was delayed somewhat by Fortescue's eventual refusal to undertake the army task. The journalist, Mr. C.T. Atkinson, was his projected successor. More difficult to surmount was the obstacle encountered by Corbett when he wished to see the 1915 secret papers. Admiral Henry Oliver[2] was most unhelpful until Corbett used Fisher's name, whereupon he appeared to soften and asked for a list of requirements.[3] When this tack proved unsuccessful, Corbett attempted to work through Slade and Graham Greene.[4] Henry Jackson, who was also attached to the War Staff, could do nothing either.[5] When Corbett was first appointed, it had been vaguely decided that he would not see 'very secret things'.[6] This could be interpreted quite broadly, and now proved to be a large roadblock. Meanwhile, Atkinson found no co-operation at the War Office, and Corbett personally visited the Office to clear the way for him. It turned out that Graham Greene was behind the ban on document consultation,[7] and Slade recommended that Corbett 'let it ride'.[8] He did so and occupied his leisure hours in writing up the various events of 1914 for which he had evidence.[9] In May, after a spell

1   Mr. J.R. Murray, Mr. A.B. Walford, Mr. R. deB. M. Layard, C.M.G.

2   Vice Admiral Oliver became C.O.S. on 4 November 1914. Marder *From the Dreadnought* II p. 92.

3   Corbett *Diary* 28.I.15.

4   Corbett *Diary* 8.II.15.

5   Corbett *Diary* 24.II.15.

6   PRO ADM. 1/8391. 18.VIII.14.

7   The influence for obscurantism of that ubiquitous functionary on the First War would repay some study.

8   Corbett *Diary* 11.III.15.

9   Corbett *Diary* 13.IV.15.

of writing in the country, Corbett happened to meet Fisher in St. James's Park and the First Sea Lord agreed to see Graham Greene about the classified papers.[1]

In the meantime, Churchill's chickens had come home to roost, for when he called his first Admiralty Board meeting of the war, his Admirals overruled him over his plans to rush the Dardanelles. It was, perhaps, time.[2] But it was too late for Fisher. His instinct to resign in January had been sound. Hankey told Corbett that the final break with Churchill had come over the question of anti-German submarine defences at the Dardanelles. Fisher wanted to keep the equipment at home, and Churchill to support his great enterprise. Fisher, Hankey claimed, revealed his megalomaniac side by demanding impossible terms before he would agree to stay on as First Sea Lord. By so doing he sealed his own fate along with that of his political chief. Both Corbett and Hankey by then were keen that the operation, poorly begun as it was, should not be given up. It was a great defect that the original operation had begun piecemeal, since Asquith, the Prime Minister, now realized that 'no one knew all that was going on'.[3] Corbett, subsequently, helped Hankey to write a memorandum to influence the Cabinet, in which he made it clear that the whole diplomatic picture ought to be considered (from the Balkans through Suez and Egypt to India) before a decision to scuttle was made.[4] There can be little doubt but that Corbett's share in this production had something to do with prolonging the Gallipoli agony, but the final decision to go ahead was made without giving it that priority status he thought necessary for success.

Meanwhile, the status of the history had not been settled beyond the collation of materials. An extra dimension was added by Lord Esher's growing interest in the form and content of Army history. This interest triggered off the question as to whether there should be a 'popular' history or not. Evidently, most previous thinking had been in terms of a restricted work. But Esher put forward the idea that he should write an army history from Sir John French's Diaries.[5] This awkward suggestion by a powerful figure was considered and countered by a suggestion that a 'popular' work be done by

---

1   Corbett *Diary* 8.V.15.

2   Corbett *Diary* 17.III.15.

3   So Hankey told Corbett. Corbett *Diary* 22.IV.15.

4   Corbett *Diary* 23, 24.V.15.

5   Corbett *Diary* 7.VIII.15.

Fortescue.[1] When Corbett reported this suggestion to Esher, he wrote of the latter's reaction — he 'did not like being bowled out by Fortescue but did not suspect me'.[2] A further suggestion was made in November that Arthur Conan Doyle's popular history (in progress) be adopted by the C.I.D. in place of Fortescue's proposed work, an idea to which the Chairman of the Historical Sub-Committee, Slade, was decidedly 'hostile'.[3] In any event, things were being brought to a head by the Treasury who then began to object to the expense of the Historical Section.[4] Some decisions were obviously necessary.

At the end of 1915, Corbett was not only collecting naval materials but he had prepared, for himself, preliminary narratives covering the events of 1914. Atkinson, for the Army, had begun collecting work in early March. Pending a change in policy that would make post-1914 papers available and some decision that would commission authors to write a history, things were at a standstill. The actual pressure for going ahead with the writing came from Lord Kitchener, who thought it time that the Army experiences be written up.[5] It has been seen that proposals involving Lord Esher and Conan Doyle had been set aside, but by January 1916 Corbett was negotiating with the Treasury to provide for an army 'interim' or 'popular' history, to be written by Fortescue, and a naval one to complement it.[6] By February, the Treasury had come to an agreement with Fortescue, and on 14 March the First Sea Lord, Sir Henry Jackson, saw Corbett and agreed that the latter should write the naval history.[7] The commissioning of a 'popular' naval history at that time did not make an immediate appeal to the First Lord, Balfour. He was won over by the argument that the Army would produce a history in any event so that Corbett's task would be 'to show (the) influence of (the) fleet on (the) war and prevent (the) army from getting out of focus'.[8] It was arranged that while Corbett's work would connect the Navy with broad strategic purposes of the war,

---

1 Corbett *Diary* 26.VIII.15. The suggestion would have been awkward because Esher might be too powerful to control. Also he was not a trained historical writer.

2 Corbett *Diary*. I.X.15.

3 Corbett *Diary* 3.XI.15.

4 Corbett *Diary* 20.XII.15.

5 See PRO CAB 24/92 *Memorandum on The Historical Section* etc. by E.Y. Daniel 3.IX.19.

6 Corbett *Diary* 17.II.16.

7 Corbett *Diary* 14.III.16.

8 Corbett *Diary* 16.III.16.

the Army history would be confined by the bounds of the campaign in France and the Low Countries. Knowing their views, the fact that Hankey and Corbett found themselves in this strong position cannot be described as accidental. Corbett, who had great contempt for the limited 'continental' viewpoint of the Army leadership, had made a strong move towards guaranteeing that its record would remain parochial, and that the naval accomplishment would stand out in the face of the public.

The actual fact was announced to the House of Commons by Asquith on 28 June, 1916.[1] He also announced that a third section, on the General Effects of War on Seaborne Trade would be written by C.E. Fayle of the Garston Foundation, who had been collecting material in co-operation with the Historical Section. But Fayle was to be paid by his foundation – not the State. The work, said the Prime Minister, was already well advanced. It is important to note that the publication arrangements were made with private publishers: Corbett's to be brought out by Longmans; Fortescue's by MacMillan; and Fayle's by John Murray. Such an arrangement provided some safeguard to the authors against any bureaucratic difficulty that might confront them, and it provided for better monetary return. Both of these points had been canvassed by Hankey as early as the autumn of 1914.

It must be remembered that Julian Corbett was not a man who wielded direct or indeed any power, in wartime. Nevertheless, it appears that he did have an influence. How much influence is a more difficult question to answer. It has been shown that his brain was both valued and used by Fisher and Hankey for specific tasks. Also, at the highest level, the Prime Ministers, Asquith, and to a lesser extent, Lloyd George, later did not hesitate to call upon his services.

Because of Hankey's position, however, and the strength of Corbett's own writing, the historian's overall strategic views seem to have had more than passing impact. It will be recalled that, in 1914, he wrote an appreciation of the first month of the war in which his view of global sea-strategy was allowed to emerge. Also, he actually drafted the general covering instructions that were sent to Jellicoe who took up the premier wartime sea appointment of Commander-in-Chief of the Grand Fleet.[2] By these means he inculcated his 'no risk' ideas both into the minds of sea officers of importance and into the thinking of senior personnel at the Admiralty. 'No risk' meant that with control

1   PRO CAB 24/4 *Memorandum on Historical Section by E.Y. Daniel 8.VI.17.*
2   Corbett called it a 'letter of information'. Corbett *Diary* 15.VIII.15.

of the North Sea secured, all consequent maritime benefits would accrue to England without fighting on a large scale *unless* this control was deliberately challenged by the enemy. His view proved accurate up to a point. In August 1914, the Germans were isolated from regular sea contact with their units abroad. These units were hunted down by the Royal Navy, and either destroyed or neutralized by the end of 1914. In European waters a rigid long distance blockade of Germany was instituted and British commerce and troop movements were made in comparative security from interference by enemy surface vessels.

Thus Corbett was opposed to any attempts to improve this beneficial position by means of moves that might endanger the security of that anchor of policy, the Grand Fleet. Any craving for spectacular action went against this principle. Thus, in the event, the Royal Navy did maintain its important stance, — even when it was threatened by the submarine, an instrument of war to which Corbett seems to have devoted little thought.

The historian also held views on the efficiency of combined operations. Indeed his historical works, taken together, constitute one long paean of praise to this type of warfare. The outstanding wartime example of this type of operation was, of course, the attack on the Dardanelles. For the Dardanelles initiative he had great sympathy, but he disliked the way in which the operation was permitted to go forward piecemeal. In particular he disapproved of permitting the Navy to attack alone without Army support. Since Churchill was the main author of this misjudgement, Corbett thought his strategic comprehension questionable. But once the operation had gone forward, Corbett was indefatigible in his efforts to point up the strategic value of success and so he supported the pro-Gallipoli men — including Churchill. Of Churchill's tip-and-run projects, he was less enamoured, thinking them projects that were too minor to draw off disproportionate enemy movement and yet involving too much in British preparation, risk and cost.

It is not to be expected that such a strong point of view regarding the central role of the Grand Fleet, a view founded upon a civilian historian's intellectual premises, would pass unnoticed. Churchill had read Corbett and both his and Fisher's North Sea strategy were Corbettian in their approach. Furthermore, they used Corbettian theory to defend themselves when attacked. It was solid logic behind which to shelter, and it survived in the thinking of their successors in the Admiralty — although most of them would have been unlikely to consciously quote Corbett if actually asked what naval policy was. Mr. Balfour, however, used Corbettian arguments when explaining

British naval policy in the war to oversea Parliamentary representatives in London. *He* understood what Corbett meant.[1] Another less eminent figure, however, knew where these ideas came from and after Jutland wrote publicly to brand them as naval heresy. The occasion was a reference to Churchill's statement that 'without a battle we have all the most victorious of battles could give us'.[2] The man who discovered the 'heretical' Corbett theory in the ex-First Lord's mouth was Reginald Custance.

Despite the fury and extent of Custance's attacks on Fisher in 1906-09, Corbett had remained on good personal terms with him, although there could be no doubt about the radical differences in their views. The same lack of balance that made him attack Fisher relentlessly, whatever the consequences, now drove him to question the whole naval policy of the war by attacking Corbett's theory. He did so by categorically claiming that the primary object of a fleet was to defeat the enemy fleet, which circumstance would cause all other advantages to follow. He did not name Corbett but he referred pointedly to the 'Green Pamphlet' of 1906-07 when he wrote that 'ten years ago another theory was enunciated', one that claimed the object of war was 'command of the sea' by which was meant 'control of communications'.[3] Such a theory concentrated on ends to the neglect of means. This was quite true of course and proves that Custance always got ends and means mixed up. He wrote 'Mr. Churchill has evidently adopted this precious theory – unwittingly it may be – and is using it to justify not destroying the German fleet if opportunity offers'.[4]

As we have seen[5] Lord Sydenham then grasped this opportunity to attack the concepts of the 'Green Pamphlet'. Aside from the attack on his doctrinal views Corbett thought Sydenham wanted to shake public confidence in the naval High Command.[6] To this Corbett objected in a private letter to Sydenham. The mischief, such as it was, had been done.

What this exchange contributes to an appreciation of Corbett shows

1 PRO ADM. 116/1681.

2 See *London Magazine*, September 1916.

3 This was *War College No. I, Notes on Strategy*. Drawn up by Corbett in consultation with Edmond Slade.

4 Custance to *The Times* 9.X.16.

5 See Chapter 3.

6 Corbett to Sydenham; CP/B7. 2.XII.16.

that Custance, Sydenham, and Corbett himself, in the way they reacted, acknowledged that the sea strategy of the war was carried on in tune with Corbett's ideas so far as main fleet strategy was concerned. Of course Hankey shared these ideas and may have arrived at them independently, and Balfour had long been exposed to Corbett's reasoning about sea-power through his close pre-war interest in the C.I.D.[1] This does not alter the fact that the first modern, rational, comprehensive, historical treatment of the theory was given to both the nation and the Navy by Julian Corbett.

Corbett was influential in another way as well. He was much concerned with the blockade policy of the Royal Navy. It requires very little imagination to comprehend that if the Grand Fleet stance gave Britain control of enemy sea communications, then a great part of the resulting power exercised depended on the vigour with which it was applied. However, it is not necessary to give a detailed description of each of Corbett's activities in support of a strong blockade policy to understand its importance, but it is necessary to understand his central reasoning. It will help this appreciation if one overcomes that rigid frustrated sense of morality characterizing so much 'peace' advocacy in our own times.

The argument was historical. Corbett's historical study had convinced him that Britain's power in previous wars was directly and primarily related to the strength of the operation of her sea power. Philip II, Louis XIV and Napoleon I had all felt its inhibiting effects. Even the effectiveness of the British Army, in European conflict, depended absolutely upon sea power for its power to act. Wellington, for instance, as he faced Napoleon at Waterloo, cast apprehensive glances past the right of his line, before 18 June, lest his communications with Ostend, the sea, the navy, and home be cut by his foes.[2] This is why talk about the relative importance of the British Army and Navy is so nonsensical. Without the Navy there would be no power to apply Army pressure anywhere but in the Island itself. But if the transportation of soldiers was important, so was continued commerce in order to maintain the financial heart and sinews of a metropolitan power complex. The third aspect was Britain's naval ability to act

---

[1] It should be noted that the communications theory was first advocated in the modern world by Sir John Colomb, but it was Corbett who gave it historical underpinnings in his books.

[2] The care he took on the day of battle, for the defence of the Hougemont Farm was partly related to this sense of unease.

against enemy communications, and of this a vital element was blockade. By the exercise of these methods, England built up a great military-industrial complex to benefit herself. In times when Europe was threatened by the domination of one military power, England saw her long range interests threatened, and reacted. Englishmen would say that this latter stance was beneficial to Europe; even as the people of various European nations did when the argument seemed appropriate. To sum up, it is clear that to have strength Britain required general pre-eminence at sea. To be *at all* effective in European and other relationships, Britain needed sea power. Of that requirement a tremendously important ingredient was blockade.

Corbett had written on this subject for propaganda purposes in 1907 to forestall possible attempts to secure an agreement on reducing the rigour of blockade, in war, at the second Hague Peace Conference.[1] During the war he continued this work. The problem facing British policymakers was delicate to begin with and became intensified as the war advanced. The Germans, of course, insisted that war made in this fashion was anti-civilian rather than anti-military, and hence a barbaric means of proceeding. In the United States of America, there were elements to whom the barbaric label made an appeal, reinforced by memories of the War of 1812 when this kind of warfare had been applied directly to all their commerce. Other sections simply demanded the end of a system that disrupted their trade with countries warring against Great Britain. The extra complication was added when President Wilson included 'Freedom of the Seas' among his morally-ambitious Fourteen Points, and, for a time, it appeared that the price of American co-operation in the war against Germany depended upon some British concession on this contentious matter.

Consequently, Corbett attempted both to strengthen the warrior-minded at home, and to counter the arguments of the pro-peace men on both sides of the ocean. In 1915, he wrote a pamphlet called 'The Spectre of Navalism' for home consumption. Another propaganda piece was written for an American audience in 1917 and applied the kind of argument summarized above to the Freedom of the Seas part of President Wilson's peace proposals.[2] The writing was done at the request of the First Lord and First Sea Lord and was issued through the Foreign Office's propaganda section.[3] The finished product was the

---

1 'The Capture of Private Property at Sea'. *The Nineteenth Century*. June 1907.

2 *The League of Peace and a Free Sea* (New York, 1917).

3 See Admiral D. Brownrigg to Corbett 25.I.17; CP/B7.

'weighty article' requested. In essence it put the question — since power regulates the relationship of nations, is it the wish of those who propose Freedom of the Sea to devalue the influence of sea powers in comparison to that of land powers? Certainly this was an argument calculated to appeal to a rising sea-power, with two sea coastlines, like the United States. Corbett handled Wilson very delicately implying that the President's viewpoint was being misinterpreted or not fully enough expressed.

Furthermore, there is evidence that Corbett, in 1915 provided arguments to help Hankey influence members of the Government in favour of a strong blockade. The eminent Foreign Office diplomat Sir Eyre Crowe suggested that perhaps Britain might give up the food blockade if Germany gave up submarines[1] Corbett wrote for Hankey a Cabinet memorandum embodying the opposite view[2] As a result, Hankey said the Foreign Office case was 'knocked out'[3] The subject did not die because late in the autumn Corbett noted in his diary that he had spent 'most of morning . . . discussing how to keep tender-hearted ministers up to blockade'[4]

Julian Corbett also sat on the Phillimore Committee, which was set up to advise the War Cabinet on historical precedents and practical difficulties in the way of a Peace League — which was obviously meant to consider coldly President Wilson's suggestions. Corbett, no doubt, was there to see that 'Freedom of the Seas' was not included and to provide historical information. Dr. J. Holland Rose, and Professor A.F. Pollard also served on this Committee, chaired by the Rt. Hon. Sir Walter Phillimore, Bart[5] Corbett thought the Committee weak mainly because of the lack of ability of its chairman. His comments on Phillimore were less than complimentary[6] Nevertheless, there can be no doubt that Corbett himself was there to provide naval backing for a 'no nonsense' line with regard to limiting British sea-power. He also wrote, in 1918, an outline of his Freedom of the Seas ideas for the Ministry of Information[7]

1 Crowe was regarded as pro-German by some during the war. He was certainly no partriotic sentimentalist during its progress.

2 Corbett *Diary* 23.VI.15.

3 Corbett *Diary* 28.VI.15.

4 Corbett *Diary* 29.XI.15.

5 The Committee also included Sir Eyre Crowe, Sir William Tyrrell, Mr. C.J.B. Hurst, and Mr. A.R. Kennedy as Secretary. See The Phillimore Reports: *Interim* 20.III.18 and *Final* 3.VII.18. War Cabinet Papers. CP/B7.

6 See among other entries, Corbett *Diary* 13.I.18.

7 Corbett *Diary* 13.IV.18.

This kind of work was, outside the history, evidence of the profound impact that this man of letters had on the prosecution of the war. It has been seen that he wrote memoranda from time to time for both Asquith and Lloyd George, but to detail each one would be to degenerate into making claims for his importance based on scattered records covering different, and often unrelated subjects.

In the New Year Honour's List of 1917, Corbett was knighted. This was a clear indication of the value of his services to the wartime government. What Fisher did not do, Hankey accomplished through Lloyd George. He, himself, was happy and his many friends were very pleased for him. A dinner was given in his honour, attended by such influential figures as the former Prime Minister, Asquith, Balfour, and of course Hankey and the C.I.D. staff. It was a well-merited honour and appropriate, considering the amount of free time and energy he had given to his beloved Navy.

By 1918, he was almost entirely absorbed by the history, which had consumed more and more of his time as 1917 advanced. One must ask then, in concluding a chapter given over to many diverse wartime activities, what did he think of British strategy and leadership in the First World War? After all, he was an extraordinarily knowledgeable strategic observer, and he stood fairly close to the corridors of power.

It is at once clear that he did not approve of a policy that tended to make land fighting in France the primary British role. He had fought against this concept before the war and had battled against enslavement to the European land-war fixation whenever his advice was asked. He was to battle it again, by stealth, in the text of the Official History. He wanted combined operations and flexibility, but he did not want them planned or led by men ignorant of the methods and potential of that kind of warfare. This accounts for his blowing hot and cold over the Dardanelles. The favourite question of the continentalists ever since — 'how else but by victory in Europe could Germany be crushed', he would never have asked. If he had been asked he would no doubt have argued that Britain was doing very well with a holding policy in France, and go on to propose effective priorities for combined operations, and advocate that the blockade should be allowed to do its work. Of the effectiveness of that blockade in the war there can be no doubt. It is seldom given enough credit in assessments of World War I. For despite the words of the 'land thrust at the heart' arguments that still are with us, it is still reasonable to think that it was possible to have maintained a more careful, less costly attitude in France. The main British Empire contribution should have concentrated on the economic strangulation of Germany. Yet Corbett realized very early on that army thinking predominated in the higher councils of the nation and that army priorities would determine, as they did, the kind of war actually fought.

Of the Army leadership he had a low opinion. Part of this was owing to their perpetual striving towards increasing their own importance as opposed to seeking to carry out the best, as opposed to their own, national policy. Personally, with a few exceptions, he found them men with closed minds who were both over-confident and anti-Navy. 'The utter stupidity of the soldiers seems to make the sailors seem quite brilliant' was his comment when he knew that Passchendaele was about to begin.[1]

What about Cabinet leadership? With regard to most of them, excepting A.J. Balfour and Winston Churchill, Corbett felt that they did not have any real knowledge of war-making in the sense that they followed any logical, strategic, or traditional policies consistently. Indeed they had little conception of such policies. Balfour, who knew something about military affairs, ran the Navy satisfactorily but not brilliantly. Carson he referred to as 'a jumpy neurotic inexperienced amateur'. Asquith he obviously liked, despite his lack of system and urgency. He seems to have shared the distrust of Lloyd George that was current amongst traditionalists, to whom that statesman appeared to be energetic if rather cunning. He was in two minds about Churchill, and saw the weakness in his overhaste at Gallipoli and his tendency to disregard ideas other than his own. Yet Corbett recognized Churchill's vitality and imagination. In March 1917, he noted that Lloyd George did not have time to do everything. In his opinion, there was no one except Churchill who could keep his eyes on everything at once and keep it all active 'but it wants a very big man to do it these days' intimating that Chatham might have found modern war trying.[2]

Hankey was a man with whom he felt deep ties of like-mindedness as we have seen. But by 1916, army control of the Cabinet's thinking had diminished Hankey's influence so as to preclude counter arguments: indeed the soldiers were in a strong enough position to resent simple requests for information concerning their activities in France.[3] By 1917, Hankey had no influence against the soldier-oriented war.[4]

There were caveats against individual amateurishness. When he

---

1 Corbett to Richmond NMM RIC/9/1 28.VII.17.

2 Corbett to Richmond NMM RIC/9/1 6.III.17.

3 Corbett *Diary* 19.V.16.

4 Corbett to Richmond NMM RIC/9/1 6.IV.17.

looked at Churchill's initial disparagement of an attack on East Africa, he found it 'disconcerting to see with what little wisdom we are governed'.[1] Similar remarks must have escaped his lips over the conduct of the Dardanelles operation.

But the general quietness of the sea-war, especially after Jutland, struck even him. He regretted Fisher's retirement, and when Jellicoe became First Sea Lord under Carson as First Lord, he began to complain of Admiralty timorousness. In a way, he was the author of this timorousness since 'no risk' meant, despite his theories, over-caution. This was owing to a number of things. First, by 1917 he, like so many, was war weary. Second, he was spending more time on the history and saw less of Hankey, so that he was somewhat out of immediate touch with current happenings. Finally, deep in his own heart there was a desire for fireworks. Consider the following as he pined for Lord Fisher, whose 'schemes take one's breath away, but he had thought them out, (and) was carefully preparing the material. There might have been an awful smash, but what a glorious smash it would have been. I wonder will the historian of our great-great-grandchildren transfer the odium that Mahan set on 1740-50 to our own day. I envy the man who is free to tell the tale 100 years hence'.[2] That passage represents the overflowing of a romantic's hope. It is not the thinking of a naval statesman.

Yet, like others at the time, he took out his frustration in condemning the First Sea Lord. Jellicoe did not impress him when they first met. 'His feet seem cold', wrote Corbett.[3] Nor did this attitude towards this man, whom he was to regard as a friend later on, stop at writing about him in the Diary. He conspired with Richmond and Hankey to get anti-Jellicoe opinions before Lloyd George in June 1917, and wrote that there was no hope of getting the navy out of the rut it was in so long as 'Jelly is where he is'.[4] It is worthy of note that this flirtation with the anti-Jellicoe faction in the Navy was encouraged by Captain Herbert Richmond with whom he corresponded in a manner that smacks of the disgruntled reformer, as Richmond then was, more than as a careful historian. No doubt there was a romantic desire to find a spectacular release from hum-drum sea progress. It is extraordinary that Corbett did not see submarine activity in this light.

1 Corbett to Richmond NMM RIC/9/1 8.VI.17.
2 Corbett to Richmond NMM RIC/9/1 6.IV.17.
3 Corbett to Richmond NMM RIC/9/1 24.IV.17.
4 Corbett to Richmond NMM RIC/9/1 18.II.17.

Finally, it is relevant that Jellicoe, at about that time, was frustrating Corbett's work as naval historian by withholding certain secret papers.[1] To the historian it seemed part of a pattern. Whatever the explanation, he seems to have condemned with insufficient facts at his disposal, in common with most of the pro-Beatty cabal with whom he would doubtless not want to be grouped.

1   'Jelly braced himself to take the risk to let me see papers which are not secret at all'. Corbett to Richmond NMM RIC/9/1 19.VI.17.

10

THE HISTORIAN AND THE CENSOR

The commissioning of the official history took place in 1916. Corbett completed the manuscript of Volume III in September 1922, just a few hours before he died. The story of the historian's relations with senior personnel in both the Government and the Naval Service who were interested in its contents, is the subject of this chapter. This is not the first time that the subject has been discussed. Captain Roskill has taken a great interest in the problems his predecessor faced, and made important information available to the present writer. This account does not seek to unravel the tangled skein of the Battle of Jutland histories that were produced by the Staff, by Captain Harper, and Corbett, except so far as they have a direct bearing on Corbett's problems as he saw them. In any event, it is probable that the crushing burden imposed on Corbett by his would-be censors was caused more by incomprehension of what standards of historical integrity were, than by a *malicious* attempt to cook the books. The heartless application of bureaucratic pressure and its resultant uncertainty were nothing more than one would expect from non-intellectual men with reputations to protect, with power to wield in secret corridors, men who had an inflated idea of their own intellectual powers. That their behaviour was vulgar in its application to the history ought to surprise no one. But it is useful to let the light of day shine on such processes from time to time.

The three books produced by Corbett are themselves a tribute to both his scholarship and his partisan cunning.[1] Some naval officers turned out to be too stupid to recognize that nobody else could have given them such prominence in a war where men in khaki were omnipresent. That does not alter the fact that the history did emphasize the naval part of the war. Corbett did this not as a humble seeker after truth, but with the deliberate purpose of 'up-grading' the naval service. It has been seen that both Corbett and Hankey thought there might be problems in publication, so they took care to arrange for the services of a commercial publisher. This turned out to be a stroke of genius. That there would be censorship they expected, and indeed Corbett had never made any bones about the value he received from having his contemporary writings, aimed at the service, read and commented on by Naval Officers. Admiral Slade, for instance, was no

---

1   For the structure of the Official Histories, see Appendix C.

mere cypher. This is to say that nothing could be further from the truth than to regard Corbett as a mere victim of prejudiced naval personnel in high places. He knew what he wanted to do, and it is true that the struggle to achieve it put him under a strain, but he neither was taken unprepared nor was he without resources. Despite the fact that after his death, the Admiralty sharply declined responsibility for what he wrote, his work largely stood intact. In this battle of Whitehall it was not the historian who lost.

Corbett was able to show how the naval theory of which he was a prime exponent worked in practice, how the power of sea warfare was global in its extent and how everything else in Britain's war effort was dependent upon the vital sea element. He had managed to get instructions that allowed him to link diplomacy and naval operation in his narrative so that his history was the comprehensive history of the war, as compared with other works which were mere campaign narratives. His strategic viewpoint, the one that Lord Sydenham had attacked, was advanced in detail showing cause and effect with clarity and brilliance. Arthur Marder had remarked, in the Preface to Volume II of *From the Dreadnought to Scapa Flow*, that there may be too much detail in those books, but Corbett never deviated from his aim of keeping description of action linked to the general narrative of the war's progress, and he arranged the details in such a way as to slip his own views into the narrative. It was on that level that the reader was invited to read between the lines. The careful student will find that the book bristles with concealed and implied judgements so skilfully masked that they escaped the men with the blue pencil.

The contents of Corbett's official history included everything down to the end of the Battle of Jutland, so that he was able to write up the overseas cruiser actions and the story of the Dardanelles. Perhaps the most vivid writing of all was that describing the myriad problems of war and the initial responses to them in 1914. Particularly interesting is the way he handled the troop contribution of the various overseas possessions. It had been the feeling of many colonies that naval defence was of no great interest to them for they thought in terms of local direct benefits, rather than in a world-wide pattern of security from which all would benefit. On the other hand, the British did not anticipate any great army support from overseas in the event of a European conflict. When the war came, both sides were proven wrong in their previews, for the soldiers came in surprising numbers and the naval dispositions were taxed to the utmost to protect overseas troops that they did not anticipate. Indeed, the heartwarming Imperial response had to be catered to by the Navy for reasons of maintaining

Imperial morale at precisely the time when the fleet was least prepared to do the escort work. It was an interesting episode in the history of Imperial defence, and Corbett set out the dilemma and the response to it with beautiful clarity, and in a way that showed his unique ability to subordinate the unexpected to a central theme.

Much of the first volume was in preliminary draft form before 1917. This was made possible by his own labours, but by 1917, he had the advantage of great assistance from Miss Edith Keate. Miss Keate was a family friend and a writer of talent who assisted Corbett at the Historical Section. She helped plan and draft a good deal of volume I of the history, and assisted Tuck and Bell in the literary side of their work.[1] He was held up by the refusal of the Admiralty to release the Grand Fleet papers and other secret papers from the post-December 1914 period. He used his time wisely, however, conducting personal interviews with officers involved in actions since the Admiralty had no system of securing written accounts with history in mind. He devoted a good deal of time to the battles of Coronel and the Falkland Islands. He interviewed Sir Doveton Sturdee who had commanded at the latter battle. The Coronel affair, he thought, reflected poorly on the Naval Staff who had served Churchill badly by sending Admiral Cradock 'ambiguous orders'.[2]

As 1917 opened, he began to press strongly for access to the papers he needed to get on with the work. Twice he tried and failed to get a favourable decision from the Admiralty Secretary, Graham Greene.[3] But his importunity resulted in an unhelpful interview with Jellicoe, the First Sea Lord, who stated bluntly that he would prefer to see the history stopped than to take the chance of any secrets escaping to the Germans. The argument that there had been a commitment to the history in the House of Commons failed to move him.[4] Hankey then persuaded Graham Greene to arrange for Corbett to see the papers 'secretly', but a road block was again thrown up by the Naval Intelligence Department, and Jellicoe pronounced that the war had to end before the documents would be released.[5] In July, the ban was eased to allow the perusal of signal logs, and Graham Greene was

---

1 Personal information from Elizabeth Tunstall, Sir Julian's daughter and wife of the late W.C. Brian Tunstall.

2 NMM RIC 9/1 Corbett to Richmond. 17.IX.16.

3 Corbett *Diary* 29.I.17. and 3.III.17.

4 Corbett *Diary* 6.IV.17.

5 Corbett *Diary* 26.IV.17

able to promise more Grand Fleet information soon.[1] Gradually he
was being allowed to see almost everything.

At the end of 1917, Jellicoe was succeeded by Admiral Sir
Rosslyn Wemyss as First Sea Lord. This made a double difference to
Corbett. First, Jellicoe became a firm friend, indeed he came to
Corbett in February of the new year and offered his services as a reader
and commentator on the history, and Corbett came to value his self-
effacing, but intelligent comments.[2] But Wemyss's appointment was to
make a great difference to the progress of the history. Wemyss was no
intellectual but he was a shrewd man of the world who had firm ideas
about what could be accomplished and what could not. Also, he
learned fast and was not overawed by politicians. On 26 February, he
sent for Corbett and gave him a mock scolding for neglecting to pay
respects to his new chief.[3] He showed his knowledge of what Corbett
was attempting by referring to the 'loss of touch between the War
Office and the Admiralty' in the war, and stating that the general
public had forgotten that we had a navy. Later in the year, he
recognized the need to change this lamentable situation by proposing
to send Naval Officers to Oxford and Cambridge so that 'Naval
Officers could be put in touch with the world'.[4] As to the history,
he had sized up the situation swiftly. Some documents would need to
remain secret, but he told Corbett that there could be no publication
until after the war in any event, since the public could not bear the
truth and since a wartime book would be 'mutilated by officialdom'.[5]

These were reasonable and perceptive remarks. But Hankey was
concerned that the naval history should come out before the army
series, and must have impressed this upon the First Sea Lord, because
by June, papers were coming to Corbett in a flood. Indeed, Hankey
was so concerned to scoop the soldiers that he allowed Corbett to see
the famous War Book that detailed the opening moves of the
conflict.[6] By July, he had written in most of the secret material and
had 'completed draft of Vol. II, I think'.[7]

1   Corbett *Diary* 13, 26.VII.17.

2   Corbett *Diary* 12.II.18.

3   Corbett *Diary*.

4   Corbett *Diary* 15.V.18

5   Also see Appendix B.

6   Corbett *Diary* 29.VII.18.

7   Corbett *Diary*.

It was at this stage that Winston Churchill crossed Corbett's path. Indeed, he stood resolutely in front of progress for the history, and stayed there for over a year, Churchill, for whom Corbett acquired an increasing respect as he investigated the ex-First Lord's part in the first year of the war, had shown an interest in the history early in 1918, when he twice took the historian out to lunch.[1] The cast of mind he revealed was both magnaminous and difficult to cope with, for he insisted on taking the large view. For instance, it has been shown that Corbett thought Churchill's performance at the time of Coronel was good, and that he had been badly served by his professional advisors. It might be thought that Churchill would welcome this opportunity to shift responsibility. On the contrary, he was aware of the problem posed for his reputation by such a course. Although he did not alter Corbett's view he pressed the point that *since he interfered continually in everything*, he could not blame his staff. In the same way, he claimed to hold nothing but admiration for Fisher.

It is not likely that Churchill took up this attitude through any undue worry about the verdict of history, although he was conscious, as always, of history. He was, after all, a young vigorous politician who had had his political career badly shaken by the events of 1915. Lloyd George had salvaged him somewhat in 1917 and made him Minister of Munitions (later Minister of Supply) and Secretary of War in early 1919. But while the war was on, Churchill was not again a member of the War Cabinet. No doubt he had already conceived the notion to write a history of the events through which he had passed as a support for his fortunes and he was very concerned that his past should not detract from his future — which, clearly, was to arrive at the pinnacle of power and hold the office of Prime Minister. There can be no doubt, looking back, with the vicissitudes of his inter-war career in mind, that he was correct to be politically sensitive and apprehensive. Yet it is entirely typical of him that he should see his problem in the round; that he should be striving for a total impression rather than the rearrangement of a few sentences. Hence, although he was concerned particularly with the performance of Admiral Milne when the *Goeben* and *Breslau* escaped in 1914, with the sinking of the ships, *Aboukir, Hogue* and *Cressy*, with the events surrounding Coronel, and with the drama of the Dardanelles, it was clearly the fact that he had a total image of himself that he wished to launch at the general public, and not these details, that made his attitude so formidable.

However, the first hint that trouble was serious reached Corbett

1   Corbett *Diary* 19, 28.1.18.

just before the war ended in 1918, when he was told that Churchill was 'dissatisfied with Volume I'. Corbett made a few amendments to try to meet the points raised. But it was not until 10 April of the next year that he found out that Churchill objected to publishing the book, claiming that the only fair way was to publish the documents.[1] Considering the fact that there were upwards of a hundred volumes of these extant for 1914 alone, it can be appreciated just how unreasonable and difficult Churchill was prepared to be.

It was a jolt. Wemyss, however, sent for Corbett and calmed him.[2] The Admiral did not think it likely that Churchill's objections would stand in the long run. He advised Corbett to proceed on the premise that an early publication would take place. To ensure ultimate success he counselled that Corbett censor his own book and delete all criticism that was merely opinion. On the other hand, no statements of fact, even if they implied criticism were to be expunged. This was solid, practical, realistic advice.

This support made Churchill's obstruction look less dangerous. It did not remove it. All progress was held up until July when the contracted publishers, Longmans, began to press for a manuscript.[3] Corbett gave this information to Hankey, who used it as a fulcrum to put the matter on the Cabinet agenda. It remained pended all during August and Corbett was kept waiting around idle.[4] Churchill seems to have been somewhat agitated in late August and actually arranged a meeting with Corbett, but failed to keep the appointment.[5] Churchill's unease was caused by Hankey's strong support for publication, and by the fact that the Prime Minister showed interest in the question. Hankey wrote a memorandum for the War Cabinet in which he set out the Government's commitment to the history. This had been made both by Asquith in 1916, and subsequently by Bonar Law for the present government, in the House of Commons on 20 November, 1918.[6] Hankey set out the commitment to the publishers, showed how Churchill's objections in detail had been met, and how unrealistic the latter's proposal (to publish all the documents) was. Probably as a result of this forceful presentation Lloyd George read the book. He

1 Corbett *Diary* For Churchill's important Memorandum see Appendix A.
2 Corbett *Diary* 10.IV.19.
3 Corbett *Diary* 9.VII.19.
4 Corbett *Diary* 15, 22.VIII.19.
5 Corbett *Diary* 25.VIII.19.
6 Secret *Memorandum for the War Cabinet,* 'Official Naval History of the War', by M.P.A. Hankey. PRO CAB 24/87 19.VIII.19.

told Hankey, early in September, that 'no one could have dealt with these difficult matters with such perfect discretion' as Corbett had.[1] For the moment, therefore, Churchill became conciliatory and sent his secretary to negotiate over details with Corbett.[2] General Sir Ian Hamilton helped Corbett by informing Churchill that Corbett wished to do him justice and that, in Corbett's words, 'he had better let me do it in my own way'.[3]

But it has been seen that the details over which Corbett had always been willing to meet him halfway were not Churchill's stumbling block. He was looking at the whole canvas, and did not like the total impression. He also probably knew that some members of the Admiralty Board were not sympathetic to Corbett, especially M.E. Browning, the Second Sea Lord, who had minuted 'I notice many personal opinions and judgements which I consider out of place . . . I think it should be fully revised by a Flag Officer'.[4] Admiral Brock, later on, assured Corbett that this criticism was 'silly'.[5]

Meanwhile, Corbett got ready to counter-attack. He secured the support of the well-known historians Sir Charles Oman, and Sir Charles Firth, with the intention of gaining public support. Firth stood ready to prepare a historian's protest, and Oman, who was an M.P., agreed to use any question Corbett drafted in the House of Commons.[6] The question was put down, but the Clerk of the House 'made a mess' of it.[7] Corbett, meanwhile, helped make a memorandum of the case against Churchill for Hankey to present to the Cabinet.[8]

By 3 November, Corbett was getting desperate and he thought he perceived, by the tenor of a conversation with Hankey, that Churchill was likely to prevail against the history.[9] The very next day, however, he heard that Churchill, at a Cabinet, 'threw up the sponge and said he

1 Corbett *Diary* 4.IX.19.

2 Corbett *Diary* 18.IX.19.

3 Corbett *Diary* 9.X.19.

4 PRO ADM. 116/2067 25.IV.19.

5 Brock told this to Corbett at a Navy League dinner. Corbet *Diary* 28.X.19.

6 Corbett *Diary* 23.X.19.

7 Corbett *Diary* 3.XI.19.

8 Corbett *Diary* 24.X.19. and See *Memorandum by the Secretary of the Historical Section of the C.I.D.* Printed for the Cabinet (October, 1919) PRO CAB 24/92

9 Corbett *Diary* 3.XI.19.

had no objection to publication'.[1]   Corbett then agreed that two
minutes, written by Churchill, be inserted in the volume as Appendix
D.[2]   The first was dated 18.IX.14, and showed Churchill's anxiety for
the safety of cruisers on the 'beat' where *Aboukir*, *Hogue* and *Cressy*
were sunk by one submarine four days later. The second was the First
Lord's minute, dated 12.X.14, on the telegram sent to the Admiralty
by Admiral Cradock before his fatal engagement off Coronel on the
first of November. It might be noted that this latter minute was not
unambiguous, but it was more precise than the instructions subsequently
sent to Admiral Cradock, who was then not sure whether he was to
protect trade or seek out and destroy the enemy, and he was not sure
exactly where he was to operate. In the text, Corbett protected both
Churchill and the Admiralty by not printing the text of the telegram
actually sent to Cradock.[3]   It has already been pointed out that
Churchill was determined not to distinguish between his staff and himself in defending the Admiralty position, and that Corbett considered
Churchill less to blame than ill-served by his naval staff. Churchill
maintained his stand when his own account was published some years
later.[4] Maurice Ashley has pointed out that he cannot entirely escape
responsibility since ' . . . Churchill was a master of words and had been
installed in the Admiralty in 1911 to overhaul the naval staff'.[5]

In any event, agreement to publish seemed settled. Churchill
approved the changes and by 14 November, Corbett heard that the
Admiralty would pass it. But Churchill again dragged his feet, and
Corbett's blood pressure shot up so that his doctor ordered rest.[6] By
the 27th, he heard that Lloyd George thought it a miracle that the
Admiralty, Churchill and Corbett had reached agreement.[7] This was the
last false dawn, for after eight more days of suspense, agreement to
publish was reached by the Cabinet.[8]   It had been a close-run thing.
The book was passed after a vote, with a majority of one for publication. The permission was only for the one volume and on its reception

1   Corbett *Diary* 4.XI.19.

2   Corbett *Diary* and *Naval Operations*, vol.I. Appendix D.

3   *Naval Operations*, vol.I, p.318. For a detail of the telegram See Geoffrey
Bennett *Coronel and the Falklands* (London, 1962), pp.86-94.   Bennet also
puts the blame on bad staff work, only slightly on Churchill pp.94-106.

4   W.S. Churchill *The World Crisis*, vol. I (London, 1939), p.379.

5   Maurice Ashley *Churchill as a Historian* (London, 1968), p. 78.

6   Corbett *Diary* 23.XI.19.

7   Corbett *Diary* 27.XI.19.

8   Corbett *Diary* 5.XII.19.

by the public was to depend the future of all the official war histories. Corbett heard privately that Balfour, Geddes, and Admiral Brock who was invited to attend to advise from the Admiralty, were against publication, but that Bonar Law had supported it since he had once given a public undertaking to do so.[1] On 11 December, the official minute reached him.[2] His blood pressure stayed high until the middle of January.

The Admiralty reaction to Volume I is not so easy to assess. Admiral Brock, for instance, had informed Corbett that objections to his book were 'silly' and yet in the event seems to have advised against publication. It is clear that Admiral M.E. Browning, the Second Sea Lord, thought the whole thing should be rewritten by a Flag Officer. But it has been seen that Wemyss met that objection by having Corbett revise the manuscript to remove judgements based on opinion. Corbett agreed to do so in consultation with Admiral Slade.[3] It was done.[4] But Wemyss retired on 1 November, and was succeeded by Beatty. It was on 11 November, that the Board of Admiralty considered Churchill's desire to have his minutes in the Appendices, and first reacted unfavourably.[5] Consequently, it appears that Corbett's support at the Admiralty ceased to be complete. Wemyss, doubtless, had been confident of his ability to hold the Board firm but Walter Long, the First Lord, had now to deal with a new uncommitted First Sea Lord, who doubtless did not wish to begin his work in controversy with politicians over what then, to him, must have been a minor matter. This impression is heightened when one realizes that Hankey had written a letter to Long, just before Wemyss left, to plead the case for the history. Corbett thought then that it was unwise to bring it before Long in that fashion. No doubt this well-intentioned move made Long nervous, and hastened a reassessment.[6]

Two things are certain: first, that Wemyss' advice and Hankey's support ultimately saved the book for publication; and second, that Corbett never questioned the right of the Admiralty to edit his text nor they that they had the right to do it. No doubt he did not like it,

1 Corbett *Diary* 8.XII.19.

2 Corbett *Diary*.

3 PRO ADM. 1/8552. 21.IV.19.

4 PRO ADM. 116/2067. 25.VIII.19.

5 PRO ADM. 167/56. 10.IX.19.

6 Corbett *Diary* 23.X.19.

but it was a fact of life. What troubled Corbett was that he was kept in an agony of suspense for nearly a year over the right to publish a book on which he had lavished much time, care and talent. He also must have been hurt that the volume, when published included a disclaimer reflecting on his judgement to the effect that 'The Lords Commissioners of the Admiralty have given the author access to official documents in the preparation of this work, but they are in no way responsible for his reading or presentation of the facts as stated'.[1] It was a hard cut, but not the last.

The good reception given to *Naval Operations,* Volume I made certain that the whole historical work would go forward, since Cabinet decision to publish *any* further official war history, either description of operations or of organization and supply, had depended upon the public reaction to Corbett's first volume. Volume II was complete in manuscript by May 1920. As soon as permission to go ahead was granted, it went through the process almost unscathed and was published in 1921. Considering the fact that the book dealt with the controversial Dardanelles operation, this was somewhat of an accomplishment, but Corbett was aware of the pitfalls and wrote with them in mind. He has written that he did his best to write it up so that an intelligent reader could deduce Corbett's real views by reading 'between the lines'.

Volume III, however, that contained a description of the Battle of Jutland, was bound to create intense interest in the Admiralty. Nevertheless, although Corbett had difficulties to surmount, the most formidable hurdle had been passed. The objection raised to the publication of Volume I had come from a Cabinet Minister, Churchill, defending his actions when he had been a member of the War Council in 1914.[2] There was some objection by members of the Admiralty Board. But the Historical Section at the C.I.D. was under the supervision of a Sub-Committee of the Committee of Imperial Defence, set up by the authority of the Prime Minister. Consequently, the final decision, to publish or not to publish, was made *not* in the Admiralty, but by the Cabinet. Hankey was well aware of both the strength and weakness of this position. The weakness was that an adverse decision would be difficult to get reversed. The strength was, that if it was passed, then other objections could be overruled from the top. It appears extremely likely that the anti-publication Ministers were won over by appreciating the political inadvisability of the public gaining the

1   It is worth noting that even Churchill, later, commented on a 'work distinguished for its care and industry'. *The World Crisis,* vol. I, p.379.

2   In 1919 Churchill was Secretary of State for War and Air.

impression that they were 'cooking the books'. It also appears likely that subsequent intensive interference from one department (viz. Admiralty) would not be likely to excite much ministerial sympathy. This is an important point, for although the Jutland controversy is a mare's nest, the powerful sailors who no doubt wished to put their version of Jutland before the British public, did not by any means hold all the good cards in the dangerous game they undertook to play.

A. Temple Patterson, in his biography of Jellicoe, and by his publication of the Jellicoe correspondence, plus the Harper Papers from the R.U.S.I. for the Navy Records Society, has let in light on many problems that seemed more sinister when repressed than they now do.[1] He has told of the relationship between the Harper Record of the battle, and the Naval Staff appreciation written by the brothers Dewar. It is not intended to repeat all of that admirable account here, but, merely, to attempt to look at the problem through Corbett's eyes. Like Mr. Temple Patterson, one is conscious of a great debt to Captain Stephen Roskill, whose interest in seeing the truth emerge without wishing to do the writing entirely himself, does him great credit.

The mass of the official Admiralty material on Jutland is contained in the file PRO ADM.116/2067. It is necessary to understand that not every document in that collection is signed. Therefore, it is sometimes not entirely clear whether Board Members', and other, comments refer to the *Official History* or the *Harper Record* for the two collections are interleaved. Secondly, it is likely that when Corbett spoke to Richmond about interference with his work, he was referring as much to the Churchill episode over Volume I as he was over the machinations involving Volume III that follow.[2]

A few words need to be said about the two British Jutland commanders and their attitude to the history of the battle. Jellicoe, in retrospect, occupies a very strong position. In battle, he forced the High Seas Fleet to retreat to its base, and Corbett and Marder,[3] the two most eminent historians to write on the subject, have vindicated his method. Also, Jellicoe did not express himself on vital matters of *opinion* as opposed to *fact* until independent investigators had pronounced on them. He corresponded with Corbett, as will be shown,

1 *Jellicoe* (London, 1969) *The Jellicoe Papers*. 2 vols. (Navy Records Society, 1966-8).

2 See *Jellicoe*, p.240.

3 Marder, *From the Dreadnought,* vol. III (London, 1966).

and agreed with him, but he did not attempt to influence him in interpretation. He had a delicate sense of propriety. Beatty, on the other hand, occupies a very weak position. The verdict of the historians mentioned has been somewhat critical of the "judiciousness" with which he acted the part of important subordinate at Jutland. The sad fact is that Beatty had emerged from the action tinged with heroism at the time, yet he subsequently found the verdict of historians going against him. The Dewars were devotees of his in 1916-17 and continued to be.[1] Richmond in 1917, thought Beatty was *the* figure of Jutland.[2] So did Corbett. Captain J.E.T. Harper, writing it up, did not. Corbett changed his mind as he saw the evidence.[3] Marder has agreed, years later. Beatty, in the 1920s, must have been outraged at what looked like a conspiracy to denigrate what, in his opinion, was his finest naval hour. This sense of injustice and a real desire that the men in *his* ships should feel no reason for shame made him react. It is regrettable that this situation led him to contemplate manipulation that under other circumstances he would have scorned. The fact is, however, that Beatty even lost the fight to save his Jutland reputation. He would not want pity, but the gallant Admiral deserves understanding.

The 1919 crisis had been hard on Corbett, but he did win through. He had learned that canniness, as well as sound scholarship, was needed to get his books before the public. When he began to consider the Jutland material, Jellicoe, with whom he had maintained good relations since 1917, had retired and was slated to be Governor of New Zealand.[4] Beatty, as we have seen, had become First Sea Lord in November, 1919. The various supporters of these two men were busy promoting their merits as actors in the Jutland drama without any direct support from either.

Meanwhile, Wemyss, when he was still First Sea Lord, commissioned Captain J.E.T. Harper, R.N. to compile a 'Record of the Battle of Jutland' for the use and consideration of the Board of Admiralty. It was Wemyss' intention that delicate problems of interpretation and the likelihood of criticism would be avoided by Harper being neutral. There does not seem to be any reason to suppose that Captain Harper was interested in producing a partisan account for their Lordships'

1 Marder, *Portrait of an Admiral;* p.238

2 *Ibid.*

3 In other words he changed his mind as his detailed knowledge increased.

4 He left to take up the appointment in August, 1920. See *Jellicoe*, p.234.

eyes.[1]   The *Record* was finished in   October, 1919, but was not considered by the Board until 1920.   Admiral Chatfield, who was Beatty's Flag Captain at Jutland, and presently D.C.N.S., Admiral O. de B. Brock, D.N.O., and Beatty, all thought the manuscript minimized the overall British achievement at Jutland, and, in particular, was unfair to the Battle Cruiser Fleet.   It is clear that pressure was applied to Harper, who altered his account to give the Battle Cruisers more credit for what honours the day had produced.

Jellicoe also saw the *Record*. He expressed himself as pleased with the charts and diagrams on which the work was based. The *Record* was not then published. Subsequently, Jellicoe learned that changes in the manuscript were being made and he claimed the right to pass on the final version, or to comment on the changes in public.[2] It will be seen that this involved Corbett.

Meanwhile, the brothers, Captain A.C. and Commander Kenneth Dewar, who admired Beatty, produced what was called the 'Admiralty Staff Appreciation' in the Staff and Training Division at the Admiralty. There was nothing sinister in this as other engagement appreciations were being written by naval officers, in the Division, acting as historians. Undoubtedly, however, its pro-Beatty tone made it appear as an antidote to Harper.[3] It is not surprising that there were different interpretations placed on events at Jutland.

Lord Fisher died in July, 1920. After attending the funeral of his old friend, Corbett went to Wales for a seaside rest and holiday. Jutland now entered his life. He received a telegram stating that Beatty wished to see him urgently.[4] When he arrived in London, a day late for the appointment, Beatty was out of town. He had missed a direct confrontation. He was informed that Beatty wished him to write an 'Introduction' to Harper's *Record* that would tend to somewhat discredit it on publication. It was desired that Corbett should explain how British gunnery at Jutland was good and that it only failed to have a decisive effect because bad British shells hit good German armour. Corbett noted that he 'meant to get out of it if I can'.[5] At this stage he had not considered the details of the battle carefully, so the offer would have been very dangerous to accept.

1   *Ibid.* pp.232-8.
2   Jellicoe to Corbett 9.V.21. CP/B7.
3   *Jellicoe*, p.236.
4   Corbett *Diary* 9.VIII.20.
5   Corbett *Diary* 12.VIII.20.

The next day, Corbett phoned Admiral Brock the D.C.N.S., and informed him that he was certain Longmans would object if the author whom they had contracted with to write the official history were to write an introduction to another history.[1]   When Brock informed Sir Oswyn Murray, Graham Green's successor as Admiralty Secretary, Murray saw the situation clearly and agreed to put this difficulty to Beatty. It turned out that Jellicoe had also been asked to write an introduction to the Harper *Record* and had refused.   He advised Corbett to do the same.[2]

As Official Historian, Corbett's problem involved more than merely not allowing himself to write the Harper introduction. He was worried that the Harper *Record,* if published, might push his own writing into the posture of a conditioned response to it. Furthermore, he wanted access to Harper's material and his conclusions.   Naturally he wished both to suppress and use the *Record.* Consequently, he put his position to Longmans, and by 22 September, he heard that they had energetically protested.[3]   Beatty gave in, but not before he requested Corbett to take over the whole production of Harper's work. Corbett declined.   The historian had been in touch with Captain Harper, and knew what was involved, for Harper was 'full of Beatty's bullying attitude'.[4]   By the 23rd of October it was agreed that not only would Harper's work be suppressed[5] but that Corbett would have access to all the *Record's* materials.   At the moment, this decision suited Harper, Beatty, Longmans, and Corbett — who had manoeuvred skilfully. The press was sniffing around the fringes of the problem, which was as Corbett informed Newbolt, a real 'mare's nest'.[6]   But he had won another victory in his defense of his official work. He was in ill health for most of that autumn.

The Jutland affair simmered until Volume II came out. By March 1921, it was made clear to Corbett that high authorities were dissatisfied with Harper's charts and diagrams which did not, it

1   Corbett *Diary* 13.VIII.20.

2   Corbett *Diary* 18.VIII.20.

3   *Ibid.*

4   Corbett *Diary* 5.X.20.

5   The Parliamentary Secretary to the Admiralty told Corbett that he would be given access to all the materials for his volume.   Corbett *Diary* 23.X.20. By suppression, I mean very restricted and not made public.

6   Beatty had later tried to get Richmond to write the Introduction to the Harper *Record.* Corbett *Diary* 13.IX.20.

appeared, agree with those used by the German Admiral Scheer.[1] Harper called on Corbett to say that he was disturbed by the development.[2] Presumably with Beatty's knowledge, it was decided that Corbett should ask Kenneth Dewar to work over Harper's diagrammatic material. This is important, for it was Dewar and his brother Alfred, who were eventually asked to do the Staff Appreciation,[3] but by selecting Dewar he had made a difficulty for himself. Certainly Beatty was still not pacified.

An odd interlude occurred when a question was asked in Parliament as to whether Corbett had access to secret material. Lord Curzon asked the question, and the motive for it is not clear. What is clear is that Corbett's position was becoming very strong. Amery, replying for the Admiralty, gave the impressive reply 'it was not considered necessary to administer an oath to Sir Julian Corbett'.[4]

Meanwhile, Jellicoe wrote Corbett that he had heard of the Admiralty Staff diagrams on Jutlands. He had seen Harper's and was prepared to accept them. These Staff ones were another matter.[5] Corbett assured Jellicoe that he had no intention of using them in the Official History, but rather Harper's.[6] He had Harper's complete confidence, for Harper then, on 15 June 1921, left in his hands 'all his papers relating to Beatty's efforts to cook the Jutland plan and the Sea Lord's comments'.[7] Obviously, Corbett and Harper were in agreement over the danger of Beatty's methods succeeding.

Corbett had written Jellicoe to ask for his help in preparing the official account of the battle, and Jellicoe agreed to provide it.[8] Still Corbett did not begin to write. He was cautious. Kenneth Dewar handed in his revised Charts in September, 1921, and Corbett let it be known that he did not mind the Admiralty having a Staff account prepared, but that Longmans would certainly object to any attempt to publish it.[9] This was an astute move, and by December he heard

---

1 Corbett *Diary* 17.III.21.

2 Corbett *Diary* 17.III.21.

3 Note that Temple Patterson in *Jellicoe* refers to it by its ultimate name – i.e. *Admiralty Narrative.*

4 *Hansard.* 12.V.21.

5 Jellicoe to Corbett 9.V.21; CP/B7.

6 Corbett *Diary* 14.VI.21. See also *The Jellicoe Papers,* vol. II, p. 411.

7 Corbett *Diary* 15.VI.21.

8 Corbett to Jellicoe 13.VI.21. CP/B7.

9 Corbett *Diary* 6, 17.IX.21.

through Kenneth Dewar, that Dewar 'had seen Beatty and Brock and they decided I was to have all there was including his (Dewar's) super secret appreciation unexpurgated'[1] He had made his position secure and a week later he began to write.

Corbett's *Diary* makes it clear that he had no fixed preconceived notion of how the battle ought to have been fought. What he wanted was a chance to study it carefully without being pressured by Beatty and those who thought like him. After all, Jellicoe was not in a position to censor the ultimate description. But it would be idle to pretend that Corbett was not more personally drawn to Jellicoe than to Beatty. After the Battle, in late June 1916, Corbett himself had drawn up an immediate appreciation of it, and Jellicoe had given him an interview.[2] When Richmond criticized Jellicoe's handling of the Battle in 1917, Corbett had not committed himself.[3] He did not finally come to a conclusion until he looked at all the materials in 1922. In the event, he supported Jellicoe. One night, late in February 1922, he explained the Battle to Admiral Richmond 'wh(ich) he had never understood before and wh(ich) confirmed Jellicoe'.[4]

He was still worried about the Staff Appreciation. There were various versions about. By 22 February, he heard that the Staff Appreciation was to be destroyed,[5] and in March, he wrote Jellicoe that he had ensured its suppression.[6] By suppression, he probably meant non-circulation until his own history was published, and it is not clear what Beatty intended to do with the Staff Appreciation, or how much Corbett could rely on assurances that it was destroyed, suppressed or locked up. For instance, one version was sent out to Jellicoe in New Zealand in August and he wrote Corbett complaining of its 'many inaccuracies and incomplete assumptions'.[7] Of the Dewars, he wrote 'I am not aware that they possess any special qualities that would fit them for such a task' and that they were 'officers with but little experience at sea and their work is careless in addition to being lacking in knowledge'.[8] The historian did not necessarily agree with

---

1   Corbett *Diary* 21.XII.21.

2   Corbett *Diary* 27, 28, 30.VI.16 and 1.VII.16.

3   See among other Richmond *Diary* 27.V.17.   RIC/9/1 *and* Marder *Portrait*, p.253. Richmond and Corbett were in constant contact.

4   Corbett *Diary* 18.II.22.

5   Corrbett *Diary* 22.II.22.

6   *The Jellicoe Papers*. vol. II. p. 413.

7   Jellicoe to Corbett 6.VIII.22. CP/B7.

8   Jellicoe to Corbett 12.IX.22. CP/B7.

Jellicoe's estimate of the Dewars' ability but he did find the 'facts' in the Staff Appreciation 'very loose'.

Meanwhile, speaking to Hankey on 26 July, Corbett explained 'how I had stopped issue of Dewar's Staff account of the battle. If he objected I could not alter. He (Hankey) said that it would have to go to Cabinet'.[1] Beatty was effectively stopped because Corbett had protected himself from the Dewars' conclusions by making sure the Admiralty would not risk giving any version of the Dewar manuscript general circulation unless Jellicoe approved of it — at least until Corbett's own account was published.[2]

By this time, Volume III was nearing completion. On 8 September, Corbett sent in the relevant chapters to Daniel at the C.I.D.[3] On 22 September 1922 he died.

It was left to Col. E.Y. Daniel at the Historical Section to see the book through its examination by the Admiralty and its final production. The changes that were made were not, in the long run, extensive. Daniel, naturally, knew that Jellicoe had seen Corbett's version of Jutland, and so he could play a fairly strong hand. Comments were made by various officers who saw the book at the Admiralty. One unsigned undated minute states that Corbett's criticism 'has been entirely confined to the conduct of the Vice Admiral Commanding the Battle Cruiser Fleet. Certain passages show a strong bias on the part of the author for which it is not easy to account. Praise, on the other hand, is reserved for the Commander in Chief and the energy, resource and daring shown by the V.A. BCF receives no recognition'.[4] Similar comments were made by other officers.[5] Nevertheless, the anti-Beatty account went to press as Corbett had been determined that it would. What Beatty himself thought of the matter is not recorded, but it is almost certain that Corbett had placed Beatty in such a position that to suppress or greatly alter the text he would have had to attend a Cabinet, as Hankey had predicted to Corbett. In any event, if he did wish to alter the account, Corbett had made it most difficult for him with Jellicoe alive and watching.

There was some difficulty over the use Corbett had been allowed to

1 Corbett *Diary,* 26.VII.22.
2 This substantially agrees with Temple Patterson's version.
3 Corbett *Diary* 8.IX.22.
4 PRO ADM. 116/2067.
5 Among them Captain Haggard the D.C.N.S.

make of intercepts of certain German W/T messages that were available to the Admiralty the night before the Battle, and which might have made Jellicoe's movements look more swift and more certain on the day of action.[1] The references were paraphrased in the first issue, and printed in an appendix of the Second Edition. Corbett thought the Admiralty knowledge was certain and that officers there were at fault for not passing all of this information on to Jellicoe.[2] The excuse for keeping them back was that it might reveal the source of British intelligence to the Germans. The real reason probably lay in Admiral Henry Oliver's comment that Corbett was wrong to think the Admiralty felt the intercepts represented clear intelligence. They produced supposition, he thought, not clear unmistakeable deductions. This was perhaps stuffy but it was a point of view.[3]

It was suggested that Corbett's constant reference to the lack of concert between army and navy was overdone.[4] Corbett was supported by Admiral Roger Keyes, who would not allow Corbett's unfavourable judgement of Sir C. Munro to be expunged.[5] In any event, the book went to press with little alteration. Corbett's literary executors were waiting for the Admiralty censors to work and then accuse them of tampering: indeed the impression amongst the Admirals was that the executors would welcome the chance to make a public outcry. Thus when Daniel wrote to object to some changes that were not of fact, but necessitated re-writing the narrative (which Daniel did not feel able to do) the Board gave in.[6] Admiral Field suggested strengthening the disclaimer, which they included.[7] It finally read:—

> The Lords Commissioners of the Admiralty have given the author access to official documents in the preparation of this work, but they are in no way responsible for its production or for the accuracy of its statements. Their Lordships find that some of the principles advocated in the book, especially the tendency to minimize the importance of seeking battle and of forcing it to a conclusion, are directly in conflict with their views.

---

1   Corbett to Jellicoe, *The Jellicoe Papers,* vol. II, p.415.

2   *Ibid.*

3   Oliver *Minute* 20.II.23; PRO ADM 116/2067.

4   *Minute* by D.O.D. 26.VIII.22; PRO ADM. 116/2067.

5   *Minute* by R. Keyes 5.I.23; PRO ADM. 116/2067. Munro had forced the abdication of Gallipoli, against Keyes' protests.

6   Daniel to Admiralty Board 22.VI.23; PRO ADM. 116/2067.

7   22.II.23; PRO ADM. 116/2067.

Presumably the reference to minimizing battle seeks to accuse Corbett of thinking Beatty too eager to fight. Certainly it is in line with Sydenham's attack on Corbett in 1916. Whatever the reason for that particular passage, it was inserted because it was the only way some members of the Admiralty Board could strike at Corbett who, from the grave, had defeated them. Corbett's intricate reasoning had rebounded on him. Looking at the whole, however, there seems to be no reason to downgrade Julian Corbett's thought concerning these matters. It is ironic that he should have been disclaimed by the Admiralty Board for upgrading the share of the Navy in the prosecution of World War I.

The official history of the war (Naval Operations) was eventually completed by Corbett's friend Sir Henry Newbolt. He, in turn, had difficulties with officialdom over censorship. But Corbett's task was done. By exercising skill in negotiations with the Government and its agents, and by the competence of his broad narrative approach, he had managed to write three books that described the navy, truly, as the 'Senior Service'. To claim that he had convinced the general public of this priority, however, would be to claim too much. Why was this so?

It would be expecting a good deal of the work of one author that he should change, single-handedly, the thinking patterns of a people. In England, during the 1914-18 war, the soldiers in Flanders and Gallipoli, together with their friends the swashbuckling fliers, captured the public imagination in a steady way. The grey ships of the Fleet on patrol, secret and busy, did not achieve the same notoriety, although on the enemy their effect was profound.

Marder has referred to 'a Jungle of Facts'. Of course, official history, with comment on the characters of its chief personnel expressly forbidden, lends itself to impersonal treatment. Yet it is true to say that Corbett, a man who thought and loved deeply, was not good at more intimate kinds of writing. Had he attempted, or been permitted, to discuss character, no doubt the important First War men would have been coldly compared to such strategists or tacticians as Drake, Pitt or Nelson. It is as likely that few could have stood the comparisons as it is unlikely that Corbett could have made their personalities live.

This work, in fact, appealed to minds trained to appreciate its purposes, method and aims. Others might, and many no doubt did, pass by on the other side. But in retrospect the purpose, method, and aims, must have their due. As this account has recorded problems, so it must record the triumphant surmounting of those problems. After the Second World War, for instance, the Official Naval Historian, Captain Roskill, distilled the wisdom scattered in a number of detailed works into shorter pieces that entrance the general reader. Corbett was not spared the time to accomplish a similar feat. Yet Roskill's broad construct, so carefully advanced in the initial pages of Vol. I. of *The War at Sea,* is Corbettian in its scope and character. His purpose was not that of chronicling the work of 'mere fighting blockheads'.

Corbett, however, if not 'popular', had provided a worthy monument to those who fought at sea. Men who had been involved in actions, or simply had to endure the routine of patrol and escort, could refer to the Official History and appreciate how their individual and ship efforts had contributed to the total overall effect. Much that must have previously appeared to have been pointless doubtless took on new significance, as sailors strove to compare the value of their service to that of their khaki brethren ashore.

The truly great achievement, however, was that those who wished to measure their personal war against the total British pattern of sea achievement could do so. Men of imagination could place their activities alongside those of Drake, Blake, Hawke and Nelson: they could understand, to slightly alter Mahan's magnificent phrase, how they, in the 'far distant storm tossed ships' on which the Kaiser's army never looked had 'stood between it and the dominion of the world'. They could see it all as a chapter in a continuous story. In the face of official interference, this was a great result for Corbett to have achieved. Reviewers all admitted the skill with which he had worked his way through the material and had given it form and shape in good solid prose. They only differed on whether he had been muzzled too much or too little — a point on which there was scope for disagreement in the face of those barbs of officialdom, the official disclaimers, which sullied the volumes.

Outside the official life herein described, Corbett had found time for other activites. In 1916, he delivered the Laughton Memorial Lecture 'The Revival of Naval History' in which he described the Renaissance in the subject to which he had made such a distinguished contribution. He also addressed the Historical Association on 'The Teaching of Naval and Military History'. The next year, he went up to Cambridge to deliver the Lees Knowles Lectures on 'Imperial Concentration — 1917' to the University. But his extra-official life thenceforth was limited by the magnitude of the commitment he had undertaken and his soul was 'fettered to an office stool' more than suited him.

For an older man unused to such a life, this naturally told on his health — as did the strain of the uncertainties described. After 1919, he was not a well man, and by the spring of 1922, the prodigious labour he put into the writing of Volume III took a heavy toll. Yet the strain of writing and protecting his book from over-censorship did not reflect in the body of the history. That work shows no fall-off in quality. Courage, high standards, good training and a prodigious effort overcame physical obstacles.

Looking at his historical writing as a whole, it is clear that he was not a 'popular' or an easy writer. Brian Tunstall, himself an expert on the period, commented that Corbett's *England in the Seven Years' War* was a specialist's book. No doubt. In many ways that book was representative. It showed his pedagogical intent, and it revealed his inability to delineate character apart from interpreting his *dramatis personae* as agents of the state's traditions. On the other hand, the vivid imagination that wove the various strands of a world wide conflict into a pattern that could be understood traditionally, without false or facile simplification, was both his strength and weakness. There are times when the reader stands amazed at the magnificent edifice erected to assist his understanding, and there are other times when the connection between cause and effect appears too elusive to really convince. Corbett's charm, and his difficulty as an historian, lie in the way he exercised this considerable talent.

Yet looking at the whole range of achievement, one is staggered by its scope. For if it is true that some of his conclusions, indeed many, have been overthrown by subsequent research, what is really amazing is the amount that has endured. Despite his tendency to glorify the dispatchers, manipulators or operators of British fleets, the main points that he made remain impressive to this day, when British sea-supremacy is not taken for granted. In 1895, he came fresh to a subject that consisted of little more than a record of the glorious exploits of the broadside bashers and the impressive growth of a nation and Empire: then the two were only vaguely linked. After upwards of twenty years' work, he left the two firmly connected through his illumination of the way in which statesmen and sailors had worked out a pattern of seapower and built on it from generation to generation. That he did not detail the influence of economic, social, and organizational factors is true. He was partly a man of his times, but by turning his back on mere heroics for their own sake, he pointed the path followed by naval historians since. He did not invent the more sophisticated approach: Mahan did that. Corbett applied it in depth and showed how Britain was a special case, not a universal representative of seapower. He transformed Mahan's insights into a scholarly occupation.

His lessons were not ephemeral. Britain required a peculiar naval organization in the Channel and North Sea to protect against invasion. Maximum effect could be gained by working the army and navy together for objects whose importance was not measured by size, and which should and could be limited. He never downgraded the army, he only wished it to maintain a British sense of proportion — a sense of proportion that he felt it had lost between 1911 and 1918. One can argue that this was inevitable, but it is not so manifest that the results were commensurate with the price paid. Above all, he was emphatic that great fleets of the past were at sea to more purpose than for the securing of prize money, or for the mere gratification of desire for military glory. Julian Corbett used history to bring the nation and the Navy together. His views still command respect and attention.

As a public figure, his contribution to his country is less obvious, but nonetheless, he was an important advisor to Admiralty and Government. His period of association with Fisher was most fruitful. At the moment when a cabal of Naval Officers and others who wished to shake confidence in the policies of Admiralty menaced the coherent direction of the Navy, Corbett acted to publicly admonish these men of the 'Syndicate of Discontent'. On top of that, though he never fully appreciated the depth of Fisher's affliction in 1908, he did help greatly in quashing the 'Invasion' trouble. If he could not cause Fisher to create a Staff it was he and Slade, through their joint labours at the War Course, who generated what non-*materièl* thought existed in the higher ranks of the Royal Navy. Churchill may have been contemptuous of his predecessors when he came to deal with the problem, but he was not capable of generating a Staff by magic. He himself wrote, after the war, that the process took time. In 1911-15, he did not appreciate this. The first real worker in that thankless vineyard was not Churchill, nor, at a lower level, was it Herbert Richmond. It was Julian Corbett in collaboration with Edmond Slade. How much they accomplished it is impossible to measure, but they understood that a Staff without staff officers was an absurdity. Fisher's understanding was even more keen. Corbett helped in the creation of staff officers. It was not easy work, but it was persevered in for a considerable time.

Assisting Fisher in the Dreadnought Age was Corbett's greatest non-historical activity. But, during the war, his great ability to produce quickly convincing argument in official memoranda, served the Navy and his country well, as has been seen. There can be no doubt that the reason for the success of both his propaganda, and his official writing, lay in the authority with which he advanced his views. It was this strength, based so solidly on his historical researches that distinguished Corbett from the large numbers of naval 'experts' who were active during the same period. It is no exaggeration to say that in this sense he was supreme, and had no rival. The men at the War Office recognized him as an enemy, and the naval service, while not always appreciating his views, understood the power of his mind, used it, and treated the man with respect. When all is said, however, it would be dangerous to try to found a high reputation for Julian Corbett by referring to his moments of official contact with the great ones of his land. On the other hand, it would be wrong to assume that because his influence was mostly literary, behind the scenes, and intermittent, it was unimportant. That was the adverse opinion of Admiral Sir Arthur Wilson in 1908. This judgement has since been repeated by practical-minded naval officers and others. To say this of a man whose ideas have largely engrafted themselves on the thinking of officers in the Royal Navy, in other navies, and on the minds of military thinkers the world over is absurd. Nothing, in the long run, is as potent as a good idea carefully developed and launched into the mental cockpit of the world. Julian S. Corbett generated more than his share. As for his total place in history, it may be said that his books stand as his sentinels.

APPENDICES

A: The Churchill Memorandum

Official Histories

I have now looked through the first instalment of the Official History of the Naval War which has been prepared by Sir Julian Corbett.

I do not in any way underrate the great care and literary skill with which this work has been conducted. As the period covered is that for which I was responsible as First Lord, I feel bound, however, to demur to its publication in its present isolated form. In my view the proper form of an official history is a full and fair selection of authentic documents — order, minutes, telegrams and memoranda — just as they were written before the event. If this is done, I see no objection to an official history, but an official history unaccompanied by the documents would be in my opinion misleading. There is very little of historic value that now need be concealed on public grounds and nothing on private grounds.

I think, therefore, that the Admiralty and the War Office should prepare a series of the authentic documents which actually were operative, and, after editing them as far as may be necessary in the public interest, should publish them with only such comments as are required to make the account fully intelligible. It will then be for the public at large and for unofficial historians to draw their own conclusions and express them at their discretion. Let the public have the facts, whatever they are.

WINSTON S. CHURCHILL

8 April 1919
PRO CAB 24/77

B: Admiral Wemyss instructions to Admiral Slade on the original Galley Proof of Official History

Admiral Sir Edmond Slade, K.C.I.E., K.C.V.O.

Attached you will find minutes by some of the Admiralty Departments on the proofs of Vol. I of the Official Naval History of the War.

It will be observed that in several places the proofs have been blue-pencilled. This was been done in many cases to call attention to passages in which criticism requires modification, and to inaccuracies of fact. As far as possible criticism should be avoided.

Will you therefore take the matter into consideration with Sir Julian Corbett.

S.D. R.E. Wemyss
5.4.19

Note on Admiral Wemyss's Minute 5.4.19 to Admiral Slade.

In compliance with this Minute I went through all the marked passages with Admiral Slade, and amended those in which he considered alteration advisable. A few of the more important ones he wished me to refer to the Admiralty. On these I took Admiral Wemyss's opinion and revised them in accordance with his personal instructions.

On the Admiral's comments as a whole the directions he gave were that all statement of personal opinion if any were to be cancelled, but that no statement of fact should be omitted merely because the statement necessarily implied criticism. On this principle I have revised the whole text as it now stands.

Since the galleyproofs were referred to the Admiralty certain telegrams relating to Coronel have been inserted verbatim at Mr. Churchill's request, permission having been first obtained from the Admiralty (See Admiralty letters 22nd April and 13th June 1919).

S.D. JULIAN CORBETT
25 August 1919

PRO ADM 116/2067

C: Plan of the Official Histories

It has been pointed out that the Historical Section at the C.I.D., after war broke out, was entrusted to a C.I.D. Committee under the Chairmanship of Admiral Sir Edmond Slade.

Its membership, in addition, comprised *by 1917:*–

Lt. Col. M.P.A. Hankey, Secretary to C.I.D. and War Cabinet
R/A Sir John F. Perry, Hydrographer of the Navy
Sir Julian Corbett
Major General Sir P.deB. Radcliffe, Director of Military
Operations, War Office

Lt. Col. F.S. Brereton, Royal Army Medical Corps
Major (Later Colonel) E.Y. Daniel (Secretary).

In the beginning, on Corbett's proposal it was suggested that Corbett should supervise the collection of naval material for the war history: that Sir John Fortescue should do the same for the military branch. The resulting history was, in accord with the prognostic for a short war, to be written by these two recognized scholars.

In the event, Sir John Fortescue declined the dual role, and in the spring Mr. C.T. Atkinson was appointed as the War Office collector and co-ordinator. However, Fortescue was still interested in writing the history itself.

But by 1916, partly on the advice and opinion of Lord Kitchener it was thought advisable to produce 'Interim' or 'Popular' histories of the War. Corbett was the choice of the C.I.D. Sub-Committee.

Fortescue soon found the work too arduous and looked for support. He left the Section in 1917. Eventually, Colonel G.S. Gordon (Professor of English Language and Literature at Leeds) was proposed for the Army writing. His appointment was finally confirmed by the War Cabinet and Treasury on 9.IV.19.

Meanwhile, a history of Seaborne Trade was desired. Mr. E.C. Fayle's name was proposed, and eventually approved on 10.IV.19. The expense of this book was to be borne by the Garston Foundation. Mr. Archibald Hurd was approved to write the history of 'The Merchant Navy in the War' on 12.VII.17. Both the above writers had been compiling materials well before their official approval dates. Sir Walter Raleigh, Professor of English Literature, agreed to write the Air History on 22.VII.18. Actually Fortescue did not complete his work, and the history of the military (Army) arm was not under Corbett's control. Nor was Raleigh's Air History.

According to CAB 24/92 'the History will be unique in English Literature'.

However, while the various specialist histories went their separate ways it was intended that the thread of statesmanship was to be provided by Corbett in the *Naval Operations*. Put another way, he was to provide what the *Grand Strategy* volumes accomplished for the history of the Second World War. For him the real history of the war was maritime history and he never thought of the Navy merely as one two or three services. His three volumes of official history reflected the consequent breadth of thought.

NOTE ON SOURCES

This book is based mainly on the Corbett Papers in the possession of Mrs. Elizabeth Tunstall and of her brother, Richard Corbett, which includes the invaluable diary. For the rest, supporting information has come from other manuscript sources, both public and private.

The printed sources that have helped have been few. The great exceptions are the work of Arthur Marder, Peter Kemp, and A.Temple Patterson, whose research dovetails with mine. In Kemp's case, for instance, my work will provide background from Corbett's side. I have made no attempt to repeat his careful work. Temple Patterson's work made the evidence concerning Corbett's involvement in the Jutland Scandal intelligible to me. Marder has provided the overall framework within which I worked.

Corbett Papers (CP) – Mrs. Elizabeth Tunstall. Printed *Catalogue of the Corbett Papers* issued in 1958 by Brian Tunstall, Peter M. Stanford and D.M. Schurman

Additional Corbett Papers (RCP) – Richard Corbett

Julian S. Corbett, in consultation with Rear Admiral Sir Edmond J. Slade, *Confidential – Maritime Operations in the Russo-Japanese War 1905-5,* 2 vols. Issued (1912-14) under the Direction of the Admiralty War Staff (not listed in *Catalogue of the Corbett Papers).*

National Maritime Museum (NMM) – Bridge Papers (BRI)
Colomb Papers (COL)
Noel Papers (NOE)
Richmond Papers (RIC)
Slade Papers (SLA)

Public Record Office (PRO) – Admiralty Papers (Adm. 1, Adm.116)
Cabinet Papers (CAB)
Committee of Imperial Defence (CID)
War Office Papers (WO)

Fisher Papers (Duke of Hamilton) Lennoxlove

Printed Sources

A.J. Marder, *Portrait of an Admiral* (London, 1952) The diary of H.W. Richmond

Fear God and Dread Nought 3 vols. (London, 1952-9). Correspondence of Admiral of the Fleet the Lord Fisher of Kilverstone

A. Temple Patterson, *The Jellicoe Papers* (NRS, 1966-8) Papers of Admiral of the Fleet the Lord Jellicoe

M.V. Brett, *Journals and Letters of Reginald Viscount Esher* 4 vols. (London, 1934)

Peter Kemp, *The Fisher Papers* (NRS. 1960-4)

Newspapers and Periodicals

In General

The Times, 1900-1922

The Monthly Review, 1900-1907

The Nineteenth Century, 1900-1907

In Particular

J.S. Corbett, 'The Teaching of Naval and Military History' *History* (April 1916)

'The Strategical Value of Speed in Battleships' RUSI *Journal* (July 1907)

'The Capture of Private Property at Sea' *The Nineteenth Century* (June 1907)

'Recent Attacks on the Admiralty' *The Nineteenth Century* (February 1907)

C.C. Lloyd, 'Royal Naval Colleges at Portsmouth and Greenwich' *The Mariners Mirror* (May 1966)

Vice Admiral P.H. Colomb, 'The Battle of Trafalgar' *United Services Magazine* (September 1899)

204

INDEX

Aboukir, HMS, 158, 180, 183
Admiral Geupratte, HMS, 103
Admiralty, 41, 42, 43; library, 24, 144, 156; staff organization, 47; encourages War Course, 48-9; building policy attacked, 64-5; attacks on, 67-71; Corbett to defend case of, 81-4, 90; spared an investigation, 94-7; Naval Intelligence Division at, 48, 49, 131-6; reactions to Corbett's writings, 183-6; Board of, 31, 72, 77, 86, 99; ultimate responsibility in wartime, 73; competency of, 129; views of, 138-41, Grahame Green, Board Secretary, 156; Churchill overruled by, 164; Board unsympathetic towards Corbett, 182, 184; record of Jutland Battle compiled for, 187-8; Staff Appreciation, 188, 190-2; Corbett disclaimed by Board, 194
Ainslie, Mr, 163
Albemarle, George Monck, Duke of, 18, 46
Albermarle, HMS, 101
Alexandretta, 162
Alexiev, Admiral, 146
Amery, Leopold S., 81, 156, 190
Anglo-Japanese Alliance (1902), 106, 146
Antwerp, 42, 158
Armada, *see* Spanish Armada
Army, British, 42, 62, 136; and defence planners, 41; leaders in strategy, 74, 75; new role for personnel, 80, 162; preventing invasion, 85, 86; territorial army, 89; Corbett made enemies in, 141; combined operations, 158, 167; history, 164-6; effectiveness dependent upon sea power, 169; leadership, 173
Army Staff College, 48
Arrogant, HMS, 101
Ashby, Dame Margery Corbett, suffragist, 4, 5
Asquith, Herbert Henry, 82, 84, 95, 96, 181; Prime Minister, 164; relations with Corbett, 166, 172, 173
Atkinson, C.T., 163
Azores, Battle of (mock battle), 37-8, 39

Bacon, Admiral R., 35
Balfour, Arthur J., 79, 80, 84, 96, 97, 159, 165; use of Corbettian argument, 167, 169; relationship with Corbett, 172, 173, 184
Ballard, Captain G.A., 66, 67, 142
Ballard Committee, 67, 82
Baltic Scheme, 159, 160, 161, 162; rejected by War Office, 42

Other volumes in this series

Copies obtainable on order from
Swift Printers (Sales) Ltd., 1-7 Albion Place, Britton Street, London EC1M 5RE